T'IEN-T'AI BUDDHISM AND EARLY MĀDHYAMIKA

Collect and protect the inexhaustible treasure—calligraphy written on New Year's Day, 1993, by Yamada Etai, the Tendai Zasu (head of the Tendai Buddhist denomination) at the age of 99 years. The point of the phrase is to emphasize that we should think not of material possessions, but of virtue, as our inexhaustible treasure. Because people are trusted based on their virtue, this is their most valuable treasure.

T'IEN-T'AI BUDDHISM AND EARLY MĀDHYAMIKA

by NG Yu-Kwan

TENDAI INSTITUTE OF HAWAII

BUDDHIST STUDIES PROGRAM

UNIVERSITY OF HAWAII

Printed in the United States of America

Library of Congress Cataloging-in-Publication Data

Wu, Ju-chün, 1946–
T'ien-T'ai Buddhism and early Mādhyamika / by Ng Yu-Kwan.
p. cm.
Includes bibliographical references and index.
ISBN 0-8248-1560-2 : $37.00. — ISBN 0-8248-1561-0 (pbk.) : $22.00
1. Chih-i, 538–597. 2. T'ien-t'ai Buddhism—Relations—Mādhyamika (Buddhism) 3. Mādhyamika (Buddhism)—Relations—T'ien-t'ai Buddhism. I. Title.
BQ9149.C457W8 1993
294.3'92—dc20 93-23160
CIP

ISBN 0-8248-1560-2 (cl.)
ISBN 0-8248-1561-0 (pbk.)

The paper used in this publication meets the minimum requirements of American National Standard for Information Sciences—permanence of Paper for Printed Library Materials
ANSI Z39.48-1984

Designed by Paula Newcomb

Distributed by
University of Hawaii Press
2840 Kolowalu Street
Honolulu, Hawaii 96822

This volume is published to celebrate the twentieth anniversary of the Tendai Mission of Hawaii.

CONTENTS

PREFACE

In my early days of studying Western philosophy and metaphysics, I was obssessed with the greatness of Kant and Hegel. Their depth and breadth seemed to have no bounds. I wondered about thinkers like Kant and Hegel: they must have had extremely high intelligence and creative power, otherwise their spectacular and fascinating philosophies would not have been constructed. When I gradually turned to the study of Buddhism, my attention was drawn to T'ien-t'ai and Hua-yen by Professor MOU Tsung-san, the celebrated Neo-Confucian scholar. He had a high appraisal of the significance of these two schools, claiming that their founders were philosophical geniuses as great as Kant and Hegel and that their philosophizing reached the highest level that the human mind can ever achieve. This was the first impression that I had of Chih-i.

Since then I have been interested in Chih-i and took every opportunity to become acquainted with his thought, but it was not until I wrote my doctoral thesis for McMaster University that I studied his system thoroughly. Because of its extremely abundant contents, it is unwise, and indeed impossible, to deal with Chih-i's whole system in a thesis. In view of the fact that I had worked on Nāgārjuna for years, and that Chih-i had a close historical relationship with early Mādhyamika doctrine, I decided to take this relationship as the focus for an intensive investigation of Chih-i. My idea was that through a comparative study of Chih-i and Nāgārjuna on selected important issues, it might be possible to find Chih-i's indebtedness to early Mādhyamika, and by locating their differences to identify the unique characteristics of Chih-i's own system. It was with this consideration that Chih-i and Nāgārjuna, two of the greatest thinkers in the Buddhist tradition, were brought together in my research.

According to this study, Chih-i's important ideas can be grouped under two main topics: one is Buddha Nature, which he identifies with No-emptiness and the Middle Way; the other is the way of realizing Buddha Nature, which includes the Four Alternatives, the Threefold Contemplation, and the Identification of the unworldly and worldly. Although both topics can be traced back to Nāgārjuna,

Chih-i's modifications of them and his own developments deserve our greatest attention since they manifest the unique characteristics of Chih-i's system.

With regard to the two main issues, Buddha Nature concerns the conception of the Truth (*shih-hsiang* in Chih-i's terminology), whereas the way of realizing Buddha Nature is a question of method. Consequently, I encountered a crucial question: Between concept and method, which aspect plays a more important role in characterizing Chih-i's system? I was aware of the fact that scholars of T'ien-t'ai Buddhism unanimously emphasized the so-called "threefold pattern" of Chih-i, failing to pay attention to his conception of Buddha Nature. I disagree with this understanding. It is true that the threefold pattern of thought—as seen in Chih-i's ideas of Threefold Contemplation, Threefold Truth, and Threefold Wisdom —is dealt with on several occasions and in considerable detail in his works. It is equally true that the concept of Buddha Nature appears in scattered references and does not seem to prompt much delineation. This does not necessarily mean for Chih-i that the issue of the threefold pattern overrides that of Buddha Nature. Rather, the threefold pattern is spoken of in methodological terms, concerning the way through which Buddha Nature or the Truth is to be realized, whereas Buddha Nature is an issue of the Truth itself. Logically speaking, the conception of the Truth precedes the way through which the Truth is to be realized. It is the understanding of the Truth that decides the way to realize it, not vice versa. In other words, Buddha Nature is more fundamental than the threefold pattern. Consequently, in the discussion of the characteristics of Chih-i's system, Buddha Nature, rather than the threefold pattern, should be given priority. In this sense I have parted company with most T'ien-t'ai scholars in my study of Chih-i, because I laid greatest emphasis on Buddha Nature.

How does Chih-i understand Buddha Nature? What are the characteristics of the Truth for Chih-i? After a long period of painstaking study, I concluded that Chih-i takes Buddha Nature to be ever-abiding, functional, and all-embracing. Consequently, the characteristics of the Truth for Chih-i are permanency, dynamism, and all-embracing nature. Among these three characteristics, dynamism is most emphasized and should deserve greatest attention. That the Truth is dynamic or functional indicates that the Truth can act. It can initiate actions. Towards what are these actions directed? For what purpose are they initiated? For Chih-i they are directed towards the actual phenomenal world so as to cause the cultivation and transformation of sentient beings. The purpose is educational and soteriological. Here is revealed in Chih-i's thought a radically pragmatic tone, carrying a deep sense of worldliness.

Hua-yen and Ch'an, the other two important schools of Chinese Buddhism besides T'ien-t'ai, also strongly advocate the concept of function. Hua-yen speaks of *li-yung* and Ch'an speaks of *tso-yung,* both indicating that the function or operation is to be imposed soteriologically upon the empirical world, a world full of suffering sentient beings longing for salvation. Here Chih-i obviously can find a common and ultimate concern, namely, care for the sentient and empirical realm. It is here that the three great schools come to terms with each other. This is indeed a significant topic deserving further investigation. Due to the limitations of space, however, the discussion of this topic is beyond the scope of the present work.

ACKNOWLEDGMENTS

The present work is a revised version of my Ph.D. dissertation submitted to McMaster University in early 1990. I wish to express my gratitude to Professors Yün-hua Jan, Graeme MacQueen and Kōichi Shinohara, who supervised the dissertation. Their instruction and comments have contributed significantly to the formation of this work. I also wish to thank Professor Kenneth K. Inada of the State University of New York at Buffalo and Professor David W. Chappell of the University of Hawaii at Manoa, the latter serving as external examiner of the dissertation. Both of them have made useful comments. My warm appreciation should be expressed to Dr. Paul Swanson of the Nanzan Institute for Religion and Culture, Japan, who has made harsh but valuable comments on the dissertation. My revision is partly a response to his comments. Particular thanks are due to my colleague, Dr. Lauren Pfister of the Hong Kong Baptist College, who has kindly gone through the entire manuscript, eliminating inconsistency and improving the English. I am grateful to the Buddhist Studies Program, University of Hawaii, the co-publisher, for assisting in editing the manuscript and preparing it for publication. In this regard, the efforts of Professor David W. Chappell, the founding director of the Program, particularly deserve my gratitude.

I also wish to thank Bishop Ryōkan Ara of the Tendai Mission of Hawaii who has founded the Tendai Institute, the other co-publisher of this book. In addition, he has arranged for the frontispiece of the book and for the financial support to make this publication possible. I am grateful to Bishop Ara's role in constantly encouraging research and publication of books in English on Tendai (T'ien-t'ai) Buddhism so that the Western world may learn and benefit from Tendai Studies. It is a great honor for me to have this book chosen to commemorate the Twentieth Anniversary of the Tendai Mission of Hawaii.

ABBREVIATIONS

Original Text in Sanskrit:

Kārikā-P	*Mūlamadhyamakakārikās de Nāgārjuna avec la Prasannapadā Commentaire de Candrakīrti,* ed. Louis de la Vallée Poussin, Bibliotheca Buddhica, No. IV. St. Petersbourg, 1903–13.

Original Texts in Chinese:

CL	*Chung-lun* of Nāgārjuna, with Commentary by Piṅgala, trans. Kumārajīva, T1564. (For the meaning of "T" see below).
FHHI	*Fa-hua hsüan-i* of Chih-i, T1716.
FHWC	*Fa-hua wen-chü* of Chih-i, T1718.
HCK	*Hsiao chih-kuan* of Chih-i, T1915.
MHCK	*Mo-ho chih-kuan* of Chih-i, T1911.
SCI	*Ssu-chiao i* of Chih-i, T1929.
T	*Taishō-shinshū-daizōkyō* (Note: This multivolume work has three columns per page referred to by letters of the alphabet, so T 38.561b.10 would refer to *Taishō-shinshū-daizōkyō,* Vol. 38, p. 561, column b, line 10.)
TCTL	*Ta-chih-tu lun, (Mahāprajñāpāramitā-śāstra),* trans. Kumārajīva, T1509.
TTSCI	*T'ien-t'ai ssu-chiao i* of Chegwan, T1931.
WMCHS	*Wei-mo-ching hsüan-shu* of Chih-i, T1777.
WMCLS	*Wei-mo-ching lüeh-shu* of Chih-i, T1778.
WMCWS	*Wei-mo-ching wen-shu* of Chih-i, Z 27–28.
Z	*Zokuzōkyō.*

Secondary References:

Andō	Andō, Toshio. *Tendaigaku: Kompon shisō to sono tenkai.* Kyoto: Heirakuji, 1968.
Hurvitz	Hurvitz, Leon. *Chih-I, An Introduction to the Life and Ideas of a Chinese Buddhist Monk.* Bruxelles: Juillet, 1962.
Inada	Inada, Kenneth. *Nāgārjuna.* Translation of *Mūla-madhyamaka-kārikā.* Tokyo: Hokuseidō, 1970.
Kajiyama	Kajiyama, Yūichi, et. al. *Kū no ronri: chūgan.* Tokyo: Kadokawa Shoten, 1969.
Kalupahana	Kalupahana, David J. *Nāgārjuna: The Philosophy of the Middle Way.* New York: State University of New York Press, 1986.
Matilal	Matilal, B. K. "Negation and the Mādhyamika Dialectic," in his *Epistemology, Logic and Grammar in Indian Philosophical Analysis.* The Hague: Mouton, 1971.
Mou 1975	Mou, Tsung-san. *Hsien-hsiang yü wu-tzu-shen.* Taipei: Student Book Co. 1975.
Mou 1977	Mou, Tsung-san. *Fo-hsing yü po-je.* Taipei: Student Book Co. 1977.
Murti	Murti, T. R. V. "Saṃvṛti and Paramārtha in Mādhyamika and Advaita Vedānta," in *The Problem of Two Truths in Buddhism and Vedānta,* ed. M. Sprung. Dordrecht: D. Reidel, 1973.
Nitta	Nitta, Masaaki. *Tendai jissōron no kenkyū.* Kyoto: Heirakuji Shoten, 1981.
Nakamura	Nakamura, Hajime. "Chūdō to kūken," in *Yūki kyōju shōju kinen: Bukkyō shisōshi ronshū.* Tokyo: Daizō Shuppan Co., 1964.
Ramanan	Ramanan, K. Venkata. *Nāgārjuna's Philosophy as presented in the Mahāprajñāpāramitā-śāstra.* Rutland, Vt. & Tokyo: Charles E. Tuttle Co., Inc.,1966.
Robinson 1957	Robinson, Richard H. "Some Logical Aspects of Nāgārjuna's System," *Philosophy East and West,* 6:4 (1957), pp. 291–308.
Robinson 1967	Robinson, Richard H. *Early Mādhyamika in India and China.* Madison: The University of Wisconsin Press, 1967.

Ruegg	Ruegg, D. Seyfort. *The Literature of the Madhyamaka School of Philosophy in India.* Wiesbaden: Harrassowitz, 1981.
Satō	Satō, Tetsuei. *Tendai daishi no kenkyū.* Kyoto: Hyakkaen, 1961.
Sprung 1977	Sprung, Mervyn. "Non-Cognitive Language in Mādhyamika Buddhism," in *Buddhist Thought and Asian Civilization,* ed. L. Kamamura and K. Scott. Berkeley: Dharma Publishing, 1977.
Sprung 1979	Sprung, Mervyn. *Lucid Exposition of the Middle Way.* London and Henley: Routledge and Kegan Paul, 1979.
Swanson	Swanson, Paul. *Foundations of T'ien-t'ai Philosophy: The Flowering of the Two Truths Theory in Chinese Buddhism.* Berkeley: Asian Humanities Press, 1989.
Tamura	Tamura, Yoshirō, et al. *Zettai no shinri: tendai.* Tokyo: Kadokawa Shoten, 1969.
T'ang	T'ang, Chun-i. *Chung-kuo che-hsüeh yüan-lun yüan-tao p'ien.* Vol. 3. Hong Kong: New Asia Institute, 1974.
Taya	Taya, Raishu, et al. *Bukkyōgaku jiten.* Kyoto: Hōzōkan, 1974.

CHAPTER I

Introduction

1. Basic questions

Nāgārjuna (*circa* A.D. 150–250) is unanimously regarded in India and China as the founder of the Indian Mādhyamika School, one of the most important schools in Mahāyāna Buddhism.[1] He is also revered in the T'ien-t'ai tradition as the founder, or at least an extremely important teacher, of this Chinese Buddhist School. Many T'ien-t'ai sources acknowledge Nāgārjuna's supreme position in the tradition. For example, in the *Mo-ho chih-kuan* of Chih-i (A.D. 538–597), the most important text of T'ien-t'ai Buddhism, it is recorded that Chih-i himself studied with Hui-ssu, Hui-ssu with Hui-wen, and that Hui-wen's conceptions were exclusively based on Nāgārjuna's *Ta-chih-tu lun.*[2] Chih-i himself is closely related to the Mādhyamika tradition, both textually and philosophically. In his works there are many Mādhyamika quotations; in addition, his philosophical conceptions are in many aspects based on Mādhyamika ideas.[3]

However, in his theory of the "classification of the Buddhist doctrines" *(p'an-chiao),* in which he groups hierarchically the various Buddhist doctrines into four categories, namely, the Tripiṭaka Doctrine *(tsang-chiao),* the Common Doctrine *(t'ung-chiao),* the Gradual Doctrine *(pieh-chiao)* and the Perfect Doctrine *(yüan-chiao),* Mādhyamika pertains merely to the Common Doctrine.[4] While acknowledging Nāgārjuna as the founding patriarch of the School, Chih-i has in many places criticized the Common Doctrine severely. He considers the Perfect Doctrine based on the *Lotus Sūtra* to be ultimate and theoretically higher than the Common Doctrine. This position brings up two important questions:

1. Why is Chih-i not completely satisfied with Mādhyamika thought?

2. Why does he seek ultimate satisfaction in the Perfect Doctrine?

These questions can be formulated in a more concrete manner. The major concern of Buddhism as a religion is, beyond doubt, liberation (Skt., *mokṣa;* Ch., *chieh-t'o*). It is commonly maintained by all Buddhist schools that liberation is to be attained in the realization of the Truth (Skt., *satya;* Ch., *ti*). However, Buddhist schools have different conceptions of the Truth and its realization. In the Mādhyamika context, for example, the Truth is Emptiness (Skt., *śūnyatā;* Ch., *k'ung*), which Nāgārjuna complements and, in fact, identifies with the Middle Way (Skt., *madhyamā pratipad;* Ch., *chung-tao*). Emptiness in Buddhism generally signifies the Truth of the non-substantiality of phenomena. Nāgārjuna's use of this concept is actually derived from the earlier *Prajñāpāramitā-sūtras.* He understands the Middle Way in terms of transcending extremes. With regard to the realization of the Truth, the Mādhyamika School proposes the method of the Four Alternatives (Skt., *catuṣkoṭi;* Ch., *ssu-chü*) and their negatives. The Four Alternatives are four possible ways in which to view an existent, i.e., is, is not, both is and is not, and neither is nor is not. Mādhyamika shows that these four alternatives are educational in leading one to approach the Truth, but from the ultimate point of view, none of these really paves the way to liberation because each has its own limitation.

Chih-i basically inherits the key concept of Middle Way and the method of the Four Alternatives and their negatives. He is, however, not completely satisfied with the Middle Way formulated in the Mādhyamika manner. He develops this concept and elevates it to a different dimension, establishing the concept of Middle Way-Buddha Nature *(chung-tao fo-hsing)* and identifying it with No-emptiness *(pu-k'ung).* This compound concept identifies the Middle Way and Buddha Nature (Skt., *Buddhatā;* Ch., *fo-hsing*). Buddha Nature is understood in the *Mahāparinirvāṇa-sūtra* as a universal endowment given to every sentient being, and is the basis of the attainment of Buddhahood or enlightenment. The Middle Way-Buddha Nature is the Buddhist Truth for Chih-i, who insists that the Truth should be spoken of in terms of both the Way and the Nature. As we understand this claim of Chih-i's, he feels that the Mādhyamika Middle Way will tend to be of a negative and static nature, denoting a state free from all extremes, whereas his Middle Way-Buddha Nature denotes a positive, dynamic and immanent nature. This compound concept is the key concept which clearly differentiates the Perfect Doctrine from the Common Doctrine. On the comprehension and attainment of this Truth, i.e., the Middle Way-Buddha Nature, Chih-i basically uses the method of the Four Alternatives, their negatives, the Threefold Contemplation *(san-kuan)* and identification *(chi)*. The Threefold Contemplation consists of the Contemplation of Emptiness *(k'ung-kuan)*, the Contemplation of the Provisional *(chia-kuan)* and the Contemplation of the Middle Way *(chung-kuan)*. In the Threefold Contemplation, one sees simultaneously the three aspects of the Truth; namely, Emptiness, Provisionality and the Middle Way. Identification *(chi)* connects *nirvāṇa* with *saṃsāra* and means that *nirvāṇa* is to be attained in *saṃsāra*. For Buddhists, *nirvāṇa* denotes the world of absolute purity, whereas *saṃsāra* denotes the impure world of life and death. When Chih-i applies these philosophical methods, all of which can be related to Mādhyamika, he does not hesitate to modify them. In such modifications, Chih-i's own interests and concerns become apparent, particularly in the Threefold Contemplation and identification. In terms of Chih-i's way of thinking, his method of the Four Alternatives and their negatives bears considerable Indian traces, whereas his Threefold Contemplation and identification are very much Chinese in character. From this understanding three questions become critical:

1. How does Chih-i understand and criticize Mādhyamika's concepts of Emptiness and the Middle Way?
2. How does Chih-i's Middle Way-Buddha Nature differ from Mādhyamika's Middle Way?
3. What are Chih-i's philosophical methods in relation to the realization of the Middle Way-Buddha Nature, and how can they be related to Mādhyamika?

The present work is devoted to the study of these questions. The third and final question is the most complicated, so its discussion will occupy more space. This study will lead to an understanding of Chih-i's thought in light of its relation to Mādhyamika and will show how Chih-i established his Perfect Doctrine by utilizing the philosophy of Mādhyamika. We shall thus be able to see how a Chinese thinker absorbed Indian Buddhist doctrines, adapted and developed them, and eventually built up a great school of Chinese Buddhism.

We may also see some differences in the ways of thinking manifested in Chinese and Indian Buddhisms.

Before proceeding to the next section, we wish to explain two terms often used in our study. First, "Truth" means the authentic nature of the phenomenal world, including our human existence. It is, as generally construed by the Buddhists, absolute and pure; for this reason it transcends all kinds of relativity and impurity. This term corresponds to *satya, tattva, tathyam* and other terms in Sanskrit. In Chinese Buddhism, it is usually called *ti, shih-hsiang, shih-chi, shih-hsing, ju,* or other names. *Ti* is Truth proper, whereas *ju* denotes the Truth as it originally is, without any distortion or perversion, and consequently refers to Suchness. *Shih* denotes the nature of ultimacy. That is, Truth is ultimate. In Chih-i's terminology, *shih* is often contrasted with *ch'üan,* which denotes the nature of expediency. On some occasions, Truth is termed *fa-hsing* (Skt., *dharmatā*), signifying the true nature or character of *dharmas* or entities. It is also termed *ti-i-i ti* (Skt., *paramārtha*), in which the nature of its supremacy is emphasized. In Chih-i's works, *shih-hsiang* is the most commonly employed term to signify the Truth, or more appropriately, the ultimate Truth.

Different Buddhist schools or masters often have their own emphases in understanding the Truth, in addition to these general meanings. For instance, as will be delineated in Chapter II, Mādhyamika specifies the Truth as Emptiness and the Middle Way, emphasizing the nature of its non-substantiality and its transcendence of extremes. In particular, Chih-i specifies the Truth as Middle Way-Buddha Nature, to which he ascribes some important characteristics to be discussed in great detail later in this work.

In our study, "Truth" or "ultimate Truth" will refer to the general meanings mentioned above. In most cases, these phrases correspond to *shih-hsiang.* However, when we speak of the Truth in a particular context, e.g., in Mādhyamika or Chih-i's system, we will specify it as Emptiness, the Middle Way, or Middle Way-Buddha Nature.

Second, the term *fa* (Skt., *dharma*) is often found in Chih-i's works. It may be translated as "thing," but this is not an ideal rendition. *Fa* or *dharma* denotes whatever is in the phenomenal world, including both sentient and non-sentient beings. "Thing" usually represents the non-sentient class of beings and excludes the class of sentient beings. Therefore, in our study we let the term remain in its original form, i.e., *dharma*. A *dharma* represents an item in the phenomenal world, whereas all *dharmas* (Ch., *i-ch'ieh fa*) represent the phenomenal world as a whole.[5]

It should be added that in his translation of Nāgārjuna's *Mūla-madhyamakakārikā*, i.e., the *Chung-lun,* Kumārajīva often renders the term *bhāva* as *fa*. *Bhāva* is usually translated as "entity" by modern scholars (in Inada and Ruegg, for instance). We will follow the modern translation and refer to *bhāva* as "entity." Essentially, there is no great difference between *dharma* and entity. Both denote the non-sentient and sentient realms of phenomena. In the present work, *dharma* and entity will often be used interchangeably.

2. Sources

It is our intention to study Chih-i and Mādhyamika through the most reliable sources. This study covers two groups of sources: the works of Chih-i and the works of the Mādhyamika, particularly by Nāgārjuna.

On Mādhyamika

Of the many works attributed to Nāgārjuna, a number are still available today.[6] The *Kārikā,* i.e., *Mūlamadhyamakakārikā,* was, no doubt, written by Nāgārjuna and is his most important work. In this work nearly all the major doctrines of the Mādhyamika School can be seen. K. Venkata Ramanan also points out that in the *Kārikā* itself one finds practically all the principal conceptions of the philosophy of Nāgārjuna.[7] This work has had a tremendous influence on Chih-i, and we shall basically understand the thought of Mādhyamika through the Sanskrit original.

The Chinese translation of the *Kārikā* is CL, *Chung-lun,* which was made by Kumārajīva (A.D. 344–413), who was also a prominent Mādhyamika scholar. Chih-i probably did not know Sanskrit. He definitely approached the *Kārikā* through the CL, and often quoted from it in his works. Indeed, in Chih-i's works we cannot find any reference to the Sanskrit *Kārikā.* Consequently, in our study we will also make use of the CL when dealing with Nāgārjuna's thought. We will, however, pay attention to the cases in which Kumārajīva's translation does not completely correspond to the original.[8]

The voluminous TCTL, *Ta-chih-tu lun (Mahāprajñāpāramitā-śāstra),* the Chinese translation of which was also made by Kumārajīva, had been attributed to Nāgārjuna for several centuries in Chinese Buddhist circles. Its Sanskrit original and Tibetan translation are not available; its authorship has been the topic of controversy among scholars for years. Étienne Lamotte refuses to admit that the TCTL was written by Nāgārjuna.[9] Yūichi Kajiyama and Ramchandra Pandeya are also doubtful about ascribing this work to Nāgārjuna. Thus, in their studies of Nāgārjuna's thought (namely, Kajiyama's *Kū no ronri: chūgan* and Pandeya's "The Mādhyamika Philosophy: A New Approach" in his *Indian Studies in Philosophy*) no references are made to this work.

However, other scholars hold opposite views. K. Venkata Ramanan, for example, strongly stands in favor of Nāgārjuna's authorship of the TCTL.[10] He claims that there is an intimate connection between the TCTL and the *Kārikā,* that almost the whole of the *Kārikā* is reproduced in fragments here and there throughout the TCTL, and thus that the TCTL can be regarded as being one piece with the *Kārikā.*[11] He is convinced that the doctrines explicated in the TCTL are a natural continuation and development of the doctrines found in the *Kārikā.*[12] Moreover, it should be noted that modern Chinese scholars have not expressed the slightest doubt on this matter. Tsung-san Mou, in his *Fo-hsing yü po-je,* understands Nāgārjuna's thought through the TCTL without any hesitation and explicitly assumes Nāgārjuna's authorship of the TCTL.

In this work, we are not in a position to discuss this issue fully nor attempt to offer a solution. Rather, we are concerned about whether or not it is appropriate to incorporate this great work into our study. Our response is quite positive and is based on the following considerations:

1. It was firmly believed in the Chinese Buddhist tradition that Kumārajīva was responsible for the translation of the TCTL. Seng-jui (A.D. 352–436), one of Kumārajīva's most eminent disciples, mentions in the preface of the TCTL that Kumārajīva abridged and translated the original Sanskrit text.[13] And, in the colophon of the work, a detailed description of how Kumārajīva translated the work is given.[14] It therefore seems safe to say, even if the issue of authorship remains unsolved, that Kumārajīva had an extremely close relation with the TCTL in its Chinese translation.

2. Kumārajīva himself was an outstanding master of Mādhyamika thought.[15] Even if one were to prove that the TCTL was not

written by Nāgārjuna—suggesting that it was forged by Kumārajīva or that he had done more than a mere translation of the TCTL—we should still hold to the fact that the work reflects Mādhyamika thought.

3. In viewing the TCTL in textual and doctrinal terms, its intimate relation to Nāgārjuna's thought can hardly be denied. The TCTL is basically a commentary on the *Pañcaviṃśatisāhasrikā-prajñā-pāramitā-sūtra,* whose unknown author had always kept Nāgārjuna's *Kārikā* in mind, as evidenced by its frequent quotation from the *Kārikā.*[16] It should be noted that many of these quotations concern extremely important issues.[17] Insofar as the doctrinal aspect is concerned, the major concept expounded in the TCTL is, undoubtedly, *pāramitā.* This concept is, nevertheless, explicated within the context of the philosophy of Emptiness and the Middle Way. As far as we can see, the conceptions of Emptiness and the Middle Way in the TCTL are in line with the ones found in the *Kārikā.* We can even go further to assert that the TCTL is a continuation and a fuller development of the *Kārikā* in this regard. The case of the Middle Way concept is particularly conspicuous.[18] We thus come to the understanding that the TCTL is a good complementary source to understanding Mādhyamika based on the *Kārikā.*

4. The relationship between the TCTL and Chih-i deserves our special attention. This work was, indeed, the central focus of his study in his youth. It was only later that he switched his interest and concern from this work to the *Fa-hua ching (Lotus Sūtra).* Despite this change, his major works still carry a tremendous amount of quotations from this text.[19] This work is, for Chih-i, a crucial text belonging to the Mādhyamika tradition. He had never doubted Nāgārjuna's authorship. In brief, this TCTL is, whether or not it was written by Nāgārjuna, an important work in Mādhyamika and a good complement to the *Kārikā.* As stated earlier, it has also had tremendous influence on Chih-i. Though our study of Mādhyamika will orient itself around Nāgārjuna, it is nevertheless not confined to him. We will thus make use of this great work, the TCTL, in our study, being convinced that it will be highly beneficial.

In addition to the *Kārikā* and TCTL, there are a few other Mādhyamika texts taught by the Chinese Mādhyamika masters. These include *Shih-er-men lun (Dvādaśamukha-śāstra), Shih-chu-pi-p'o-sha lun (Daśabhūmika-vibhāṣā-śāstra)* and *Pai-lun (Śata-śāstra).* Both the

Shih-er-men lun and *Shih-chu-pi-p'o-sha lun* are attributed to Nāgārjuna, while the *Pai-lun* is attributed to Āryadeva, Nāgārjuna's direct disciple. All of these works were translated by Kumārajīva. It is also interesting to note that both the Sanskrit originals and the Tibetan translations of these three works are not available. Obviously, there also exist in these cases problems with authorship, particularly with regard to the *Shih-er-men lun* and *Shih-chu-pi-p'o-sha lun.* Chih-i does not seem to be much impressed by these works and mentions them only on rare occasions.[20] With regard to Nāgārjuna's *Vigrahavyāvartanī,* the Sanskrit original and its Chinese and Tibetan translations are all available. In his major writings, Chih-i makes no mention of it at all. None of these works will be our central concern, inasmuch as we wish to cover only those sources in which a close connection exists between Chih-i and Mādhyamika.

There are several commentaries to the *Kārikā.*[21] Within Chinese Buddhist circles, however, only the one done by Piṅgala was widely read. This commentary was translated by Kumārajīva, its Sanskrit original and Tibetan translation being unavailable. Chih-i was, to some extent, influenced by this commentary. He quoted from it a few times,[22] including one important reference to the Middle Way.[23] This commentary will therefore be consulted in our study. One comprehensive commentary of the *Kārikā* is Bhāvaviveka's *Po-je-teng lun-shih (Prajñāpradīpa)* . Chih-i does not seem to be attracted to this work, but, we will consult it in our study because it provides important clues to the understanding of Nāgārjuna's Four Alternatives.

On Chih-i

When we approach the issue of the sources related to Chih-i, the situation is a little complicated. There are numerous works attributed to him, but some of these include forgeries. These works were supposed to have been written in two periods, which Prof. Tetsuei Satō has identified as the "early" and the "later." Chih-i first studied with Hui-ssu in Ta-su Mountain of Kuang-chou. He then went to Ching-ling at the age of 31 and remained in Wa-kuan Monastery for eight years. At age 38 he moved to T'ien-t'ai Mountain and remained there for eleven years in seclusion. This is what Satō calls the "early period." At 50 he returned to Ching-ling, where he lectured on the *Fa-hua ching* in Kuang-chai Monastery. At 56 he went to Ching-chou, his hometown, whrere he resided until his death. This is the "later period."[24] In our study, we will use only those works which can undoubtedly represent his own thought, most of which were written in the later period. First, let us consult Tetsuei Satō's *Tendai daishi no kenkyū* for a precise understanding of Chih-i's works. Among the huge bulk of works attributed to Chih-i, twenty-eight are lost and forty-six are extant. The forty-six works can be classified into three categories:

1. Works written by Chih-i himself. They include works established in his early period, such as the *Fa-chieh tz'u-ti ch'u-men, Fa-hua-san-mei ch'an-i, Fang-teng ch'an-fa* and *Chüeh-i san-mei.* They also include the ten-chapter *Ching-ming hsüan-i,* written in his later period.[25]

2. Works representing Chih-i's thought, which can further be divided into two groups:

   a. Works by Chih-i's followers, recording what he had delivered orally and subsequently submitting the draft to him for correction and approval. These works include the *Tz'u-ti-ch'an men* in his early period, and the thirty-one-chapter *Ching-ming-ching shu* in his later period. The one-chapter *Kuan-hsin lun,* which was recorded shortly before his death, should also be placed here.[26]

   b. Notes taken of Chih-i's lectures by his followers, particularly Kuan-ting (A.D. 561–632). The drafts were made available after Chih-i's death, and thus do not bear his stamp of approval. Among these works are the celebrated *San ta-pu* ("Three Great Works"), i.e., FHHI *(Fa-hua hsüan-i),* FHWC *(Fa-hua wen-chü)* and MHCK *(Mo-ho chih-kuan),* all of which were recorded by Kuan-ting.

3. Works publicized under Chih-i's name. These works were actually written by scholars after Chih-i. They include a few outright forgeries, and works whose contents are mixed with Chih-i's writings. These works include, to name a few, the *Chin-kuang-ming-ching hsüan-i, Chin-kuang-ming-ching wen-chü, Kuan-yin hsüan-i, Kuan-yin i-shu, Ch'ing-kuan-yin-ching shu, Ssu-nien ch'u* and the works related to Pure Land Buddhism.[27]

Satō also discusses particularly the *Wu hsiao-pu* ("Five Small Works") of T'ien-t'ai, i.e., *Kuan-ching shu, Chin-kuang-ming-ching hsüan-i, Chin-kuang-ming-ching wen-chü, Kuan-yin hsüan-i* and the *Kuan-*

yin i-shu. He strongly doubts Chih-i's authorship of any of them, even though they were traditionally attributed to him.[28] With regard to the *Jen-wang-ching shu,* which allegedly contains Chih-i's expression of the Threefold Truth *(san-ti),* Satō remarks that it was written by a T'ien-t'ai scholar after Chih-i's death.[29]

Satō also mentions the following works, which may be attributed to Chih-i. The *Ch'an-men k'ou-chüeh* and *Cheng-hsin lun* were written in the early period and so may represent Chih-i's early thought. The *Ch'an-men yiao-lüeh* and *Ch'an-men chang* were written in the later period and were probably published after Chih-i's death. Both works reflect to some extent Chih-i's views developed in the later period. The *Kuan-hsin-shih fa, Kuan-hsin-sung-ching fa, Kuan-hsin shih-er-pu-ching i* and *Tso-ch'an fang-pien-men* are works concerning psychological and technical problems that involve the Ch'an practitioner. It is difficult to decide whether or not they represent Chih-i's views.[30]

So far we can see that only those works listed in the first two categories and a few mentioned in the previous paragraph are sources reliably representing or reflecting Chih-i's views. Satō, on many occasions, stresses the division of Chih-i's thought into two periods,[31] which is in fact a division between his early attention to the Emptiness of the Prajñāpāramitā literature and his later attention to the ultimate Truth *(shih-hsiang)* of the *Fa-hua ching.* From the early to the later period, there is a manifest progress of thought in Chih-i's life. This progress can be seen in his classification of Buddhist doctrines, in which he considers the *Fa-hua ching* to be more perfect than the thought expressed in the Prajñāpāramitā literature. He expressed his great concern for the *Fa-hua ching* even at the moment of death.[32] Generally speaking, works written in the later period of a thinker are more mature and thus deserve more attention. We will, in our study, pay more attention to works established in the later period.

Consequently, the sources on Chih-i in our study will be basically confined to the following: The FHHI (T. 1716), FHWC (T. 1718), MHCK (T. 1911), HCK (T.1915), *Kuan-hsin lun* (T. 1920), *Ch'an-men yiao-lüeh* (Z. 99), *Ch'an-men chang* (Z. 99), *Ching-ming hsüan-i* and *Ching-ming-ching shu.* In our study we refer to these sources as Chih-i's major works. Among these works, the FHHI and MHCK are the most important because they reflect comprehensively Chih-i's most mature thought and cover nearly all of the key concepts and philosophical methods involved in the study of our basic questions.

A brief explanation is in order concerning the *Ching-ming hsüan-i* and *Ching-ming-ching shu.* Both are commentaries of the *Wei-mo ching (Vimalakīrti-nirdeśa-sūtra),* in which Chih-i was very much interested during his old age. The ten-chapter *Ching-ming hsüan-i* was written by Chih-i in A.D. 595, at the invitation of Yang Kuang (A.D. 569–618), who was then the Crown-Prince of the Sui Dynasty. This text survives in part as the twelve-chapter SCI (*Ssu-chiao i,* T. 1929), which is now widely read. The thirty-one-chapter *Ching-ming-ching shu* was written at a later date, after Chih-i returned to T'ien-t'ai Mountain. This work is actually the composition of two independent works, namely, the six-chapter WMCHS (*Wei-mo-ching hsüan-shu,* T. 1777) and the twenty-five-chapter WMCWS (*Wei-mo-ching wen-shu,* Z. 27–28), which was later abridged into the ten chapter WMCLS (*Wei-mo-ching lüeh-shu,* T. 1778) by Chan-jan (A.D. 711–782), an outstanding thinker in the T'ien-t'ai tradition. In our study, we will use SCI, WMCHS, WMCLS and WMCWS.

Finally, we will make a special exception and include the *Fa-chieh tz'u-ti ch'u-men* (T. 1925) in our study. This work was, as pointed out previously, written in Chih-i's early period. The work, however, contains a few important ideas which Chih-i developed fully in the later period. These ideas include the theory of classification of Buddhist doctrines,[33] the concept of Middle Way-Buddha Nature,[34] and the two approaches to Emptiness.[35] The two approaches are *t'i-fa,* i.e., to realize Emptiness directly in the *dharmas* or phenomena, and *hsi-fa,* i.e., to realize Emptiness through disintegrating and eradicating the *dharmas* or phenomena. They are ascribed by Chih-i in his classification of Buddhist doctrines to the Common Doctrine and Tripiṭaka Doctrine, respectively. Satō proposes that, because of its discussion of the classification of Buddhist doctrines, this work should be taken to be the last one written in the early period. He argues that the idea of the classification of Buddhist doctrines hardly appeared in Chih-i's early works, and that it was formed in his later period, when he established his Buddhist conceptions based on the *Fa-hua ching.*[36] It therefore seems safe to presume that Chih-i was approaching maturity in thought when he wrote the *Fa-chieh tz'u-ti ch'u-men.*

CHAPTER II

Emptiness and the Middle Way in Mādhyamika

The first of our basic questions concerns Chih-i's understanding and criticism of Mādhyamika's Emptiness and Middle Way. Although Mādhyamika's concepts of Emptiness and Middle Way have been widely and deeply studied by modern scholars based on Sanskrit, Tibetan and Chinese sources, we would like to examine the meaning of Emptiness and the Middle Way, especially through the *Kārikā,* TCTL and Piṅgala's commentary of the *Kārikā,* in view of the fact that Chih-i basically understood these concepts through these works. We will try to situate our examination in the context of previous scholarship where necessary, but our primary intention will be to emphasize the issues that enhance our study of Chih-i's thought in light of his relation to Mādhyamika, the *Kārikā* and TCTL in particular.

Emptiness is, without much controversy, the central concept in the Mādhyamika system of thought, as has been pointed out by many scholars.[1] Indeed, the entire *Kārikā* can be regarded as an exposition of this concept; the aim of the arguments in the *Vigrahavyāvartanī* is no more and no less than eliminating the concept of Self Nature *(svabhāva)* and establishing the nature of Emptiness. What, then, is Emptiness for the Mādhyamikas? Nāgārjuna's declaration in the *Kārikā*—that whatever is of Dependent Origination *(pratītyasamutpāda)* is Emptiness—naturally comes to mind.[2] In this declaration, Emptiness is related to the causal relationships of all entities and is identified with Dependent Origination. These issues are critically important in understanding the meaning of Emptiness. However, this approach to Emptiness is insufficient because it seems to be endorsed by most Mahāyāna Buddhist schools; consequently, it does not reflect the particular meaning of Emptiness in Nāgārjuna's and Mādhyamika's contexts. Moreover, in the declaration, Emptiness is treated as a predicate of Dependent Origination, which is the subject matter. Nāgārjuna, obviously, does not intend to explicate Emptiness positively. For this reason, we will not focus on this declaration in our discussion of Emptiness. We intend to undertake a more sophisticated project through which we may show Nāgārjuna's argumentative and practical interests. Nevertheless, reference to the relationship between Emptiness and Dependent Origination will be made whenever necessary.

The meaning of Emptiness, as found in the *Kārikā,* can be summed up as the negation of Self Nature and false views. The negative implication of this concept is obvious, regardless of which aspect we consider.[3] As a matter of fact, this understanding has been expressed by Ruegg, who speaks of *śūnyatā* (i.e., Emptiness) both as Emptiness of "own being" (i.e., Self Nature) and as release from all speculative dogmatic views.[4] He refers to speculative views as *dṛṣṭi,* or "false views".[5] Since he does not elaborate this understanding in detail, we will handle this issue in a more thorough manner to delineate the implications of these claims.

1. Emptiness as the negation of Self Nature

Nāgārjuna does not explicitly define Emptiness in the *Kārikā.* Instead, he basically expresses this concept in terms of the negation of Self Nature, by making reference to the concept of Dependent Origination. Still, he does not explicitly state that Emptiness is the negation of Self Nature.

In order to understand Nāgārjuna's concept of Emptiness, we must first examine the concept of Self Nature. Self Nature (Skt., *svabhāva;* Ch., *hsing,* meaning Nature, as translated by Kumārajīva in the CL, but literally it should be rendered *tzu-hsing,* meaning Self Nature) denotes the unchangeable and thus permanent substance, or substantiality. Nāgārjuna, however, does not positively mention in detail what Self Nature is. He prefers to express it negatively, as can be seen in the following two verses of the *Kārikā:*

> How is it possible for the self-nature to take on the character of being made? For, indeed, the self-nature refers to something which cannot be made and has no mutual correspondence with something else.[6]

> If existence is in virtue of a primal nature, then its nonexistence does not follow. For, indeed, a varying character of a primal nature is not possible at all.[7]

It can be seen that Nāgārjuna regards Self Nature as what cannot be made or manipulated (Skt., *akṛtrima;* Ch., *wu-tso*); it is devoid of "varying character" (Skt., *anyathābhāva;* Ch., *i-fa*). With regard to the understanding that Self Nature refers to something which cannot be made, Ruegg offers the following observation:

> In the course of the discussion and refutation of it in the MMK [i.e., *Mūlamadhyamakakārikā*] and the rest of the Madhyamaka literature, *svabhāva* "own being, self-nature, aseity" has been defined as some thing unproduced *(akṛtrima)* which is independent of all other things *(nirapekṣaḥ paratra);* those who postulated a *svabhāva* have indeed conceived of it as not produced through causal conditioning.[8]

The Sanskrit term for Self Nature in the two verses above is *svabhāva* and *prakṛti,* respectively. Kumārajīva translates both as *hsing,* making no difference between them. *Svabhāva, prakṛti* and *hsing* all express the nature of unchangeability, so that entities that have this quality are not subject to the transition from a state of existence to one of non-existence or nothingness. Therefore, whatever is in possession of Self Nature will not undergo nothingness (Skt., *nāstitā;* Ch., *wu*). Nāgārjuna approaches Self Nature in terms of the negative nature of being made, of varying character and of non-existence, all of which are attributes usually ascribed to what is empirical or phenomenal. Consequently, we can say that Nāgārjuna reveals Self Nature through negating the phenomenal.

From the negation of Self Nature, Emptiness is introduced, as seen in the following verse:

> From the perception of varying natures all entities are without self-natures. An entity without self-nature does not exist because all entities have the nature of *śūnyatā.*[9]

In this verse, having no Self Nature (Skt., *niḥsvabhāvatva;* Ch., *wu-hsing*) and having Emptiness *(śūnyatā)* are brought together to describe entities. That is, entities are, on the one hand, devoid of Self Nature, whereas on the other, they are empty. Two propositions can now be affirmed: namely, entities are devoid of Self Nature, and entities are empty.[10] From the two propositions, we cannot directly infer that the empty nature or Emptiness is identical to the negation of Self Nature. However, as both Emptiness and the negation of Self

Nature are used to describe entities, there must be a close relationship between them.

This relationship is strengthened through the concept of Dependent Origination. Nāgārjuna declares in the *Kārikā* that whatever is of Dependent Origination is Emptiness. He also says elsewhere: "Any entity which exists by virtue of relational origination is quiescence in itself."[11] Nāgārjuna regards quiescence (Skt., *śānta;* Ch., *chi-mieh*) as the nature of relational origination or Dependent Origination. This "quiescence" can be viewed as a synonym of "Emptiness," as seen in Piṅgala's comment on the above verse:

> Entities originated from various causes do not have Self Nature, and are therefore quiescent. Quiescence is called "nothingness." . . . Entities originated from various causes do not have Self Nature. It is because they have no Self Nature that they are empty.[12]

Here, "quiescence" is identified with "nothingness" *(wu),* and we have no way of knowing the original Sanskrit term in Piṅgala's commentary. Elsewhere in the *Kārikā,*[13] however, Kumārajīva translates *śūnyatā* as "nothingness." It seems safe to infer that here, in Piṅgala's commentary, the original Sanskrit term for "nothingness" is *śūnyatā.* From this, we can assume that Piṅgala identifies quiescence with Emptiness. Kajiyama also remarks that quiescence is the state of having no Self Nature, and that it is used as the synonym of Emptiness.[14]

In view of this identification of quiescence and Emptiness, we are convinced that the half verse of the *Kārikā* quoted previously expresses the same thing as Nāgārjuna's declaration: whatever is of Dependent Origination is Emptiness. Both texts stress the identity of Dependent Origination and Emptiness. Furthermore, as shown below, Emptiness is associated with the negation of Self Nature through the concept of Dependent Origination.

In another verse, Nāgārjuna deals with Self Nature and causes: "If you perceive the various existences as true beings from the standpoint of self-nature, then you will perceive them as non-causal conditions."[15] Here, one is warned not to see existences or entities in terms of Self Nature, otherwise entities will be causeless; in so doing, the principle of causality will be violated. An opposition between Self Nature and causality is manifest here. With regard to entities, if one maintains the principle of causality, one has to refute the supposition of Self Nature. It is not possible for both to be maintained at the same time. Piṅgala makes a helpful comment on this verse:

> If entities determinately have Self Nature, then they should not originate and extinguish. Why then should there be causes for them? If entities originate from causes, then they will not have Self Nature. Thus, if entities determinately have Self Nature, then they will not have causes.[16]

Piṅgala points out that the concept of Self Nature contradicts the concepts of origination and extinction, which form the phenomenological basis of causality. Thus, the concept of Self Nature also contradicts the principle of causality. If 'a' is causality and 'b' is Self Nature, then, logically,

$$a \supset \sim b, \; b \supset \sim a$$

In other words, 'a' implies the negation of 'b,' 'b' implies the negation of 'a;' 'a' and 'b,' or causality and Self Nature, cannot stand together. They logically reject each other.

The Buddhist expression of causality is Dependent Origination. From the above discussions, we see that Nāgārjuna identifies Emptiness with Dependent Origination, the latter of which is incompatible with Self Nature. It therefore seems natural to Nāgārjuna that Emptiness is likewise incompatible with Self Nature, and that they cannot be maintained simultaneously. In order to realize Emptiness, Self Nature must be negated. Nāgārjuna obviously understands Emptiness in terms of the negation of Self Nature, although he does not state this understanding explicitly. Piṅgala's assertion that entities are empty because they have no Self Nature (cf. note 12) also expresses this understanding.

We have said earlier that Nāgārjuna understands Emptiness in relation to Dependent Origination. This relation is extremely important. Dependent Origination refers to a principle that prescribes how entities arise. Entities must come from causes; their existence depends on causes. Because they are from causes, they are naturally of the nature of being made (Skt., *kṛtrima;* Ch., *tso*). Entities are subject to change including disintegration, since the causes, which make the entities as they are, may themselves disappear. These entities are manifestly devoid of Self Nature, which defies changeability. They are, indeed, empty.[17] It is in this context that Nāgārjuna speaks of Emptiness. Emptiness therefore denotes the true aspect of entities. Dependent Origination is nothing but the nature of the empirical world, the phenomenal world, in which all entities are formed by causes. What is important to note is that Nāgārjuna's Emptiness is the Emptiness of the phenomenal world, or more explicitly, the Emptiness of the Self Nature of phenomena, not an Emptiness spoken of in general.

Ramanan remarks briefly that *śūnyatā* is the comprehension of the non-substantiality of things in their mundane nature.[18] This statement also points to our emphasis on the phenomenal or mundane world in comprehending Emptiness. "Non-substantiality" is just another expression referring to the state of being devoid of Self Nature.

The close relationship between Emptiness and the phenomenal world can also be described in a logical manner. We have seen that Nāgārjuna speaks of Self Nature in terms of the negation of phenomena. We now know that he sees Emptiness as the negation of Self Nature as well. If 'p' represents the phenomena, then Self Nature will be '$\sim p$,' and Emptiness will be '$\sim(\sim p)$,' which logically equals 'p.' Emptiness in this manner finally returns to the phenomena, or the phenomenal world. This means that Emptiness cannot be established apart from the phenomenal world.

Emptiness conceived in this way is, for Nāgārjuna, the Truth; and the Truth is the non-substantiality, or non-self nature, of the phenomenal world. This conception of Emptiness is more explicitly and fully discussed in the TCTL:

> The various entities originate from the combination of causes. As these entities [originating] from combination do not have determinate nature, they are empty. Why? Entities originating from causes are devoid of Self Nature. Because they are devoid of Self Nature, they are ultimate Emptiness. This ultimate Emptiness is originally empty, not being made by the Buddha or anyone else.[19]

It is clearly shown in this passage that things originating from causes do not have Self Nature and are consequently in the nature of Emptiness. That is, "being devoid of Self Nature" and "Emptiness" are identified with each other, both being spoken of in the context of things originating from causes.

Elsewhere in the TCTL the concept of "Nature Emptiness" *(hsing-k'ung)* is proposed:

> "Nature" *(hsing)* is called "self-existence," and it does not rely on causes. If it relies on causes, then it is something made, and is not named "Nature." In the various entities there is no Nature. . . . The Nature of all entities cannot be found. This is called "Nature Emptiness."[20]

From the definition of Nature Emptiness—that the Nature of all entities cannot be found—it is easy to see that Emptiness is the negation of Nature, which means the lack of an enduring, uncaused essence called Self Nature. It should also be noted that this Emptiness, or Nature Emptiness, is spoken of with regard to the phenomenal realm; this suggests that no nature as such is to be found in various entities.[21]

2. Emptiness as the negation of false views

Nāgārjuna also discusses Emptiness in terms of the negation of false views. He states:

> The wise men (i.e., enlightened ones) have said that *śūnyatā* or the nature of thusness is the relinquishing of all false views.[22]

The implication here is that, from the Buddhist point of view, Emptiness is the relinquishing or negation of false views *(dṛṣṭi)*. For the Buddhists, all views are partial and relative and thus have limitations. They tend to be false with regard to understanding of the Truth. But what exactly do these false views denote? Nāgārjuna does not explicitly and fully respond to this question in the *Kārikā*. Piṅgala, however, explicates it in his commentary:

> The Great Saint preached Emptiness in order to refute the sixty-two various views *(dvāṣaṣṭi-dṛṣṭi)* and defilements such as ignorance, love, etc.[23]

This explication occurs right after the above verse, indicating that for Piṅgala, the false views in question denote mainly the sixty-two various views. These views are, in the Buddhists' eyes, false views of the self and the world assumed by non-Buddhists. They are, like such defilements as ignorance and love, obstruction to our understanding of the Truth.[24]

Although Nāgārjuna does not specify the false views in the *Kārikā,* he tends to associate them with conceptualization, discrimination and differentiation:

> Non-conditionally related to any entity, quiescent, non-conceptualized by conceptual play, non-discriminative, and non-differentiated. These are the characteristics of reality.[25]

Here, the characteristics of Reality or the Truth are enumerated, including non-conceptualization, non-discrimination and non-differentiation. It can be inferred that the opposites of these characteristics—such conceptual acts as conceptualization, discrimination and differentiation—are either incompatible with the Truth or obstructive to attainment of the Truth. In view of the fact that Nāgārjuna here also speaks of the Truth in terms of quiescence (which, as pointed out earlier, is used as the synonym for Emptiness), we are certain that by the "Truth" he means Emptiness or the "Truth of Emptiness."

Therefore, both false views and such acts as conceptualization, discrimination and differentiation are harmful to attainment of Emptiness. The close relationship between them cannot be denied; in fact, it is possible that false views arise from such acts. Discrimination and differentiation, which are based on the use of concepts and thus promote conceptualization, will tend to initiate a dichotomy that will destroy the wholeness and absoluteness of the Truth, which Nāgārjuna regards as non-discriminative and non-differentiated. When Nāgārjuna mentions false views, we believe he is referring to perversive views that split the Truth. Nāgārjuna's vehement refutation of concepts and conceptualization is vividly seen in the dedicatory verses with which he begins the *Kārikā:*

> I pay homage to the Fully Awakened One, the supreme teacher who has taught the doctrine of relational origination, the blissful cessation of all phenomenal thought construction.
>
> (Therein, every event is "marked" by:) non-origination, non-extinction, non-destruction, non-permanence, non-identity, non-differentiation, non-coming (into being), non-going (out of being).[26]

The passage above contains the famous Eight-Nos or Negations, which have been widely studied by scholars. What we want to point out is that the meanings of the concepts in the "Nos" are established unanimously in a relative and dependent sense. For example, the meaning of origination is relative to and dependent on that of extinction, and *vice versa.* This relative and dependent nature of the concepts cannot reveal the Truth of events, that is, Emptiness in its absoluteness and wholeness. Rather, it discriminates, differentiates and consequently bifurcates the Truth into dichotomous falseness.

Conceptualization (in the form of discrimination, differentiation and bifurcation) may also induce false views and obstruct us from attaining the Truth in the sense that the concepts used are bound to form a duality of extremes—being and nothingness—both of which are irrelevant to the Truth. Taking an event occurring in the empirical world as an example, one is likely to apply the opposite pair of definite concepts, being and nothingness, to describe it and assert that the event exists or that it does not exist. However, from the standpoint of Dependent Origination, we can only say that the event exists causally, and that it is devoid of Self Nature and consequently is in the nature of Emptiness. This is the Truth of the event. To assert that the event exists or does not exist on the basis of the definite concept of being or nothingness will miss this Truth. Such assertions are false views.[27]

There is in Buddhism a specific term for conceptualization, viz., "conceptual play" (Skt., *prapañca,* Ch., *hsi-lun*), which is expressive of the character of mental fabrication and of its irrelevance to Reality or the Truth. Inada's rendition of the Sanskrit *prapañca* as "thought constructions" in the first verse above conveys the same message. Because conceptual play causes false views, the negation of false views, in terms of which Nāgārjuna understands Emptiness, naturally entails the negation of conceptual play. In fact, the insistence that conceptual play be banished is seen throughout the *Kārikā.*

3. Further reflections

So far we know that Nāgārjuna's Emptiness has two objects to negate: Self Nature and false views, and that his understanding of Emptiness is revealed in the negation of these two aspects. As seen in section 1 above, Nāgārjuna, Piṅgala and the TCTL all see Emptiness as the negation of Self Nature; they all stress the incompatibility of Self Nature with the concept of causality or Dependent Origination; thus they arrive at the need to refute Self Nature. They have little interest in metaphysical issues and do not undertake an extensive study of the characteristics of Self Nature. What they are concerned about is that Self Nature renders the relational origination, and consequently the changeability of the empirical world, impossible because anything in possession of the unchangeable and self-sufficient Self Nature will defy causal formation. Since Self Nature will destroy the world of Dependent Origination, the need to refute it is therefore unavoidable and shows a deep concern with the empirical world. This concern will be unpacked a bit more in section 8, when we refer to the TCTL in the discussion of the harm caused by attachment to being and nothingness. Moreover, the discernment of Emptiness as the negation of Self Nature enhances our understanding of the empirical world: that is, in this discernment, we are asserting the very Emptiness of the empirical world in the sense that the empirical world is devoid of Self Nature. Accordingly, this discernment bears an epistemological implication with regard to the empirical. In the negation of false views, however, the concern is very much practical and soteriological: that is, Emptiness is to be realized as the Truth through relinquishing false views; enlightenment is attained in the realization of Emptiness.

The negation of Self Nature tends to respond to the question "What is the meaning of Emptiness?" The answer will also convey the meaning of "being devoid of Self Nature." The manner in which to deal with the question is to reveal what is absent rather than what is present. It is important to note that the negation of false views tends to respond to the question "How is Emptiness to be realized?" Strictly speaking, the negation as such concerns mainly an educational method rather than a meaning, namely, how to achieve a soteriological goal. As a matter of fact, with regard to the half verse,

> The wise men (i.e., enlightened ones) have said that *śūnyatā* or the nature of thusness is the relinquishing of all false views,

the Sanskrit version understands Emptiness in terms of the negation of false views, whereas Kumārajīva modifies his Chinese translation significantly:

> The Great Saint taught the doctrine of Emptiness in order to free [sentient beings] from various [false] views.[28]

This modification emphasizes the pragmatic and educational aspect of teaching the doctrine of Emptiness. Piṅgala's comment on the same verse also reveals a similar emphasis.[29] We thereby know that both Kumārajīva and Piṅgala are aware of the pragmatic implication of Nāgārjuna's understanding of Emptiness as the negation of false views.

In view of the point that the negation of Self Nature and the negation of false views correspond to different questions with different concerns, these two negations must be clarified carefully, or, the understanding of Nāgārjuna's Emptiness is bound to involve confusion. One way to understand these differences is that Nāgārjuna is not merely a great thinker, but also a great practitioner and teacher. In his explication of the philosophy of Emptiness, he is not merely concerned about the meaning of the Truth of Emptiness; he is also concerned about how to realize it. The negation of Self Nature ("being devoid of Self Nature") reveals what he means by Emptiness. Yet Nāgārjuna also asserts that Emptiness should be realized in the relinquishing of false views to complement to the understanding of Emptiness in a practical and educational sense.

Although how the negation of false views is related to the negation of Self Nature is not explicitly delineated in the *Kārikā,* the close relationship between the two negations is not difficult to perceive. The false views undoubtedly include a view of Self Nature, in which Self Nature is conceptualized and substantiated. That is, Self Nature, which is essentially a mental fabrication, is taken as a concept having its own existence in the external and empirical world. The substantiation of Self Nature is likely to induce attachment to the empirical world, which will in turn cause defilements. Nāgārjuna's advice is that this false view—i.e., the substantiation of Self Nature—must be relinquished or negated. For him, Self Nature is mentally fabricated, devoid of any external existence whatsoever. This is the negation of Self Nature, which is what Emptiness denotes.

4. Emptiness itself is not to be adhered to

In response to the concept of Emptiness as the negation of Self Nature and as the negation of false views, one is apt to ask two questions. First, does Emptiness itself as the negation of Self Nature have any objective reference, or does it correspond to something in the substantive world? Second, in view of the negative tone of the understanding of Emptiness, one is also apt to see Emptiness from an annihilative angle and take it as an equivalent of nothingness. Is Emptiness really annihilative? These doubts arise from an inappropriate understanding of Emptiness, which should be refuted. The Mādhyamika School proposed the well-known thought that Emptiness itself is not to be adhered to. It is highly likely that this thought was aimed at dealing with these doubts. That Emptiness itself is not to be adhered to is clearly expressed in the *Kārikā:*

> The wise men (i.e., enlightened ones) have said that *śūnyatā* or the nature of thusness is the relinquishing of all false views. Yet it is said that those who adhere to the idea or concept of *śūnyatā* are incorrigible.[30]

The passage above mentions the false idea or concept, or false view of Emptiness *(śūnyatādṛṣṭi),* which is to be negated.

Piṅgala's commentary also speaks of the view of Emptiness in negative terms. He says that the Buddha teaches Emptiness in order to prevent people from developing the sixty-two various views and defilements such as ignorance, love, etc. Yet when one holds a view of Emptiness, one will not be subject to religious cultivation.[31] Piṅgala proposes the well-known expression, "Emptiness is to be emptied" *(k'ung i-fu k'ung).*[32] His advice, no doubt, is made in the context of the thought that Emptiness itself is not to be adhered to, meaning that the "false view of Emptiness" is not to be adhered to.

What precisely the false view of Emptiness denotes is not expounded by Nāgārjuna. It seems reasonable, however, to relate it to the distortion that may arise from the understanding of Emptiness as the negation of both Self Nature and false views. This distortion can be shown as follows. First, one is apt to see Emptiness as something that can initiate the act of negating other things; this might suggest that one substantiates and objectifies it. Emptiness eventually becomes a substantive object.[33] This understanding is false for Mādhyamikas. A substantive object is so only in a relative and individual sense. To take Emptiness as a substantive object will degrade it to the realm of relativity and individuality and deprive it, as the Truth, of the significance of absoluteness and wholeness.

Modern scholars warned against the distortion of Emptiness as a substantive object. For example, Tsung-san Mou says:

> "Emptiness" is a descriptive word, not a substantive word. It is spoken of in the context of describing the meaning of Dependent Origination. If we should assert that it is an entity, a concept or an idea, for example, it can only be an entity in the nominal sense and in the secondary order. It cannot be an entity originated from causes which would be of the primary order.[34]

The late Richard Robinson also pointed out that Emptiness is not a term in the primary system referring to the world, but a term in the descriptive system (meta-system) referring to the primary system, and that Emptiness has no status as an entity.[35] By "primary order" or "primary system" they refer to the substantive entities in this actual world. Both Mou and Robinson take Emptiness to be of a descriptive nature, without any independent substance of its own. That is, it is descriptive about something. For instance, Emptiness describes the empirical world as being devoid of Self Nature. There is, however, no substantive object or entity called "Emptiness" in the actual world. The view that takes Emptiness to be a substantive object in the actual world must be refuted.

Second, as hinted above, the negative tone in the understanding of Emptiness may induce one to view Emptiness in annihilative terms, i.e., as nothingness. This annihilative understanding of Emptiness is by all means false. The negation of Self Nature and false views should not be confused with nothingness in any way. Even in the Buddha's time, there were still Buddhist disciples who took an annihilative and nihilistic view of Emptiness.

The "false view of Emptiness" consequently signifies the fact that Emptiness can be falsely understood in various ways, particularly as a substantive object or as nothingness. A substantive object is an item in the actual world that is in possession of existence or being. Accordingly, to take Emptiness as a substantive object is not different from taking it as being. Nothingness defies Dependent Origination which governs the formation of the phenomenal world and is identical with Emptiness. To take Emptiness as nothingness will tend to miss its close connection with the phenomenal world. In an excellent article on the Middle Way and the view of Emptiness (Jp., *kūken*), Hajime Nakamura points out that the so-called "view of

Emptiness" is a distortion of the original meaning of Emptiness as non-being and non-nothing. This distortion reduces Emptiness to being *(bhāva)* and nothingness *(abhāva)*.[36] Nakamura tends to regard the view of Emptiness as being and nothingness as a false understanding of Emptiness, which is in fact in line with the analysis given above. His "view of Emptiness" is simply the "false view of Emptiness."

We believe that it is in the context of avoiding the false view of Emptiness that Nāgārjuna advises us not to adhere to Emptiness. In this respect, Nakamura also understands the expression "Emptiness is to be emptied" to be the refutation of the false view or distortion of Emptiness in which Emptiness is taken as either being or nothingness.[37]

It is a regret that Nāgārjuna did not elaborate on the false view of Emptiness in the *Kārikā.* Nevertheless, our understanding of this issue is justified by other sources, including Piṅgala's commentary. He comments on the verse quoted above, in which Nāgārjuna advises one not to adhere to the false view of Emptiness:

> A person whose guilt is heavy, whose greed and attachment are deep in the mind, and whose wisdom is obtuse, takes [false] views on Emptiness. On the one hand, he says that there is Emptiness [as a being]. On the other hand, he says that there is no Emptiness [i.e., Emptiness is nothingness]. [These views of] being and nothingness in turn initiate defilements.[38]

Candrakīrti, an authoritative commentator of the *Kārikā,* also speaks of the false view of Emptiness in terms of taking Emptiness as being or nothingness.[39]

5. Emptiness of Emptiness

The radical expression that Emptiness itself is not to be adhered to is called the "Emptiness of Emptiness" (Skt., *śūnyatā-śūnyatā;* Ch., *k'ung-k'ung*). This idea originally appeared in the Prajñāpāramitā literature and was fully expounded in the TCTL. In this idea, Emptiness is not merely that from which to be detached, but it is also to be "emptied" or relinquished. Emptiness denotes here the "false view of Emptiness" or the "Emptiness" that causes disaster. It is only when Emptiness causes disaster that it must be relinquished; before the need of relinquishing arises, Emptiness can be pragmatic and instrumental. The TCTL expounds the instrumental character of Emptiness, the idea of the Emptiness of Emptiness, in the following manner:

> Emptiness destroys all entities. There is only Emptiness tenable. Having destroyed all entities, Emptiness itself should also be relinquished. Hence the need of Emptiness of Emptiness. Moreover, Emptiness deals with all entities, whereas Emptiness of Emptiness deals with Emptiness alone. For instance, even though a strong person can beat all thieves, there is still somebody who can beat this strong person. The same is true with Emptiness of Emptiness. [That is, Emptiness can tackle all entities, and also Emptiness of Emptiness can tackle Emptiness.] In the example of taking medication, the medication can overcome the disease. After the disease is overcome, the medication should leave [i.e., be relinquished]. If it does not leave [i.e., if it is taken continuously], it will itself induce disease. We use Emptiness to cure the disease caused by various defilements. Being concerned that Emptiness may in turn cause disaster, we use Emptiness to relinquish Emptiness. This is called "Emptiness of Emptiness".[40]

In this delineation, it is shown that Emptiness and Emptiness of Emptiness deal with different subject matter. On the one hand, Emptiness deals with entities, or, to be more precise, entities understood falsely. How they are understood falsely is not elaborated. It is possible that they are taken as having Self Nature, the negation of which is denoted by Emptiness. The purpose of (the doctrine of) Emptiness is to lead people to a correct understanding of the entities; that is, that they are devoid of Self Nature. On the other hand, the Emptiness of Emptiness deals with Emptiness after the latter has completed its purpose and caused disaster. From the analogy of medication which shows that even medication can be harmful when treated improperly, it can be inferred that Emptiness can likewise be harmful when treated or understood improperly. What is to be emptied or relinquished is not plain Emptiness, but the Emptiness that causes disaster.

In the analogy of Emptiness to medication, Emptiness is taken as an effective measure to deal with entities, or more appropriately, to eradicate the attachment to or incorrect views of entities. This is done by releasing sentient beings from attributing Self Nature to entities. Emptiness, with its implication that entities are devoid of

Self Nature, can certainly rectify any supposition of Self Nature in entities. Indeed, this is the very aim of Emptiness. When this goal is attained, Emptiness will lose its reason to persist and should be set free. Emptiness is, in this sense, very much of a pragmatic and instrumental character. It persists not for its own sake, but for a pragmatic use. This is an interesting but important facet of Emptiness, which does not seem to attract much attention from modern scholars.

In certain circumstances, obviously, Emptiness may be treated improperly and cause disaster. The TCTL says elsewhere:

> The practitioner sees being as hindrance. So he goes on to eradicate being with Emptiness, but in so doing in turn values the latter. In clinging to Emptiness, one falls into [the realm of] annihilation. With this [disaster] in mind, one should employ Emptiness to eradicate being, but one should not cling to Emptiness either.[41]

"Being" in this passage does not denote plain being or phenomenal existence; rather, it denotes an incorrect understanding of being as having Self Nature. Emptiness, as the negation of Self Nature, can be employed to erase such an incorrect understanding. But this pragmatic and instrumental implication of Emptiness may be overemphasized, and Emptiness may be clung to. When this occurs, one will tend to employ Emptiness uncontrolledly and without limits. That is, one will blindly overthrow everything, without distinguishing between the correct and false, the pure and impure. This will unavoidably result in complete annihilation, which is vehemently refuted in Buddhism. It is this disaster that Emptiness may cause, necessitating both the warning that Emptiness itself is not to be adhered to and the need for the Emptiness of Emptiness.

6. Emptiness as the true state of entities as such

From the above discussions, we conclude that Emptiness is, for Nāgārjuna and his followers, the true state of entities as such, free from all human fabrications, which include the supposition of Self Nature and taking false views. These entities are what we face in our daily life and are causally originated. The doctrine of Emptiness basically reveals the true situation or state of entities: the lack of permanent Self Nature. This state is revealed in a negative manner, rather than in a positive one. That is, it does not convey what the entities are, but what the entities are not: namely, they are not in possession of Self Nature. Moreover, this state is purely descriptive, without any substantive or objective reference whatsoever. That is to say, there is absolutely no such thing called "being devoid of Self Nature" or "empty state" at all, whether it be a thing in the phenomenal sense, or a thing in the noumenal sense (a thing-in-itself).

This approach to Emptiness is clearly epistemological in character, with a practical and soteriological purpose behind it. In proposing this doctrine of Emptiness, the Mādhyamikas were concerned not merely with teaching people how to see the world, but also with teaching them how to act toward the world. When people understand that the world is in essence empty, devoid of Self Nature and the permanency they are so eager to seek, they will naturally cease to cling to anything and will control their thirst for worldly objects. Perversions and defilements can eventually be avoided. This freedom from clinging is, as the Mādhyamikas and Buddhists in general understand, crucial to enlightenment.

In relation to the practical and soteriological purpose of Emptiness, we should pay attention to two points. First, Emptiness is pragmatic in the sense that it helps people erase their attachment to and false understanding of entities, yet it has nothing to do with annihilation of entities. This is the positive significance of Emptiness. This significance, however, has its restrictions. That is, Emptiness is pragmatic insofar as there are attachments and false understandings. When the latter are erased, Emptiness will have no object to work upon and thus should not be made to persist any longer. Unconditional persistence of Emptiness will tend to direct one to annihilation and nihilism. To decide whether or not one should make Emptiness persist is, indeed, a matter of wisdom and experience.

Second, the understanding of Emptiness in terms of relinquishing false views shows Nāgārjuna's deep practical concern for Emptiness. The idea of the Emptiness of Emptiness can also be construed in this practical context, because the Emptiness to be refuted refers to the false view of Emptiness. Because the false view of Emptiness denotes a view that regards Emptiness as a substantive object or a view that sees Emptiness as nothingness, the aim of this idea is, to be sure, to prevent people from substantializing, objectifying or annihilating Emptiness. Paradoxically, this "Emptiness" of Emptiness can likewise be substantialized, objectified or annihilated by false views. If the Emptiness of Emptiness is treated in this way, it must again be emptied or negated. Thus, theoretically speaking, the negation of Emptiness can go on *ad infinitum,* and the practitioner has to remind himself constantly of the nature of Emptiness: it denotes the true state of entities. In addition, he must not abide in this nature of Emptiness by mistaking it for a substantive object or nothingness.

The nature of Emptiness as a state has been pointed out by scholars, but without much elaboration. Inada sees *śūnyatā* or Emptiness as the "the state of *śūnya.*"[42] Sprung translates *śūnyatā* as the "absence of being in things,"[43] in which "being" refers to Self Nature or a permanent element. Ruegg speaks of *śūnyatā* in terms of the true state of affairs.[44]

Our understanding of Emptiness as the true state of entities is reminiscent of a crucial question regarding Emptiness, namely, whether or not Emptiness refers to the Absolute. This has been a controversial problem among scholars for a long time. Our position is that Emptiness is revealed in the refutation of false views that originate from our attachment to relative concepts (being and nothingness, for example). In this manner, Emptiness transcends the realm of relativity and is absolute. Kalupahana also remarks:

> (Emptiness) helps the individual to attain freedom from views and upholding it as the absolute or ultimate truth without any reference to the "empty" would be the last thing either the Buddha or Nāgārjuna would advocate.[45]

We have spoken of Emptiness in terms of absoluteness and wholeness in section 2 above, but we must note that this understanding of Emptiness applies mainly in a practical and soteriological context. Its absolute sense should not be related to metaphysical substantiality or Substance, with which the Absolute is apt to be associated. As far as the present work is concerned, we do not sense a need to discuss the controversial problem of the relationship between Emptiness and the Absolute, much less work out a solution of it. The conclusion that Emptiness denotes the true state of entities will suffice for our purposes.

7. The Middle Way as a complement to Emptiness

The Middle Way is an important concept in the Buddhist system whose emphasis can be traced back to a very early period.[46] It also played a crucial role in formulating the Mādhyamika philosophy, as can be seen from the fact that this very name is used to identify the Mādhyamika School and its doctrine. In the corresponding Sanskrit term, *madhyamā pratipad, madhyamā* means middle, and *pratipad* or *prati-pad* means road or track. *Mādhyamika,* then, assumes the abstract meaning of "middle." In the *Kārikā,* however, Middle Way is mentioned only once. In order to denote the proper meaning of the Middle Way, we will first determine its relationship to Emptiness. Kumārajīva's translation of the verse in the CL that refers to the Middle Way reads:

> I declare that whatever is of Dependent Origination is Emptiness (nothingness); it is also a Provisional Name; it is also the meaning of the Middle Way.[47]

According to Chinese grammar, this verse should be seen as describing the relationship of Dependent Origination to Emptiness, to the Provisional Name and to the Middle Way, respectively. Dependent Origination is the subject throughout, whereas Emptiness, the Provisional Name and the Middle Way are equal predicates, the latter three assuming the same position toward the former. That is, the Middle Way and Emptiness are coordinates.

But the original verse is somewhat different in its grammatical structure. The Sanskrit runs:

> *yaḥ pratītyasamutpādaḥ śūnyatāṃ tāṃ pracakṣmahe, sā prajñaptirupādāya pratipatsaiva madhyamā.*[48]

In the former half verse, *yaḥ* corresponds to *tām,* the pattern being that of correlative and relative, and *tām* refers to *śūnyatām.* Therefore, the half verse means: "We declare that whatever is of Dependent Origination is Emptiness." This is the same as Kumārajīva's translation, with Dependent Origination as subject and Emptiness as predicate. The latter half verse is, however, quite different. Here, the subject is *sā,* which is feminine singular and thus refers to the *śūnyatā* of the former half, which is also feminine singular. And *upādāya* or *upā-dāya* is the pattern of "because. . . . therefore," expressing a reason. Hence we have the meaning of the latter half as:

> Because this Emptiness is a Provisional Name, therefore it [Emptiness] is indeed the Middle Way.

Here, the subject is Emptiness, and Provisional Name and Middle Way are predicates. We can see that the Sanskrit original has not placed these three concepts in parallel positions; rather, it stresses the meaning of Emptiness as the Middle Way because of its provisionality. That is, the Middle Way, with the indication that Emptiness itself is provisional but not ultimate, serves as a complement to a better understanding of Emptiness. The idea that Emptiness is provisional and not ultimate will be elaborated later. What we want to point out here is that the Middle Way in this passage is subordinate to Emptiness. It can be appropriately accounted for only in the context of the latter. Indeed, in the assertion that Emptiness is the Middle Way, the Middle Way is used as a predicate to describe the subject, Emptiness, and enhance our understanding of the latter. The complementary implication of the Middle Way with regard to Emptiness is beyond doubt.[49]

It is true that the Middle Way is identified with Emptiness in the verse, but the identification is made on the basis of the Middle Way as a complement that provides a more thorough understanding of Emptiness. Clarification of this point is important because we know by means of it that Nāgārjuna does not assertively take the Middle Way as the Truth independent of the Truth of Emptiness. Consequently, the endeavor to elevate the Middle Way to a level of a Truth higher than the Truth of Emptiness, as the T'ien-t'ai School does, cannot be justified from Nāgārjuna's standpoint.

8. The Middle Way in terms of transcendence of extremes

What does the Middle Way denote in the Mādhyamika context? This is a subtle question that needs careful study. As stated above, the *Kārikā* mentions this concept only once and gives no explication of it. Nevertheless, it is not impossible to detect the meaning of the Middle Way from the *Kārikā* and Piṅgala's commentary. From the above-quoted verse, we see that Emptiness is identified with the Middle Way because it is a Provisional Name; that is, because of its provisionality.[50] The meaning of the Middle Way has to be understood in the context that Emptiness is a Provisional Name. How can Emptiness and the Provisional Name introduce the emphasis of the

Middle Way and its identification with Emptiness? The assertion that Emptiness is a Provisional Name may lead one to speak of Emptiness in reserved terms; that is, as provisional and not ultimate. This reservation toward Emptiness may be related to the latter's restriction and the denial of its unconditioned persistence as described in the previous section. It may also refer to the descriptive character of Emptiness, as delineated by Mou (see the quotation in section 4 above), namely, a descriptive word revealing the state of entities, with their lack of Self Nature. With regard to the issue of the Middle Way, we wish to argue as follows:

a. The assertion that Emptiness is a Provisional Name entails a warning: Emptiness should not be adhered to as something ultimate. This assertion also implies that Emptiness should not be distorted in meaning, and it is possible to avoid adhering to Emptiness simply by understanding Emptiness properly.

b. Because the Middle Way must be understood in the context of the assertion that Emptiness is a Provisional Name, which is closely associated with the non-distortion of Emptiness, it follows that the meaning of the Middle Way cannot be found apart from the non-distortion of Emptiness.

c. Distortion of Emptiness indicates a false view of Emptiness, while non-distortion of Emptiness can be taken as a relinquishing of false views. As pointed out earlier, Nāgārjuna understands Emptiness in terms of the relinquishing of false views. It follows that Emptiness can be understood by means of clarifying the non-distortion of Emptiness itself.

d. From the above arguments, we can conclude that both the Middle Way and Emptiness can be understood by means of clarifying the non-distortion of Emptiness.

e. According to our previous study and Nakamura's suggestion, the distortion of Emptiness may be situated in the context of the so-called "false view of Emptiness," i.e., *śūnyatādṛṣṭi,* which denotes the false understanding of Emptiness as being or nothingness. In other words, the distortion of Emptiness may, more specifically, denote the distortion of Emptiness as being or nothingness, and the non-distortion of Emptiness may be taken as the transcendence of this distortion. In view of the fact that this distortion is based on the discrimination or duality between being and nothingness, the non-distortion of Emptiness manifestly consists in the transcendence of this duality.

f. It therefore can be inferred that both the Middle Way and Emptiness are, as far as their meanings are concerned, closely related to the transcendence of the duality of being and nothingness. This transcendence of being and nothingness is the basis on which the Middle Way and Emptiness are identified with each other.

Therefore, we may respond to our question raised in the beginning of this section and conclude that Nāgārjuna's Middle Way denotes the transcendence of being and nothingness. This understanding is supported by Piṅgala, who comments:

> When the various causes assemble and combine, the thing originates. This thing belongs to the various causes. Therefore it is devoid of Self Nature. In view of this, it is empty. Emptiness is also to be emptied. However, for the sake of educating sentient beings, it is taken as a Provisional Name to explicate [the nature of the things]. The transcendence of the two extremes of being and nothingness is called the "Middle Way."[51]

In this passage, the subject matter is Emptiness or the nature of entities. This nature is revealed in terms of causal origination or Dependent Origination and the lack of Self Nature. There are two important points. First, Piṅgala relates the assertion that Emptiness is a Provisional Name to the expression that even Emptiness is to be emptied, tending to explain the former through the latter. However, it should be noted that Piṅgala's comment was made on the Sanskrit text of the *Kārikā,* not on Kumārajīva's translation. Accordingly, the claim that Emptiness is to be emptied should correspond to the claim that Emptiness is a Provisional Name; not the case that whatever is of Dependent Origination (entities) is a Provisional Name, as in Kumārajīva's translation. Piṅgala has explicated Nāgārjuna's assertion that Emptiness is a Provisional Name in terms of the advice that Emptiness is to be emptied. As delineated above in section 4, the advice that Emptiness is to be emptied is made in the context of the thought that Emptiness itself is not to be adhered to; in this context, Emptiness refers to the false view of Emptiness, or the distortion of Emptiness. Accordingly, Piṅgala tends to take the assertion that Emptiness is a Provisional Name to entail a warning against any adherence to the distortion of Emptiness, and thus against any distortion of Emptiness as well. In doing so, he significantly justifies our association of the assertion that Emptiness is a Provisional Name with the non-distortion of Emptiness. Second, Piṅgala explicitly speaks of the Middle Way in terms of the transcendence of being and nothingness. This is exactly the position we reached in our arguments above.

But we must pay attention to a crucial point: Nāgārjuna identifies Emptiness and the Middle Way in the assertion that Emptiness is a Provisional Name, focusing on the provisionality of Emptiness. How one moves from the provisionality of Emptiness to the identification of Emptiness and the Middle Way is ignored by many scholars; and needs some elaboration. Even Piṅgala does not divulge any explicit hint. As shown in our arguments, we infer from the provisionality of Emptiness the implication of the non-distortion of Emptiness as being or nothingness, and consequently move to the further implication of the transcendence of being and nothingness. We take this transcendence of being and nothingness as the basis for the identification of Emptiness and the Middle Way.

We are convinced that this is the most appropriate way to deal with the issue of the Middle Way, if we wish to stick to the Sanskrit text of the *Kārikā* and account for the identification of Emptiness and the Middle Way in the context of the verse at hand. In supporting this position, it is important to note that Kumārajīva's translation of the verse is not only questionable in grammar, but also vague in meaning with regard to the issue of the Middle Way. It says that whatever is of Dependent Origination is the Middle Way and tends to identify Dependent Origination with the Middle Way. But in what sense are the entities of Dependent Origination the Middle Way? This question is not dealt with. There is no way in this perspective to figure out the meaning of the Middle Way at all.

In regard to Nāgārjuna's understanding of the Middle Way in terms of the transcendence of being and nothingness, it should be added that he has warned that both being and nothingness are devoid of independency; consequently he strongly advocates the need to transcend both of them. This can be seen from the following verses in the *Kārikā:*

> If existence does not come to be (i.e., does not establish itself), then certainly non-existence does not also. For, indeed, people speak of existence in its varying nature as non-existence.[52]

> Those who see (i.e., try to understand) the concepts of self-nature, extended nature, existence, or non-existence do not perceive the real truth in the Buddha's teaching.[53]

> According to the Instruction to Kātyāyana, the two views of the world in terms of being and non-being were criticized by the Buddha for similarly admitting the bifurcation of entities into existence and non-existence.[54]

The issue in these three verses is about being and nothingness, or existence and non-existence. The supposition of being and nothingness that represent the two extremes of existent nature and non-existent nature will, as seen by Nāgārjuna, bifurcate the world and entities, obstructing us from intimating the undifferentiated Truth. Specifically, the world and entities as such are formed on the basis of Dependent Origination. They are devoid of Self Nature and thus subject to change. This is the undifferentiated Truth of Emptiness. The world and entities are not being in the sense of possessing a permanent substantiality; neither are they nothingness, because they arise from causes. To ascribe the extremes of being and nothingness to them will be to completely miss their basis in Dependent Origination and to bifurcate the Truth of Emptiness into duality.

It is important to note that being and nothingness here merely symbolize two extremes. What Nāgārjuna vehemently rejects is, no doubt, all kinds of extremes, which he believes would bifurcate the undifferentiated Truth into duality. This justifies his rejection of the distinction made between Self Nature *(svabhāva)* and extended nature ("other nature", *parabhāva*), both of which tend to form a self-other duality and express two extremes. Although the term "Middle Way" is not specified in these verses, it is very likely that the issue of rejecting or transcending extremes refers to this concept. In other words, Nāgārjuna understands the Middle Way in terms of the transcendence of extremes.

With regard to this understanding of the Middle Way, Ruegg also states:

> (The Middle Way) falls neither into annihilationism by denying what originates in dependence, nor into eternalism by hypostatizing as real what are constructs and designations originating in dependence and, consequently, empty of own being.[55]

Apparently, both annihilationism and eternalism are the results of taking the world and entities, which are based on Dependent Origination, as nothingness and being, respectively. They are extreme views strongly refuted by Nāgārjuna and his followers.

This understanding of the Middle Way receives more definite and detailed expositions in the TCTL. First, the TCTL repeatedly stresses that the Middle Way is the detachment from the two extremes, and that it is revealed in the liberation from the two extremes.[56] Second, the TCTL specifically identifies these two extremes as being and nothingness.[57] Third, the TCTL also specifies other items than being and nothingness, such as pleasure and suffering, eternalism and annihilationism, commencement and noncommencement, identity and differentiation.[58] The second of these three points requires some further explanation. In identifying the two extremes as being and nothingness, the TCTL details the harm caused by attachment to being and nothingness:

> In such ways, sentient beings attach to the views of being and of nothingness. These two views are false and untrue, and can destroy the Middle Way. It is like one walking on a narrow road. On one side [of the road] is deep water; on the other, a large fire. Both sides can cause death. Both the attachment to being and the attachment to nothingness are faulty. Why? Because, if the various entities are determinately real, then there will be no major and subsidiary causes. . . . If, however, there are no entities that are real, then there will be no difference between evils and merits, bondage and liberation. Neither will there be any difference between various entities.[59]

The TCTL attempts to clarify two points. First, the supposition of the extremes of being and nothingness destroys the doctrine of the Middle Way, so the doctrine of the Middle Way must be established on the transcendence of these extremes. Second, such a supposition also contradicts the nature of the Dependent Origination of the entities. The arguments are that if the entities are taken as being—in the sense of having Self Nature—then the entities will originally be there, without undergoing any causal origination. On the contrary, if the entities are taken as nothingness—as completely unreal in the annihilative sense—then everything will be the same as nothingness, whether they be evils, or merits, or any other significant entities. In this case, causal origination cannot "originate" entities that are different from each other, and will then be functionless or meaningless.

In either case, the supposition of being and nothingness destroys Dependent Origination. This point exactly reveals the harm caused by ascription of the extremes of being and nothingness to the world and entities.

9. The Middle Way as a state complementing Emptiness

It is obvious that the Middle Way understood in the above manner refers to a state of detaching from or transcending extremes. Logically speaking, when a pair of extremes is negated, what is really negated is not merely the two extremes, but the whole realm pertaining to these extremes. In the case of the Middle Way, which is established by the negation of being and nothingness or other extremes, being and nothingness are relative in nature. What is negated is the whole realm of relativity. When relativity is transcended, the absolute significance of the Middle Way will be revealed. The Middle Way therefore refers to a state of absolute meaning, which is still spoken of (as with the term Emptiness) in a descriptive sense. The Middle Way is not a way as such; it does not have any substantive reference. Neither does it denote a concrete position, a position between two things or extremes, as does the Aristotelian mean. It denotes a total spiritual state that one must realize for a soteriological purpose.

Like Emptiness, the Middle Way also bears a deep practical implication. It is not merely an absolute state to be cognized, but also a method or practice through which such a state can be attained. This practical implication is mostly emphasized in the TCTL:

> The Buddhist disciples relinquish the two extremes and act in accordance with the Middle Way.[60]

> The two views of being and nothingness being relinquished, [one] employs the wisdom of non-conceptual play and acts according to the Middle Way. This is called "the wisdom eye."[61]

There are many occasions in which one is urged to act in accordance with the Middle Way,[62] or warned against falling into the extremes of being and nothingness.[63] In either case, the message is the same: one should do one's best to transcend all extremes and overcome the attachment to extremes.

The Middle Way as the state of transcending extremes reveals the nature of entities, as being originally free from all sorts of duality and dichotomy formed by extremes, being and nothingness in particular. This is the Truth of the entities. But does this Truth differ from the Truth of Emptiness? Can there be two Truths, namely, the Middle Way and Emptiness? Our response is negative; the authentic Truth is not relative, but absolute in nature. It is undifferentiated. The Middle Way cannot be different and separate from Emptiness.

As a matter of fact, the transcendence of extremes, which the Middle Way indicates, is embraced by Emptiness. This is seen through two perspectives. First, as delineated earlier, Emptiness is revealed in the non-distortion of Emptiness itself, which is the transcendence of being and nothingness. That is, Emptiness is revealed in the transcendence of being and nothingness, which are extremes. We may certainly say that Emptiness embraces the transcendence of extremes. Second, Nāgārjuna understands Emptiness in terms of the negation of false views, including, no doubt, the views of being and nothingness as extremes or the attachment to extremes. In this sense, Emptiness may imply the transcendence of extremes.

Accordingly, in the Middle Way, an important aspect of Emptiness—the transcendence of extremes—is reflected. Nāgārjuna obviously employs the Middle Way to emphasize this aspect of Emptiness, and it is in this sense that we assert that the Middle Way is a complement to Emptiness. As a state of transcending extremes, the Middle Way can be taken completely as the Truth. Still, it is not a Truth different and separate from Emptiness; it complements Emptiness by emphasizing a particular aspect of the latter among many others. This aspect is the transcendence of extremes.

This understanding of the Middle Way in terms of the transcendence of extremes is, incidentally, not confined to Nāgārjuna and his followers. It is commonly maintained in many Buddhist texts, such as the *Saṃyutta-nikāya,* the Prajñāpāramitā literature and the *Satyasiddhi-śāstra,* among others. Nakamura[64] has made many relevant quotations from these texts to reveal this point clearly. However, the relationship between the Middle Way and Emptiness is seldom discussed carefully in these sources. It is Nāgārjuna who brings the Middle Way into the context of Emptiness and proposes the complementary relationship of the former to the latter. This should be taken as a new element added to the traditional understanding of the Middle Way.

CHAPTER III

Chih-i on Mādhyamika

With some fundamental understanding of the Mādhyamika concepts of Emptiness and the Middle Way, we may now proceed to deal with our first basic question: How does Chih-i understand and criticize those Mādhyamika concepts? This question is closely related to Chih-i's theory of the classification of Buddhist doctrines, which is the backbone of his system of thought. In this theory we can see how Chih-i understands the different Buddhist doctrines and what standpoint he himself takes. This is particularly true in dealing with the question of Chih-i's interpretation of Emptiness and the Middle Way. Only after we have a clear idea about how he classifies the important Buddhist doctrines can we be in a better position to find out how he evaluates and accommodates the Mādhyamika.

1. Chih-i's classification of Buddhist doctrines

Among Chih-i's major writings—viz., those which reflect his mature thought—the descriptions of his classification of Buddhist doctrines are found in many places.[1] The SCI, in particular, gives an extremely detailed and systematic analysis of this theory.[2] Like most original Chinese thinkers, who initiated new ideas but were always reluctant to claim authorship under their own names, Chih-i let it be known that the theory of classification was not his own creation; he stated that its basic idea could be found in a number of Mahāyāna *sūtras* and *śāstras*.[3] As a matter of fact, there had been various theories with regard to classifying the Buddhist doctrines before Chih-i proposed his own.[4] Yet the comprehensiveness and clarity of his theory, and thus its supremacy over others, should not be neglected.[5] This theory reveals Chih-i's unique way of digesting or crystallizing the Buddhist doctrines and his view on what the perfect Buddhist doctrine should be.

Chih-i's classification of Buddhist doctrines has been amply studied by modern scholars (for example, Andō and Tamura in Japan and Hurvitz in the West).[6] However, as will be clearly explicated below, Buddha Nature (or more appropriately, Middle Way-Buddha Nature) is the key concept in Chih-i's system of thought, in which the classification of Buddhist doctrines is an important item. These scholars do not pay attention to this concept and so, in our opinion, fail to provide a precise understanding of Chih-i's theory of classification. To be specific, both Andō and Tamura make no mention of Buddha Nature, much less Middle Way-Buddha Nature. Hurvitz, in the main body of his work discussing Chih-i's classification, does not mention Buddha Nature either. He merely introduces the three aspects of Buddha Nature *(san-yin fo-hsing)* in a footnote in order to explain the feature that the cause is separate; this is one of the features that made Chih-i distinguish and designate the "Separate Teaching" (which we shall refer to as "Gradual Doctrine") *pieh-chiao.*[7] This footnote reflects Hurvitz's lack of awareness of the importance of Buddha Nature in Chih-i's classification. As for the recent works on T'ien-t'ai, Swanson and Nitta in particular, the former makes no mention of the Middle Way-Buddha Nature, while the latter does mention this concept a few times, without, however, laying any emphasis on it.

We are aware of the fact that among the important works of Chih-i used here, the FHHI, FHWC and MHCK were actually recorded by Kuan-ting, and the WMCLS was abridged by Chan-jan from the WMCWS. It is possible that Kuan-ting might have made some accretions with reference to the sources of other schools, the San-lun School led by Chi-tsang (A.D. 549–623) in particular. With regard to the explication of Buddha Nature or Middle Way-Buddha Nature, we find that the FHHI, FHWC and MHCK are, in the main, quite in line with the SCI, WMCHS, WMCLS and WMCWS, the commentaries on the *Vimalakīrti-nirdeśa-sūtra (Wei-mo ching)* written by Chih-i himself in his later days. We therefore do not think that there should be serious problems with Kuan-ting's possible accretions in the understanding of Chih-i's Buddha Nature or Middle Way-Buddha Nature. Further, the incidence of Buddha Nature or Middle Way-Buddha Nature is much greater in these commentaries than in the FHHI, FHWC and MHCK, manifesting a deeper concern with the Buddha Nature or Middle Way-Buddha Nature on Chih-i's part in his old age. The delineation of the Buddha Nature or Middle Way-Buddha Nature should also be taken as representing Chih-i's mature thought.

In view of our dissatisfaction with the understanding of Chih-i's theory of classification revealed by modern scholars, we will proceed to undertake an original study of this theory. Chih-i classifies the Buddhist doctrines into four types in accordance with the difference in contents that the Buddha preached. This classification is called *Hua-fa ssu-chiao,* in contrast to the *Hua-i ssu-chia,* which was also proposed by Chih-i to classify the four types of methods the Buddha was supposed to have undertaken in his preachings. These four types of doctrine are the Tripiṭaka Doctrine, the Common Doctrine, the Gradual Doctrine and the Perfect Doctrine.[8]

The leading issues that govern Chih-i's classification of the Buddhist doctrines are *shih-hsiang* ("the Truth") and the way to realize it. For Chih-i, the Truth explicated in both the Tripiṭaka Doctrine and the Common Doctrine is Emptiness, while the Truth explicated in both the Gradual Doctrine and the Perfect Doctrine is the Middle Way. With regard to the way to realize the Truth, Chih-i maintains that the Tripiṭaka Doctrine proposes to analyze, disintegrate and eliminate *dharmas* in order to enter into the state of Emptiness, while the Common Doctrine advocates that one should realize Emptiness in the nature of *dharmas,* without destroying anything whatsoever. On the other hand, the Gradual Doctrine teaches people to penetrate the Middle Way through a gradual process, while the Perfect Doctrine advises that one should realize the Middle Way instantaneously. The expressions to show these four different ways are: *hsi-fa ju-k'ung* (Tripiṭaka Doctrine), *t'i-fa ju-k'ung* (Common Doctrine), *tz'u-ti ju-chung* (Gradual Doctrine) and *yüan-tun ju-chung* (Perfect Doctrine).[9]

2. The Tripiṭaka Doctrine and the Common Doctrine

The Truth of the Tripiṭaka Doctrine and the Common Doctrine is termed a "partial Truth" *(p'ien-chen)* in contrast to the "Perfect Truth" *(yüan-chen)* of the Gradual Doctrine and the Perfect Doctrine.[10] This is because Chih-i regards the Emptiness of the Tripiṭaka Doctrine and the Common Doctrine as negative, static and transcendent, whereas the Middle Way of the Gradual Doctrine and the Perfect Doctrine is positive, dynamic and immanent. The point is that for Chih-i the Emptiness spoken of in this context is mere Emptiness *(tan-k'ung);*[11] the Middle Way, on the other hand, is identified with Buddha Nature, which is characterized by permanence, function and the ability to embrace all *dharmas* that express positive, dynamic and immanent dimensions.[12]

What, then is the difference between *hsi-fa* (to analyze and disintegrate *dharmas*) of the Tripiṭaka Doctrine, and *t'i-fa* (to embody *dharmas*) of the Common Doctrine? Chih-i's interpretation is that people who advocate the Tripiṭaka Doctrine tend to see *dharmas* as something real. They therefore analyze and even disintegrate *dharmas* in order to reach the point at which they find nothing left and realize that all *dharmas* are empty. On the contrary, people advocating the Common Doctrine understand that *dharmas* are dreamlike and empty by nature. These people consequently attain the Truth of Emptiness right in the nature of *dharmas,* without analyzing and destroying anything.[13]

In the midst of this comparison, Chih-i applauds the way of *t'i-fa* and denounces the way of *hsi-fa.* In his opinion, the Tripiṭaka Doctrine confuses the unreal with the real, the non-substantial with the substantial. In order to attain the Truth of Emptiness, *dharmas* would have to be disintegrated and eliminated. This way is described as inappropriate and "dull" (*cho,* literally, "awkward") by Chih-i. On the contrary, the Common Doctrine is right in understanding *dharmas* as essentially empty or non-substantial. Emptiness or non-substantiality can be attained in such a way as to keep *dharmas* as they are. We need not touch or disturb, much less eliminate, them. Chih-i considers this way as appropriate and "skillful" *(ch'iao).*[14]

It should be noted that *hsi* (to "disintegrate") in *hsi-fa* and *t'i* (to "embody") in *t'i-fa* are used as methodological terms. Chih-i in many places also employs the terms *hsi-men* and *t'i-men,* i.e., the "door of disintegration" and the "door of embodiment."[15] From his explanation that *men* (door) is what one "passes through,"[16] Chih-i emphasizes the term's methodological implications.

To penetrate deeper into the issue of Truth, it is necessary to introduce the idea of the Twofold Truth *(erh-ti),* which was very much on Chih-i's mind. In the Buddhist circle, it was generally accepted that the realm of entities or phenomena is causally conditioned and represents the worldly Truth; consequently, the absolute nature of Emptiness represents the transcendent Truth. With regard to the two Truths, Chih-i undoubtedly appreciated the maintenance of both, rather than sacrificing one in favor of the other, as is clearly shown in his severe criticism of the Tripiṭaka Doctrine, in which he states:

> When entities are present, there is no [attainment of the] transcendent; and when entities are eliminated [and the transcendent attained], there is no [recourse to the] conventional.[17]

He concludes that, in the Tripiṭaka Doctrine, the idea of the Twofold Truth cannot be established.[18] Chih-i's point is that, for the Tripiṭaka Doctrine, the transcendent *(chen)* Truth (Emptiness) and the conventional *(su)* or worldly Truth cannot stand together: Emptiness can only be attained by the elimination of all entities or the worldly realm. The conclusion is precisely the result of *hsi-fa ju-k'ung*.

On the contrary, in the Common Doctrine, phenomena and Emptiness do not contradict each other; consequently, the worldly Truth and the transcendent Truth can be established simultaneously. This is possible because, in this viewpoint, phenomena and entities do not hinder Emptiness. Rather, they are the very realm where Emptiness is to be realized. That is, Emptiness is the Emptiness of entities; it is attained relative to entities. Consequently, in order to attain Emptiness, entities would have to be maintained as they are, rather than being eliminated. Therefore, Chih-i's depiction of this characteristic of the Common Doctrine with regard to the relation of the worldly entities and Emptiness runs as follows:

> The transcendent [is realized] right in the conventional nature of entities.[19]

And:

> The transcendent [is realized] right in the embodiment of *dharmas*.[20]

Indeed, this depiction with regard to the realization of the transcendent or Emptiness in the Common Doctrine can be seen here and there in Chih-i's works. The word *t'i* ("embodiment") in *t'i-fa ju-k'ung* prevents the elimination of *dharmas* or entities.

3. The Gradual Doctrine and the Perfect Doctrine

For Chih-i, Emptiness as the Truth, whether in the Tripiṭaka Doctrine or the Common Doctrine, is negative. He refers to this Truth by the conventional term "partial Truth" or "one-sided Truth" *(p'ien-chen)*.[21] When Chih-i speaks of the Truth, he usually uses *chen* to refer to Emptiness, which he takes to be the Truth of the Tripiṭaka Doctrine and the Common Doctrine, and *chung* to refer to the Middle Way, which he regards as the Truth of the Gradual Doctrine and the Perfect Doctrine.[22] Emptiness and the Middle Way tend to be identified with each other in the *Kārikā;* at least, the Middle Way is taken to be the complement of Emptiness. They are, however, not at all the same for Chih-i. He thinks that Truth should be spoken of in such positive terms as No-emptiness *(pu-k'ung),* which is the Truth relative to the Gradual Doctrine and the Perfect Doctrine.[23] This No-emptiness is nothing but Buddha Nature,[24] which Chih-i identifies with the Middle Way.[25] In this context, he introduces the concept of Middle Way-Buddha Nature, which he also refers to as Buddha Nature-Middle Way. The point here is that Buddha Nature as the Truth is an extremely important concept that is the characteristic feature of the Gradual Doctrine and the Perfect Doctrine. This concept is, in fact, what distinguishes the Gradual Doctrine and the Perfect Doctrine from the Tripiṭaka Doctrine and the Common Doctrine: while the former relates to the Buddha Nature, the latter does not.[26] When Chih-i makes reference to the four Doctrines, he usually relates the Tripiṭaka Doctrine to the worldly *dharmas,* the Common Doctrine to the unreality of *dharmas,* and both the Gradual Doctrine and the Perfect Doctrine to the Buddha Nature. This understanding is revealed throughout his major works.

The Buddha Nature is proposed in contrast to Emptiness, which, as Chih-i sees it, obviously tends to be negative. He approaches this Buddha Nature in terms of permanency, dynamism and immanence. It is permanent because it is itself the spiritual Dharma Body (Skt., *dharmakāya;* Ch., *fa-shen*), which, unlike our physical bodies, is not subject to change. It is dynamic in the sense that it is capable of functioning. It is immanent because it by nature embraces all *dharmas.*[27] This approach to Buddha Nature is very important, in the sense that Chih-i identifies Buddha Nature with the Middle Way, which is the Truth and it follows that Truth is permanent, dynamic and immanent as well. Chih-i ascribes this Truth to the Gradual Doctrine and the Perfect Doctrine exclusively, a new conception of Truth that was a great contribution to the development of Buddhist thought in China.

In his voluminous work on the T'ien-t'ai doctrines, Andō discusses the Gradual Doctrine in terms of the Middle Way and takes the Middle Way to be the central principle of the Gradual Doctrine.

The Middle Way of the Gradual Doctrine, he claims, transcends both extremes of being and nothingness and is consequently different from either of them.[28] Andō does not mention the Buddha Nature at all. In the discussion of the Perfect Doctrine, he does not mention the Buddha Nature either, but refers to the principle of the Middle Way. He regards this Middle Way of the Perfect Doctrine as not detached from being and nothingness.[29] This approach to the Gradual Doctrine and the Perfect Doctrine in terms of the Middle Way is proper except that the understanding of the Middle Way is insufficient. The major point of Chih-i's conception of the Middle Way of both the Gradual Doctrine and the Perfect Doctrine lies in the identification of the Middle Way with Buddha Nature, which, as noted earlier, is permanent, dynamic and immanent. Therefore, the Middle Way as the Truth assumes permanence, dynamism and immanence. In our opinion, the Middle Way cannot be properly understood without reference to Buddha Nature. This novel conception of the Middle Way is, in fact, original and highly inspiring.

The Gradual Doctrine and the Perfect Doctrine share a view that regards the Middle Way as the permanent, dynamic and immanent Truth. They part company, however, with regard to the manner in which the Truth is realized. For the Gradual Doctrine the manner is gradual; and for the Perfect Doctrine, instantaneous or sudden. In the Gradual Doctrine, the term that expresses the gradual manner is *li-pieh,* or *tz'u-ti,* meaning "undergoing gradations." That is, ignorance is to be eradicated and the Truth attained by a step-by-step process from the lower position to the higher. The Gradual Doctrine even goes so far as to declare that one has to "undergo cultivation for *kalpas*" *(li-chieh hsiu-hsing),* an interminably long period of time, before the final goal can be attained.[30] It should be noted that the word *pieh* in *pieh-chiao,* i.e., "Gradual Doctrine," has two denotations according to Chih-i. The first is "different," in the sense that the Doctrine in question is different from the other three Doctrines. The second is "gradual," in the sense that this Doctrine advocates the gradual manner in which one attains the Truth.[31] Some scholars, Leon Hurvitz for instance, adopted the first denotation and translated the Doctrine as "Separate Doctrine."[32] In the present work, we emphasize the second denotation and translate the Doctrine as "Gradual Doctrine" because, in our opinion, the word "gradual" transmits the true characteristic of the Doctrine, whereas the word "separate" does not.

In the Perfect Doctrine, the term that expresses the sudden manner is *yüan-tun,* meaning "perfect and sudden." The term *pu tz'u-ti* is also used, meaning "non-gradual,"[33] to signify the fact that ignorance can be overcome and the Truth attained suddenly or instantaneously, without undergoing gradations. It should be added that *tz'u-ti* and *pu tz'u-ti* are also employed with methodological implications as evidenced by the use of the terms *tz'u-ti men* and *pu-tz'u-ti men,* or the "gradual door" and "non-gradual door," as seen in FHWC.[34] As pointed out in the previous section, *men* or "door" is what one "passes through."

Of the two Doctrines, as would be expected, Chih-i views the Perfect Doctrine as superior. He says that although both Doctrines teach No-emptiness, the gradualism of the Gradual Doctrine does not possess ultimacy; only the Perfect Doctrine realizes ultimate reality without the slightest reservation.[35]

4. General Observations

Chih-i's classification of the Buddhist doctrines is comprehensive, clearcut and systematic. The following points deserve our special attention. The correct understanding of Truth and thus the attainment of enlightenment were the major concerns of all Buddhist schools. Among the four types of doctrine, the difference between the former two (the Tripiṭaka Doctrine and the Common Doctrine) and the latter two (the Gradual Doctrine and the Perfect Doctrine) is crucial: namely, they differ in terms of the Truth conceived in static and transcendent sense, and the Truth conceived in dynamic and immanent sense.

Second, the difference between the former two types of doctrine and between the latter two is equally methodological. That is, the Tripiṭaka Doctrine's disintegration of *dharmas* and the Common Doctrine's embodying of *dharmas* are both concerned with the way in which the Truth is to be realized. The same can also be said about the gradualism of the Gradual Doctrine and the suddenness of the Perfect Doctrine.

Third, logically speaking, the conceptualization of the Truth precedes the way to realize it. Chih-i's scheme of the four types of doctrine is articulated in such a way that they are placed on two different levels, rather than on parallel positions. The primary level is concerned with the nature of Truth itself, while the secondary level is concerned with the method of practice. The method of practice is closely related to or dependent on the conception of the Truth.

Finally, Chih-i always enumerates the four types of doctrine in an ascending order: from the Tripiṭaka Doctrine to the Common Doctrine, then to the Gradual Doctrine, and finally to the Perfect Doctrine. This hierarchy has axiological implications; that is, the elevation from the Tripiṭaka Doctrine to the Perfect Doctrine, *via* the Common and Gradual Doctrines, should be understood in valuational and soteriological terms. This is evidenced by Chih-i's concepts of *ch'uan,* which means "expedient" or "makeshift," and *shih,* which means "ultimate." He sees what is *ch'uan* as being for merely temporary purposes and assigns what is *shih* to finality.[36] With the contrast of these two concepts made, Chih-i classifies the Perfect Doctrine as ultimate and relegates the other Doctrines to the realm of expediency.[37] In other words, the previous three Doctrines have instrumental values that lead to the final and ultimate Perfect Doctrine. Thus, in light of the Perfect Doctrine, Chih-i maintains the positive significance of the previous three Doctrines, rather than downplaying them. Consequently, all Buddhist doctrines, no matter how different they seem to be from each other, are integrated under the Perfect Doctrine. This classification, indeed, deserves much appreciation from the viewpoint of Buddhist Dharma as a totality.

5. Mādhyamika as Common Doctrine

In order to answer our first basic question concerning Chih-i's understanding and criticism of Mādhyamika's Emptiness and the Middle Way, we must first examine how Chih-i understands the Mādhyamika in the context of his classification of Buddhist doctrines. Our concern here will focus on the *Kārikā* and the TCTL, the major texts of the Mādhyamika. Specifically, we will examine the position of these two texts in Chih-i's classification of Buddhist doctrines.

This concern is logically preceded by another question: do the major Mādhyamika texts have a place in Chih-i's classification? The answer is yes. Chih-i states that the four types of doctrine were initiated by the Buddha to accommodate all *sūtras,* and furthermore, all *śāstras* are commentaries to the *sūtras*. Therefore, no scripture can exceed the realm of the four types of doctrine.[38] There is no reason to believe that the major Mādhyamika texts, which were regarded as being so important to the Buddhist tradition, should be excluded from this classification.

Unfortunately, Chih-i never explicitly classifies the *Kārikā* and TCTL in the scheme of the four Doctrines, although he does identify the *Prajñāpāramitā-sūtra* and *Fa-hua ching* with the Common Doctrine and the Perfect Doctrine respectively. Though the classification theory is extremely important in formulating Chih-i's whole philosophical system, he is not much concerned about the direct correlation of the four types of doctrine relative to particular *sūtras* and *śāstras*. In some places, however, Chih-i discusses the four Doctrines in conjunction with many important Buddhist texts; in these contexts, we can judge vaguely which text belongs to which Doctrine. But the position of the *Kārikā* and TCTL is not clear.[39] Nevertheless, from the doctrinal point of view, we can reasonably be sure that the *Kārikā* and TCTL belong to the Common Doctrine. Hurvitz also suggests that the Common Doctrine (he uses the term "pervasive teaching") may be virtually identified with the Mādhyamika philosophic system.[40] Nevertheless, he does not elaborate this suggestion. Our ascription of the *Kārikā* and TCTL to the Common Doctrine can be argued as follows:

First, the fundamental concept of the *Kārikā* is Emptiness, the nature of Truth. As pointed out previously, this Truth indicates the nature of causal origination of entities and is realizable directly in these entities. This conception of the Truth entails a positive thought in the realization of the Truth by which entities of the nature of origination and extinction can and should be maintained as they are, rather than being eliminated entirely. This thought, undoubtedly, corresponds mostly to the Common Doctrine, which is characterized by the assertion of *t'i-fa ju-k'ung* (i.e., the Truth of Emptiness is to be attained in the context of embodying the entities or *dharmas*). This manner of thinking with regard to the realization of the Truth has nothing in common with the Tripiṭaka Doctrine, which advocates the disintegration and elimination of *dharmas*.

It is not easy to relate the *Kārikā* to the Gradual Doctrine and the Perfect Doctrine, especially with regard to the issue of Truth. The difficulty is that the *Kārikā* speaks of the Truth in terms of Emptiness, a state revealed in the negation of both Self Nature and false views; the Gradual Doctrine and the Perfect Doctrine speak of the Truth in terms of Buddha Nature, which possesses positive contents and dynamic functions. This concept will be explicated in the next chapter; here it can be mentioned that, for Chih-i, Emptiness is very different from Buddha Nature, which is comparable to No-emptiness. The implications of Buddha Nature contain those of Emptiness and to a great extent exceed them.

Second, the doctrine of the Four Noble Truths (Skt., *catuḥ-satya;* Ch., *ssu-ti*) is always mentioned in Chih-i's major works. What attracts our attention is that he expounds this doctrine in the context of his classification theory. That is, he classifies the methods to realize the Four Noble Truths into four types and matches them with the four Doctrines, respectively. According to Chih-i, the realization of the Four Noble Truths employed in the Common Doctrine is by No-origination, or *wu-sheng.*[41] He understands the meaning of No-origination as follows:

> If *dharmas* have origination, they will have extinction. As *dharmas* essentially do not originate, they will not extinguish.[42]

Apparently, Chih-i is speaking of No-origination in the context of the Truth; this refers to the ultimate nature of *dharmas,* which transcends all extremes, including origination and extinction. No-origination then transcends origination as an extreme view, which is exactly what Nāgārjuna's Middle Way implies. Nāgārjuna himself seems to ascribe special significance to the transcendence of origination and extinction, beginning his *Kārikā* with a verse on the Eight Negations *(pa-pu),* which includes the negation of origination and extinction.[43] In addition, he immediately argues for the concept of No-origination by using an important logical method, the negative of the Four Alternatives.[44]

The concept of No-origination also entails the following message of transcendence: as *dharmas* essentially do not originate and extinguish themselves, there is no need to eliminate them in order to attain the Truth. Chih-i also points out in his FHHI that the nature of No-origination with regard to the attainment of the Truth is that Truth is realizable right in the events, but not after their elimination.[45] This nature of No-origination closely conforms to the *Kārikā*'s conception of Emptiness, which advises (as in section 1 of the previous Chapter) that Nāgārjuna's Emptiness is the Emptiness of the phenomenal world, not Emptiness spoken of in an isolated sense. Consequently, the realization of Emptiness occurs in the phenomena or events, not apart from them.

We see, therefore, that Chih-i explicates the Common Doctrine's manner of realizing the Truth in terms of No-origination, which is also a crucial concept in the *Kārikā*. Chih-i himself is also clearly aware of the extreme importance of this concept in the *Kārikā*, as he asserts,

> Every chapter in the *Chung-lun* has its own goal. Yet all of them converge in the concept of No-origination.[46]

Chih-i summarizes the twenty-seven chapters of the *Kārikā* in terms of their converging *(hui)* in No-origination, indicating that all chapters in the *Kārikā* are expressive of No-origination. It is clear that the family resemblance between the Common Doctrine and the *Kārikā* cannot be denied. Not only are we able to conclude that the *Kārikā* pertains to the Common Doctrine, but also that the *Kārikā* itself is an important text expressive of the Common Doctrine.

Third, the affiliation of the Mādhyamika with the Common Doctrine can be justified by reference to Prajñāpāramitā thought. Chih-i clearly states in his SCI that the various *Prajñāpāramitā-sūtras* pertain to the Common Doctrine.[47] On the other hand, there is an extremely close doctrinal relationship between Nāgārjuna and the Prajñāpāramitā literature.[48] With regard to this relationship, Chih-i himself also states as follows:

> [Nāgārjuna] destroys all closures and clingings with the unattainable Emptiness and advocates the non-substantiality of all *dharmas*. This is called conformity to the *prajñāpāramitā*.[49]

This passage indicates a recognition of doctrinal intimacy between Nāgārjuna and Prajñāpāramitā literature. We will, of course, not forget the fact that Chih-i is well aware that the TCTL is an important commentary to a great *Prajñāpāramitā-sūtra*. It therefore seems beyond controversy that the Mādhyamika, which is closely related to Prajñāpāramitā thought, which is clearly the Common Doctrine for Chih-i, is to be seen as Common Doctrine as well.

In examining the above arguments, we are confident that Mādhyamika is, in Chih-i's view, the Common Doctrine. Accordingly his criticism of the Common Doctrine should be regarded as applicable to Mādhyamika. Chih-i is highly critical of the Common Doctrine, as can be seen throughout his major works. This criticism comes from the standpoint of the Perfect Doctrine, reminding us of Chih-i's dissatisfaction with the *Kārikā* in light of the *Fa-hua ching,* which he ascribes to the Perfect Doctrine. In his FHHI, a commentary on the *Fa-hua ching,* Chih-i states twice that the *Kārikā* is not comparable to the *Fa-hua ching.*[50] He also states that Nāgārjuna in the TCTL praises the profoundity of the *Fa-hua ching.*[51] These statements indicate Chih-i's parting of company with the Mādhyamika, asserting at least his preference for the Perfect Doctrine over the Mādhyamika.

Yet on most occasions when Chih-i criticizes the Common Doctrine, he seldom makes reference to the Mādhyamika. This does not mean that he does not see Mādhyamika as the Common Doctrine. We may rather infer that Chih-i is reluctant to explicitly criticize Mādhyamika because of Nāgārjuna's supreme position in the T'ien-t'ai tradition. Nevertheless, his underlying dissatisfaction with the *Kārikā,* as expressed in his criticism of the Common Doctrine, cannot be denied.

6. Emptiness in its relationship to Dependent Origination

With the understanding that the Mādhyamika belongs to the Common Doctrine, we come to a discussion of how the Mādhyamika Emptiness is viewed by Chih-i. As stated before, Chih-i speaks of the Common Doctrine's Emptiness in terms of *t'i-fa;* this means that Emptiness is to be realized in the context of embodying *dharmas*. The nature of *t'i-fa* should also be applicable to the Mādhyamika Emptiness. Chih-i himself clearly specifies the Mādhyamika Emptiness only a few times in his major works. In one of these references, he regards the first half of the famous verse in the *Kārikā*—in which the concepts of Dependent Origination, Emptiness, Provisional Name and Middle Way are introduced—as expounding the Common Doctrine.[52] This part of the verse reads,

> I declare that whatever is of Dependent Origination is Emptiness.[53]

This passage is expressive of the identification of Dependent Origination with Emptiness, appearing to speak of Emptiness in the context of Dependent Origination. That is, Emptiness is the negation of Self Nature, the falsely ascribed nature of *dharmas* that are causally originated. The presumption is that Emptiness is to be properly understood in light of its relationship to Dependent Origination.

Second, Chih-i praises Nāgārjuna with regard to the treatment or employment of Emptiness:

> [Nāgārjuna] destroys all closures and clingings with the unattainable Emptiness. . . . After purifying various *dharmas,* he specifies Emptiness to explicate the *dharmas* and concludes [the explication] with the aspects demonstrated by the Four Alternatives.[54]

In Chih-i's view, Nāgārjuna teaches the doctrine of Emptiness to rid people of false understanding of and clinging to *dharmas.* "Unattainable Emptiness" *(pu-k'o-te k'ung)* by no means signifies that Emptiness cannot be attained or realized. Rather, it signifies that Emptiness cannot be grasped and attached to as an object. This is reminiscent of the thought of Emptiness of Emptiness and the thought that Emptiness is not to be adhered to, as discussed in the previous chapter. The assertion that Nāgārjuna destroys all closures and clingings with unattainable Emptiness clearly shows that Chih-i is well aware of the pragmatic and instrumental character of Emptiness, which is demonstrated in the TCTL and explained in detail in our previous chapter, section 5. This character indicates that Emptiness can be taken as an effective measure to eradicate the clinging to, or incorrect view of, *dharmas.* Chih-i believes Nāgārjuna to be the author of the TCTL and highly appreciates this character of Emptiness.

The statement that Nāgārjuna specifies Emptiness to explicate the *dharmas (tien-k'ung shuo-fa)* should particularly attract our attention. It entails the message that *dharmas* appear as *dharmas* on the basis of Emptiness. That is, it is due to the nature of being devoid of Self Nature that *dharmas* can remain causally originated and by that means assume the character of Dependent Origination. In brief, this is to speak of the *dharmas* of Dependent Origination in terms of Emptiness and is, in fact, comparable to an important verse in the *Kārikā:*

> Whatever is in correspondence with *śūnyatā,* all is in correspondence (i.e., possible). Again, whatever is not in correspondence with *śūnyatā,* all is not in correspondence.[55]

Inada notes after his translation of this passage that the meaning conveyed is that *śūnyatā* is the basis of all existence, and that without *śūnyatā* nothing is possible.[56] All existence (Skt., *sarvam;* Ch., *i-ch'ieh fa*) denotes, of course, the entities or *dharmas* that are causally originated. This verse has also been frequently quoted by Chih-i in his works.

From the above two occasions, we see that Emptiness and Dependent Origination are mutually dependent on each other. This is one of the important points in understanding the identification of Dependent Origination and Emptiness. Chih-i seems to be happy with Nāgārjuna's Emptiness as related to Dependent Origination, in that he does not isolate the Truth of Emptiness from the causally originated *dharmas*. This approach to Emptiness closely conforms to the Common Doctrine's nature of *t'i-fa,* whereby *dharmas* are perceived together with the realization of Emptiness.

7. Emptiness is not No-emptiness

At the same time that Chih-i affirms the pragmatic use of Emptiness, he is critical of the Emptiness taught in the Common Doctrine. In FHHI, he comments on the Common Doctrine:

> The wise sees Emptiness. He should also see No-emptinesss. How can he steadfastly abide in Emptiness?[57]

On one occasion, Chih-i criticizes the Prajñāpāramitā as the teaching of no-characteristic *(wu-hsiang chiao),* asserting:

> The teaching of no-characteristic expounds Emptiness and eradicates characteristics. It still belongs to [the realm of] impermanence as it fails to expound the permanence of Buddha Nature.[58]

This is actually a criticism directed at the Common Doctrine, to which the Prajñāpāramitā belongs. As pointed out earlier, Chih-i's criticism of the Emptiness of the Common Doctrine should also be applicable to that of the Mādhyamika. What then is No-emptiness? It is, for Chih-i, nothing but Buddha Nature.[59] Consequently, Chih-i's criticism of the Emptiness of the Common Doctrine or the Mādhyamika is essentially that it refers to mere Emptiness, not No-emptiness and not Buddha Nature. As far as the literal meaning is concerned, Emptiness is of course not No-emptiness, but Chih-i is not concerned about this point. Rather, he believes that the Truth, no matter what name it goes by, should not only include what Emptiness entails, but also what No-emptiness or Buddha Nature involves.[60]

Emptiness is negative in nature. No-emptiness should signify a positive implication, but unfortunately, Chih-i does not explicitly elaborate upon this idea. Nevertheless, it is possible to detect what he ascribes to No-emptiness in his explanation of the Twofold Truth teaching based on his classification of the Buddhist doctrines. Specifically, he divides the Twofold Truth teaching into seven types. Four of them are from the viewpoints of the Tripiṭaka Doctrine, the Common Doctrine, the Gradual Doctrine and the Perfect Doctrine, respectively. The rest of them are from the viewpoints of "the Gradual directing the Common" *(pieh chieh t'ung),* "the Perfect directing the Common" *(yüan chieh t'ung)* and "the Perfect directing the Gradual" *(yüan chieh pieh). Chieh* is *chieh-yin,* meaning to direct one from a lower spiritual stage to a higher one. The major purpose of this division of the Twofold Truth is to show the interrelationship among the four Doctrines.[61]

In mentioning the three types of Twofold Truth teaching from the viewpoints of the Common Doctrine, "the Gradual directing the Common" and "the Perfect directing the Common," Chih-i proposes three kinds of No-emptiness:

> Eradicating the clinging to Emptiness, we therefore speak of No-emptiness. When the clinging to Emptiness is eradicated, one may merely see Emptiness, without seeing No-emptiness. Those of sharp faculties say that No-emptiness is a wondrous existence, and so teach No-emptiness. Those of sharpest faculties, upon hearing somebody speak of No-emptiness, say that it is the *tathāgatagarbha,* and that all *dharmas* move toward the *tathāgatagarbha.*[62]

Here, the No-emptiness resulting from the eradication of the clinging to Emptiness reminds us of the Mādhyamika thought of the Emptiness of Emptiness.[63] This No-emptiness is the No-emptiness of the Mādhyamika, which Chih-i does not view as the authentic No-emptiness because it merely emphasizes the negative side, namely, its eradicating character. What Chih-i is in favor of is the other two kinds of No-emptiness: that which is a wondrous existence, and that which is the *tathāgatagarbha,* which all *dharmas* move toward. It is obvious that these latter two are the No-emptiness of the Gradual Doctrine and the Perfect Doctrine, respectively. To be specific, Chih-i relates the wondrous existence to practitioners with sharp faculties, who assume, in this context, the viewpoint of "the Gradual directing the Common." From this viewpoint, the Gradual Doctrine dominates the Common Doctrine. It is therefore obvious that the wondrous existence is ascribed to the Gradual Doctrine. Similarly, Chih-i relates the *tathāgatagarbha,* which all *dharmas* move toward, to practitioners with the sharpest faculties, who assume the viewpoint of "the Perfect directing the Common." From this viewpoint, the Perfect Doctrine dominates the Common Doctrine. It is therefore obvious that the *tathāgatagarbha* is ascribed to the Perfect Doctrine. Mou, referring to the above quotation, also states that the first No-emptiness pertains to the Common Doctrine, the second to the Gradual Doctrine, and the third to the Perfect Doctrine.[64]

We now see that Chih-i speaks of No-emptiness in terms of *miao-yu,* or "wondrous existence," and *i-ch'ieh-fa ch'ü ju-lai-tsang,* or "all *dharmas* moving toward the *tathāgatagarbha.*" What then is *miao-yu?* Chih-i does not define it clearly in his major works. According to Yogācāra and Tathāgatagarbha thought, this concept refers to the realm of beings or *dharmas* which are viewed as empty in nature, without any clinging or attachment. Consequently, the emphasis of *miao-yu* would imply an affirmative but non-attaching attitude toward the *dharmas* in the world.[65] As for *i-ch'ieh-fa ch'ü ju-lai-tsang,* Chih-i relates it to the embracing of all Buddhist *dharmas (chü i-ch'ieh fo-fa).*[66] That is, all Buddhist *dharmas* move toward the *tathāgatagarbha.* Consequently, all Buddhist *dharmas* are embraced in the *tathāgatagarbha,* which is what makes Buddha a reality and is thus called the Buddha Nature. It is apparent that both *miao-yu* and *i-ch'ieh-fa* refer to the realm of experience, the realm of phenomena, bearing heavy worldly implications. It is in this context of bearing heavy worldly implications that Chih-i speaks of No-emptiness. It is also in this context that we consider that No-emptiness carries a positive tone.

So far it is clear that Chih-i is critical of the Mādhyamika concept of Emptiness as the Truth because it is negative in character and lacks worldly connection. That is, it fails to refer to the wondrous existence and does not embrace all *dharmas.* For Chih-i, wondrous existence and embracing *dharmas* are attributes ascribable to the Truth *(shih-hsiang).*

Does this criticism do justice to the Mādhyamika? In response, we make the following points:

1. It seems too much to assert that the Mādhyamika Emptiness lacks worldly connection. The intimate relationship between Emptiness and Dependent Origination, as held by Nāgārjuna, gives evidence against Chih-i's position. Rather, we should assert that Nāgārjuna strongly defends the importance of worldly connection to the realization of Truth. He argues in the *Kārikā* that the supreme Truth, Emptiness, should be attained in common practices performed in the phenomenal world. Apart from these common practices, no Truth is realizable. This point will be discussed in full detail in Chapter VII below.

2. The concept of "wondrous existence" may also be ascribed to the Mādhyamika. In various places in the TCTL, the attitude of "non-clinging and non-forsaking" *(pu-cho pu-she)* expressed toward the phenomenal world is very much present. This attitude is one of the major components of Prajñāpāramitā thought, of which the TCTL is a good example and explication. This attitude is quite conformable to the concept of a "wondrous existence," which teaches of the strength in non-clinging and non-attachment to entities.

3. From the viewpoint of the Perfect Doctrine, which speaks of the Truth in terms of Buddha Nature, Chih-i's criticism certainly makes sense; for in this context, all worldly entities are embraced *(chü)* and are therefore included in the Truth itself, rather than in a realm in which the Truth is to be realized, as seen in the *t'i-fa* thinking. Speaking from an ultimate viewpoint, the worldly entities in the Perfect Doctrine are inseparable from the Truth; they are not inseparable in the Common Doctrine or the Mādhyamika. The concept of "embrace" *(chü)* in Chih-i's system of thought implies "having as a part of itself," and thus "being inseparable from." To distinguish the Perfect Doctrine and Mādhyamika in terms of worldly connection, we can at least say that the former's worldly connection is closer and much more rigid than that of the latter.

4. The distinction between separability and inseparability is based on whether or not the Buddha Nature can be established as the Truth *(shih-hsiang)*. The concept of "embrace" discussed above is spoken of merely in the context of the Buddha Nature. As we will see in the next chapter, the Buddha Nature as the Truth is one of the most important concepts in Chih-i's system of thought. It is, however, ignored in the major Mādhyamika texts and, for instance, is not mentioned in the *Kārikā* at all.[67]

8. The Middle Way revealed in the transcendence of extremes

We now come to a discussion of Chih-i's understanding and criticism of the Middle Way as presented in the Mādhyamika. We wish, first of all, to note that he has in mind two kinds of Middle Way. One is the Middle Way revealed in the transcendence of extremes; the other is the Middle Way spoken of in terms of Buddha Nature. Chih-i is quite aware of the difference, as he states:

> That which transcends annihilation and eternalism is called the Middle Way. It is, however, not the Buddha Nature-Middle Way.[68]

That is, he makes a sharp distinction between the Middle Way in reference to the transcendence of extremes and the Middle Way as manifested in the Buddha Nature. There is a regretful tone in what he says about the Middle Way in reference to the transcendence of extremes.

The concept of Middle Way revealed in the transcendence of extremes appears quite often in Chih-i's works,[69] and the extremes to be transcended are akin to those specified in the Mādhyamika texts. For example, when Chih-i raises the issue of negation of being and nothingness, origination and extinction—terms Nāgārjuna often enumerates as extremes—he states,

> If being is not determinate, it is non-being. If nothing is not determinate, it is non-nothing. What is called non-being is non-origination. What is called non-nothing is non-extinction. That which transcends the level of being and nothingness is called the Middle Way. This is identical with the *Chung-lun*.[70]

This quotation shows a conception of the Middle Way that is identical with that mentioned in the *Kārikā*. To the extent of transcending extremes, Chih-i's understanding of the Middle Way indeed conforms to that of the Mādhyamika, and he is well aware of the fact that it is equivalent to the Mādhyamika way of understanding the Middle Way.

In the previous chapter, it was pointed out that Nāgārjuna's Middle Way is a complement to his Emptiness, and that he does not assert that the Middle Way as the Truth is independent of the Truth of Emptiness. This conception of the Middle Way is affirmed by Chih-i in his discussion of the two Truths, i.e., *paramārtha-satya (chen-ti)* and *lokasaṃvṛti-satya (su-ti),* the "absolute Truth" and the "relative Truth." As explicated in the Common Doctrine, he says that Emptiness and the Middle Way are combined in the absolute Truth,[71] that the Middle Way itself is incorporated into the absolute Truth.[72] In the context of the Common Doctrine, the absolute Truth is referred to as Emptiness, while the relative Truth is referred to as provisionality. It seems clear that Chih-i does not consider the Middle Way to be an independent Truth distinguished from Emptiness, but sees it rather as a subordinate conception and thus a complement to Emptiness. In view of this, we may say that Chih-i has a proper understanding of the complementary character of the Mādhyamika Middle Way as pointed out in the previous chapter.

We have also mentioned the Mādhyamika thought of the Emptiness of Emptiness in the previous chapter. Corresponding to this thought is Chih-i's discussion of the Emptiness of the Middle Way *(chung-tao k'ung).* The purpose of this Emptiness of the Middle Way is exactly the same as that of the Emptiness of Emptiness. That is, the Middle Way, being identical to Emptiness, is not to be adhered to; otherwise, it becomes a hindrance.[73] As pointed out earlier,[74] Chih-i is well aware of the Mādhyamika thought of the Emptiness of Emptiness as the Truth; it is only natural that he now speaks of the Emptiness of the Middle Way as the complement of the Truth itself. This Emptiness of the Middle Way in all respects conforms to the Mādhayamika spirit of advising against clinging to anything, including the Truth itself.

There is no doubt that Chih-i is well-versed in the Mādhyamika conception of the Middle Way as the transcendence of extremes. He also appreciates its import, but does not accept it without reservation. His criticism is shown in the following section.

9. The Middle Way is devoid of functions and does not embrace *dharmas*

We have mentioned that Chih-i has in mind two conceptions of the Middle Way, one revealed in the transcendence of extremes and the other as a manifestation of the Buddha Nature. He constantly criticizes the former from the standpoint of the latter. It is interesting to note that, as the former is expounded in the Mādhyamika, which

Chih-i regards as Common Doctrine, he on many occasions goes so far as to accuse the Common Doctrine of not understanding the Middle Way at all.[75] What he means by the Middle Way is, of course, identical to the Buddha Nature. He asserts in various places in his works that the Middle Way is conceived in this way only in the Gradual Doctrine and the Perfect Doctrine.

Chih-i's criticism of the Middle Way explicated in the Common Doctrine is that it is devoid of functions and does not embrace *dharmas.* This criticism is made in Chih-i's division of the Threefold Truth teaching into five types. In section 7 above it was mentioned that Chih-i divides the Twofold Truth teaching into seven types. This Twofold Truth refers to the absolute Truth, or *chen-ti,* and the relative Truth, or *su-ti.* The absolute Truth in turn refers to Emptiness, and the relative Truth to provisionality. These seven types of Twofold Truth will become seven types of Threefold Truth, if the Truth of the Middle Way is added. Chih-i thinks, however, that the Tripiṭaka Doctrine and the Common Doctrine, to which the first two types of the Twofold Truth teaching belong, respectively, do not fully understand the Middle Way. This Middle Way is spoken of in terms of the Buddha Nature, which, for Chih-i, is not explicated in these two Doctrines. Therefore, Chih-i speaks of only five types of the Threefold Truth teaching: "the Gradual entering the Common" *(pieh ju t'ung),* "the Perfect entering the Common" *(yüan ju t'ung),* the Gradual Doctrine, "the Perfect entering the Gradual" *(yüan ju pieh)* and the Perfect Doctrine.[76] In describing the first type—the Threefold Truth teaching from the viewpoint of "the Gradual entering the Common"—Chih-i states:

> The Middle Way explicated in the doctrine in question only differs from Emptiness. This Middle Way is devoid of functions and does not embrace various *dharmas.*[77]

In this quotation, Chih-i is speaking about the Threefold Truth in the context of the Gradual Doctrine's nature of entering *(ju)* or directing *(chieh)* the Common Doctrine. Chih-i uses the word *ju,* as in *pieh ju t'ung,* and the word *chieh,* as in *pieh chieh t'ung,* interchangeably.[78] In the above passage, the Middle Way is specified and criticized. As far as Chinese grammar is concerned, this Middle Way may be related to either the Gradual Doctrine or the Common Doctrine, both of which are doctrines in question *(tang-chiao).* But from the context of this type of Threefold Truth, in which the Common Doctrine is to be guided by the Gradual Doctrine, we can be sure that this type of the Middle Way under criticism should be related to the Common Doctrine.[79] Indeed, this is a rare occasion in Chih-i's major works, in which the Middle Way of the Common Doctrine is clearly criticized.

The Middle Way criticized is also the Middle Way of the Mādhyamika, and is thus related to the transcendence of extremes. But what does Chih-i's criticism mean? And what are the nature of "a function" and the "embracing of *dharmas*?" These questions will be dealt with in detail in the next chapter. In order to avoid repetition, we wish to say that both "functions" and "embracing *dharmas*" are usually spoken of in the context of the spatio-temporal world. That is, functions are what are imposed on this actual world in order to initiate any transformation within it; what are embraced are actually nothing but worldly entities. In Chih-i's view, "functions" and "embracing *dharmas*" are truly expressive of the dynamism and immanence of the Middle Way, respectively. Indeed, dynamism and immanence are the two attributes of Buddha Nature, which is identical with the Middle Way.[80]

In summary, Chih-i's criticism of the Mādhyamika Middle Way points out that it is not dynamic and immanent; consequently, it tends to be interpreted as transcendent of this world. Does this criticism do justice to the Mādhyamika? We would have to answer in the affirmative, especially in view of the understanding that the Mādhyamika Middle Way is revealed in the transcendence of extremes and is therefore no more than a true principle or state of the entities. This type of Middle Way tends to be static and transcendent, in the sense that it, as a principle or state, merely provides a method by which to avoid commitment to the extremes. It does not have much to do with the unique force by which one can act upon and transform the phenomenal world.

It may be helpful to relate this criticism of the Middle Way to Chih-i's comment on the Twofold Truth teaching:

> The Twofold Truth is devoid of the substance of the Middle Way. Therefore, when the absolute [Truth] is clarified, it is eternally quiescent as Emptiness. When being is clarified, it resembles the gold existing in a rock. Both the rock and the gold are beings, yet are different.[81]

Here, Chih-i is referring to the Common Doctrine. However, the Twofold Truth teaching is clearly discussed in the *Kārikā;*[82] it would seem that Chih-i should have been aware of it. In view of these points, it seems safe to assume that the above comment is directed at Nāgārjuna. As shown in the *Kārikā,* Nāgārjuna's Twofold Truth is composed of the relative and absolute Truth. The absolute Truth is Emptiness, complemented by the Middle Way. Chih-i's comment that the Twofold Truth is devoid of the substance of Middle Way does not infer that Nāgārjuna does not understand the Middle Way. Rather, he is criticizing Nāgārjuna's Middle Way as a state derived from transcending extremes, a criticism based on the Middle Way as related to Buddha Nature. Tsung-san Mou also points out that Nāgārjuna's Middle Way pertains to the *t'i-fa* thought of the Common Doctrine.[83] As we have noted before, this thought does not expound the concept of the Buddha Nature. The word "substance" *(t'i)* in the concept of the "substance of the Middle Way" *(chung-tao t'i),* which Chih-i prefers, suggests that the Middle Way so conceived is more than a state. Though this Middle Way does not necessarily denote substantiality or a metaphysical substance, concepts strongly refuted by all Buddhist schools, it has something to do with the source of actions and functions. The term *t'i* here is reminiscent of a pair of important categories in classical Chinese philosophy: *t'i* and *yung* ("function"). These two categories express the two aspects of entities: their potentiality and their manifestation or function, respectively. We are not in a position to discuss in detail these two categories here. Nevertheless, it is certain that *chung-tao t'i* is spoken of here in the context of potentiality and function. We are convinced that the source of actions and functions can be related to the Buddha Nature, which, for Chih-i, can initiate functions as such. It is therefore quite understandable that Chih-i raises the concept of the substance of the Middle Way in contrast to the expression of the "eternally quiescent as Emptiness." "Quiescence" *(chi)* in Chinese usually denotes a transcendent state that lacks function and dynamism. For Chih-i, the Mādhyamika Middle Way is no more than a static type of Emptiness. He earnestly believes that the authentic Middle Way, as *shih-hsiang* or the ultimate Truth, should be identical to No-emptiness and dynamic at all times.

CHAPTER IV

Middle Way-Buddha Nature as the Truth

Having discussed above the first basic question, let us now deal with the second one: namely, how does Chih-i's Middle Way-Buddha Nature differ from the Mādhyamika's Middle Way? To a limited extent, we responded to this question, when we explicated Chih-i's understanding and criticism of the Mādhyamika's Middle Way in the above chapter. That is, Chih-i is dissatisfied with the Mādhyamika's Middle Way in the sense that it is devoid of functions and does not embrace *dharmas*. This dissatisfaction is equally applicable to the Mādhyamika concept of Emptiness as Truth, which Chih-i regards as partial or one-sided *(p'ien)* and without direct and strict connection with the empirical world. Therefore, for Chih-i, the Truth expounded in the Mādhyamika and the Common Doctrine, whether it be termed "Emptiness" or "Middle Way," tends to be negative, static and transcendent. He thinks Truth should be permanent, dynamic and all-embracing.

It has been mentioned before that Chih-i speaks of Truth in terms of the Middle Way-Buddha Nature. Indeed, he himself is well aware of the fact that Middle Way-Buddha Nature is an issue of Truth, with deep soteriological implications:

> The Tripiṭaka Doctrine and the Common Doctrine contemplate [the nature of] Origination and No-origination respectively, penetrating the one-sided Principle, which they call the True and Ultimate. On the other hand, the Gradual Doctrine and the Perfect Doctrine contemplate [the nature of] Immeasurability and No-creation, respectively, penetrating the Middle Way-Buddha Nature, which they call the True and Ultimate.[1]

Here Chih-i is discussing the four ways of understanding the Four Noble Truths in Primitive Buddhism in the context of his classification theory. He ascribes the nature of Origination *(sheng),* No-origination *(wu-sheng),* Immeasurability *(wu-liang)* and No-creation *(wu-tso)*[2] to the Tripiṭaka Doctrine, Common Doctrine, Gradual Doctrine and Perfect Doctrine, respectively. The term *chen-shih,* or "True and Ultimate," explicitly signifies that the issue in question is about the Truth, or the ultimate Truth.

In the WMCLS, chap. 8, Chih-i states that "What is called liberation is the realization of the Middle Way-Buddha Nature."[3] In the following chapter, Chih-i shows the extreme importance of penetrating the Middle Way as the path to Buddhahood by remarking that the penetration of the Gradual and Perfect Doctrines into the Middle Way is the Buddha Way.[4] As this Middle Way is spoken of in the context of the Gradual and Perfect Doctrines, it is, no doubt, the Middle Way-Buddha Nature.[5] In view of the understanding that the Middle Way-Buddha Nature is what is to be penetrated and realized in order to attain Buddhahood and liberation, Chih-i undoubtedly regards it as the Truth, or the ultimate Truth.

As has been pointed out earlier, the concept of Middle Way-Buddha Nature compounds and identifies the Middle Way and Buddha Nature. This identification is, in fact, mentioned by Chih-i himself in his FHHI, in his discussion of Buddhist merits.[6] This compound concept appears very often in Chih-i's most important works, *viz.,* MHCK, FHHI, SCI, WMCWS and WMCHS. It appears occasionally in the WMCLS and once in the *Fa-chieh tz'u-ti ch'u-men.*[7] Sometimes the concept is termed "Buddha Nature-Middle Way" *(fo-hsing chung-tao)* rather than "Middle Way-Buddha Nature."[8] There is, however, not the slightest difference between these two terms.

Although Chih-i does not explicitly enumerate the characteristics of the Middle Way-Buddha Nature, from a wide study of his major works we are able to find out that this concept has three characteristics, which, for Chih-i, are entirely lacking in the Mādhyamika's Middle Way. They are, in Chih-i's own terminology, "ever-abidingness" *(ch'ang-chu),* "meritorious function" *(kung-yung)* and "embracing various *dharmas*" *(chü chu-fa).* Only after all these characteristics are fully accounted for can we have a clear picture of the differences between the Middle Way-Buddha Nature and the Mādhyamika's Middle Way. Because these differences are extremely significant to an understanding of Chih-i's system of thought, the three characteristics must be delineated in detail.

Incidentally, although the Middle Way-Buddha Nature assumes a crucial position in Chih-i's thought, it is widely ignored by modern scholars in T'ien-t'ai Buddhism. Not only is there no examination of its characteristics, the concept is not even mentioned in the works of Andō, Satō, Tamaki, Tamura, Hurvitz and Swanson listed in our bibliography. Accordingly, the study of this concept is all the more necessary for a proper understanding of Chih-i's thought.

1. The ever-abidingness of the Middle Way-Buddha Nature

Ever-abidingness denotes the nature of permanence, which is not subject to change. Whatever has this nature is able to abide by itself and persist forever. Chih-i basically ascribes this nature to the Dharma Body (Skt., *dharmakāya;* Ch., *fa-shen*) and the Buddha Nature.[9] On the one hand, as seen in the final section of the previous chapter, he criticizes Nāgārjuna's Twofold Truth as "devoid of the substance of the Middle Way." On the other hand, he often raises the issue of the ever-abidingness of the Buddha Nature and the Dharma Body, which, as we will soon discover, he identifies with the Middle Way. It seems that Chih-i is in favor of the Middle Way as a body or substance, which is for him the Buddha Nature or the Middle Way-Buddha Nature; he therefore ascribes the ever-abiding nature to the Middle Way-Buddha Nature as an important characteristic.

The nature of the ever-abidingness of the Dharma Body is often stated by Chih-i in contrast to the physical body, which obviously pertains to the realm of life and death and is consequently impermanent. This is mainly done in his FHHI, where Chih-i remarks:

> The Vairocana Buddha stays on the lotus flower sea with the great bodhisattvas. All of them are not human beings subject to life and death.[10]

What Chih-i wants to convey is that the Vairocana Buddha and the great bodhisattvas all have the form of the Dharma Body, which is different from the physical body that undergoes birth and death. Consequently, he further remarks:

> What is quiescent is liberation. Liberation necessarily involves a person. This person is [spoken of in terms of] the Dharma Body, which is not the actual [physical] body.[11]

The ever-abidingness seems to refer to something spiritual, something with a permanent nature. This point, that the Dharma Body is spiritual and permanent, is described in a most detailed manner in the WMCLS. There, Chih-i speaks of two kinds of body, namely, *sheng-shen* and *fa-hsing shen*. *Sheng-shen* is the corporeal body in the nature of life and death, while *fa-hsing shen* is the body in reference to the Truth. The Sanskrit for the term *fa-hsing* is *dharmatā,* or *dharmatva,* which means the true nature or Truth of *dharmas*. The difference, according to Chih-i, is that *sheng-shen* is affected by nine kinds of defilement (Skt., *kleśa;* Ch., *fang-nao*): hunger, thirst, cold, heat and other ailments. When these troubles come, the body has to be cured; for example, when hungry, one should drink some milk. On the other hand, *fa-hsing shen* is free from these troubles. It is in fact the Dharma Body, which is in the nature of a diamond and is everlasting.[12] Chih-i later positively asserts that the authentic Dharma Body is devoid of the nine ailments.[13] He elaborates this assertion with an analogy between the Dharma Body and a diamond:

> The body of the *tathāgata* has the substance of a diamond. This is the permanent body of the Dharma Body. The purpose of the analogy [of this Dharma Body] with the diamond is [to indicate] that the substance [of this Body] is indestructible, that its functions are beneficial, and that it penetrates completely into Reality. The "indestructibility" suggests that the Dharma Body is not infected by the impurities of illusion, defilement and life and death, remaining ever-abiding and unchangeable. The "beneficence" suggests the quality of wisdom belonging to the Dharma Body. The merit of illumination of the *prajñā* [wisdom over phenomena] is all-inclusive. And the "complete penetration into Reality" suggests the power of the severance of the Dharma Body. The liberation attained is ultimate and the hindrance of defilements is completely severed.[14]

It should be noted that the analogy of the Dharma Body with a diamond does not mean that both are of the same dimension. The diamond, no matter how "indestructible" it may be, is still destructible as an item within the realm of Dependent Origination. Rather, this analogy signifies that Chih-i is inclined to speak of the Dharma Body in terms of its permanent, functional and ultimate nature. The permanent nature refers to indestructibility *(chien),* the functional nature to beneficence *(li),* and the ultimate nature to Reality *(pen-chi)*.

Chih-i also ascribes the ever-abiding nature to the Buddha

Nature. When he does so, he usually mentions without much elaboration the expression "Buddha Nature is ever-abiding" *(fo-hsing ch'ang-chu)*, or "the ever-abiding Buddha Nature" *(ch'ang-chu fo-hsing)*.[15] Nevertheless, he identifies the Middle Way and the Dharma Body[16] and even coins a compound term, "Middle Way-Dharma Body" *(chung-tao fa-shen)*, to express this identification.[17] It is thus clear that, for him, the Middle Way, Dharma Body and Buddha Nature all denote the same subject: the Middle Way-Buddha Nature. It is also clear that the ever-abiding nature he ascribes to the Dharma Body is also ascribed to the Buddha Nature. He creates a rather complicated statement, "Buddha Nature-Dharma Body is ever-abiding" *(fo-hsing fa-shen ch'ang-chu)*, to express this idea.[18]

In view of the identity of the Dharma Body and the Middle Way-Buddha Nature, it is certain that the latter also has the ever-abiding nature, which is expressed in terms of substance *(t'i)*, function *(yung)* and Reality *(pen-chi)*. It is also certain that the Mādhyamika, as the Common Doctrine, is devoid of this nature. On some occasions, Chih-i criticizes the Common Doctrine for failing to understand the permanent nature.[19] Mou also points out that the *Chung-lun* is devoid of the idea of the permanence of the Buddha Nature.[20] This is expected because this permanent nature is spoken of only in the context of the Buddha Nature, a concept which is lacking in the Mādhyamika, as we mentioned earlier.

2. The functional nature of the Middle Way-Buddha Nature

Chih-i also ascribes a functional nature to the Middle Way-Buddha Nature as a characteristic, and he places much stress on this nature, as is evidenced in the following points. First, Chih-i vehemently criticizes the Middle Way explicated in the Mādhyamika and Common Doctrine as being devoid of functions and lacking the nature of "embracing *dharmas*," as described in the previous chapter.[21] Apparently, this criticism is made from the standpoint of the Perfect Doctrine, the highest Buddhist doctrine for Chih-i. Consequently, it can be inferred that the functional nature must, in Chih-i's view, play an important role in the establishment of the concept of Middle Way-Buddha Nature, which is the Truth as the Perfect Doctrine. Second, as mentioned earlier, Chih-i speaks of the Dharma Body in terms of *t'i* and *yung*, i.e., substance and function. On some occasions, he speaks of this function as "the great function without limits" *(wu-fang ta-yung).* For example, he divides liberation into two types: conceivable and inconceivable, remarking that the latter has this "great function without limits," whereas the former does not.[22] This inconceivable liberation is the authentic one and is attained in the realization of the Middle Way-Buddha Nature.[23] Chih-i also relates the "great function without limits" to the *tathāgata,*[24] which is the potential state of the Dharma Body.[25] This, it should be remembered, is another expression of the Middle Way-Buddha Nature. Therefore, we see that Chih-i speaks of the Middle Way-Buddha Nature in terms of function, which is great and without limits.

To signify this functional nature, Chih-i proposes three terms in his major writings: *kung-yung, li-yung* and simply *yung.*[26] Generally speaking, these three terms all refers to the same thing, namely, the function or functions exerted toward this empirical world. Once one penetrates more deeply into the issue, however, a seemingly slight but actually very significant difference can be discerned. That is, Chih-i divides *kung-yung* and *li-yung* into *kung* and *yung, li* and *yung,* respectively. With regard to *kung-yung,* he states:

> *Kung* refers to self-cultivation, while *yung* refers to the benefit to entities [or others]. If taken together, they signify the transformation of others.[27]

With regard to *li-yung,* he specifically refers to *li* as the power of wisdom which enables one to understand the Principle or the Truth; by *yung* he refers to the function of wisdom in transforming others.[28] This reference is further reflected in Chih-i's discussion on the part of function *(yung)* in his FHHI. As a matter of fact, the FHHI, one of Chih-i's most important works, is composed of five parts dealing with five topics, the fourth of which is devoted to the discussion of function. This demonstrates Chih-i's emphasis on the concept of function in his system.[29]

As we have just seen, *kung-yung* and *li-yung* can be divided into two components. Both divisions further indicate that the functional nature can be realized and completed in two steps, respectively: self-cultivation and the transformation of others. It is natural to cultivate oneself sufficiently before exerting oneself in transforming others, a point of which Chih-i is clearly aware. He remarks that the *yung* is deeply influenced by the *kung,* just as in the case of trees: Only when trees are deeply rooted can their branches, flowers and leaves flourish.[30] Here, *kung* is associated with the roots, while *yung* represents the branches, flowers and leaves.

Given these differences between *kung* and *yung,* and *li* and *yung,* Chih-i nevertheless views *yung* alone as expressive of the functional nature of the Middle Way-Buddha Nature, and he greatly emphasizes the aspect of the transformation of others. In a brief but precise explanation of the five topics dealt with in the five parts of the FHHI, he simply enumerates *yung* as the topic of the fourth part, stating that *yung* transforms others.[31] Later, he adds that *yung* is benefitting others.[32] In view of this, we will employ in the following discussions the term *yung* (or "function") to signify the functional nature of the Middle Way-Buddha Nature. This term is, if not otherwise specified, expressive of the above-mentioned implications of *kung* and *li.*

Chih-i asserts that this functional nature is to be realized in relation to the actual world of space and time. That is, one has to enter this actual world and engage oneself in its affairs. This is the so-called *ju-chia,* or "entering the provisional [realm]." This *ju-chia* is an indispensable step in benefitting others, as Chih-i states:

> If [one] abides in Emptiness, that will never be beneficial to sentient beings. If [one] aims at benefitting others, that is the meaning of entering the provisional.[33]

The expression *ju-chia* appears quite often in the MHCK, chapter 6.[34] Indeed, Chih-i devotes ample space in this chapter to discussion of the motivations and circumstances *(yin-yüan)* of *ju-chia*[35] and the process to complete it,[36] which are usually related to the bodhisattvas. In this connection, Chih-i also mentions *ch'u-chia.*[37] In Chinese, *ch'u,* "to leave," is commonly used as the opposite of *ju,* "to enter." Interestingly enough, in the context in which *ch'u-chia* appears, it means exactly the same as *ju-chia,* i.e., to "enter the provisional world." This can be inferred from the MHCK, which states:

> Originally, the bodhisattva practised Emptiness, not because he values Emptiness, but for the sake of sentient beings. He does not value Emptiness, therefore he does not abide [in it]. For the sake of benefitting sentient beings, he has to enter [their realm].[38]

The word for "enter" here is *ch'u*. Sentient beings stay in the empirical or provisional world. In order to benefit them, the bodhisattva has to enter this world, *ch'u-chia*. Chih-i does not distinguish between *ch'u-chia* and *ju-chia*. Indeed, both *ch'u* and *ju* mean "enter" in the context in question. Yet it should be noted that whether one enters the provisional with or without Emptiness makes a big difference. To enter the provisional with Emptiness entails a non-attachment to the substantiality of the provisional, while entering without Emptiness does not. As will be seen in Chapter VI below, Chih-i speaks of the Contemplation of the Provisional *(chia-kuan)* in terms of "entering into the Provisional from Emptiness" *(ts'ung-k'ung ju-chia)*. This Contemplation embraces the Contemplation of Emptiness *(k'ung kuan)*; it is likely that entering the provisional or *ju-chia* in the present context is integrated with Emptiness.

Chih-i understands *ju-chia* or entering the provisional in terms of benefitting others, which denotes mainly the saving of sentient beings, who suffer constantly in this world of life and death. That is to say, the function in question is basically confined to saving sentient beings. This can also be inferred from Chih-i's statement that if one does not save sentient beings, one is not capable of functioning.[39]

3. To put sentient beings into correct places with the perfect function

The issue of the function in question is that the function has to be performed in the world, which is by nature provisional. Consequently, one has to enter this world to save sentient beings. Here, then, a crucial question arises: How does the function operate? Or, more specifically, how are sentient beings to be saved? In response to this issue, Chih-i offers an explanation in the context of describing the Perfect Doctrine:

> The bodhisattva hears the perfect Dharma, awakens the perfect faith, establishes perfect actions, abides in the perfect position, decorates himself with perfect merits, and puts sentient beings into correct places with the perfect function. . . . How does he place sentient beings perfectly? He may shed light, enabling sentient beings to benefit from the wisdom of penetrating the identity of Emptiness, the Pro-

visional and the Middle Way, and to acquire the method of the Four Alternatives. Or they may attain [the goal], whether they are walking, standing, sitting, lying, speaking, remaining silent or working. . . .

[The Dragon King] makes various kinds of clouds, thunder, lightning and rain. The Dragon stays in his own palace, yet he is able to make all of these without the slightest movement himself. The bodhisattva is likewise. Penetrating into the identity of Emptiness, the Provisional and the Middle Way, he enables [sentient beings] to obtain various kinds of benefit and acquire various kinds of ability, yet with no effect on the Dharma Nature. This is called "putting sentient beings into correct places with the perfect function."[40]

This is a beautiful and lively elaboration of the bodhisattva's function with respect to saving sentient beings. "The Bodhisattva hears the perfect Dharma, . . . decorates himself with perfect merits" corresponds obviously to *kung,* "self-cultivation"; while "putting sentient beings into correct places with the perfect function" corresponds to *yung,* signifying the benefitting of others. The function in the statement that the bodhisattva "put(s) sentient beings into correct places with the perfect function" is the function of the Middle Way-Buddha Nature. This is because a bodhisattva is a sentient being who has attained enlightenment and liberation already. As pointed out in the beginning of this chapter, liberation is the realization of the Middle Way-Buddha Nature. Accordingly, all performances in benefitting others should emanate from this Middle Way-Buddha Nature. The treatment of sentient beings with this function is manifestly soteriological: what benefits the sentient beings are the wisdom of the Threefold Contemplation (i.e., penetration into the identity of Emptiness and the Provisional and the Middle Way) and the method of the Four Alternatives. Both are, for Chih-i, closely related to the realization of the Truth and attainment of liberation.[41]

To put sentient beings into correct places with the perfect function concerns an endeavor to cope with the afflictions (defilements and ignorance) with which sentient beings are confronted. With regard to this endeavor, Chih-i proposes three steps by means of a medical analogy dealing with the curing of diseases: to diagnose the diseases, to select the medicine, and to distribute the medicine.[42] With respect to the diagnosis of diseases, Chih-i remarks that diseases are closely analogous to the attachment to false views of self *(wo-chien)* that arise from the delusive mind *(huo-hsin).* This delusive mind can initiate numerous false views, all of which are conducive to various kinds of evil conduct, trapping one in the realm of transmigration.[43] With respect to the selection of the medicine, Chih-i points out that just as there are numerous diseases, there are also equally numerous medications.[44] He states:

> Every *dharma* has various names, characteristics and efficacies. All bodhisattvas who enter the provisional world should distinguish and understand [them]. For the sake of [saving] sentient beings, they collect various *dharma*-medications like the sea-instructors. Whoever does not understand [the *dharma*-medications] cannot benefit [the world of] entities. In order to understand [them], [the bodhisattvas] practise cessation, contemplation, great compassion, vow-taking and the power of persistent exertion whole-heartedly and thoroughly.[45]

With respect to the distribution of the medicine, Chih-i remarks that this should be done in terms of the talent of sentient beings. He divides the talent of sentient beings into four categories and proposes the distribution of "medicine" in the context of his theory of the classification of the Buddhist doctrine. That is, the medicine of the Tripiṭaka Doctrine is distributed to those of low talent, that of the Common Doctrine to those of medium talent, that of the Gradual Doctrine to those of high talent, and that of the Perfect Doctrine to those of supreme talent.[46]

The diseases and their remedies are, of course, symbolic; they are spoken of in an entirely soteriological sense. What is important is that the soteriological goal—liberation of sentient beings—must be achieved by means of actions. These actions, usually undertaken by the bodhisattvas, must be imposed upon the spatio-temporal world of life and death, "the world of sufferings."[47] The bodhisattvas, who are capable of the attainment of *nirvāna,* must leave the transcendent state of Emptiness, enter the provisional world *(ju-chia)* and undertake actions. The functional nature of the Middle Way-Buddha Nature can be spoken of only in these actions. In light of this functional nature, we can also speak of the dynamism of the Middle Way-Buddha Nature.

The concept of function—whether it be termed *yung, kung* or *li*—appears very frequently in Chih-i's works. Interestingly enough, Chih-i occasionally employs a compound term, *ta-yung-kung-li,*[48] uniting *yung, kung* and *li* to express their greatness. Chih-i's stress on function is undeniable. From the function's extremely close relationship with the empirical world, Chih-i's emphasis on this world is also clear. This emphasis deserves our attention even more in view of Chih-i's comparison of function with the Transformation Body, one of the three bodies of the Buddha. We will end this section with a delineation of this point.

The theory of Three Bodies (Skt., *trikāya;* Ch., *san-shen*) states that the Buddha has three forms of body: the Dharma Body (Skt., *dharma-kāya:* Ch., *fa-shen*), the Bliss Body (Skt., *saṃbhoga-kāya;* Ch., *pao-shen*) and the Transformation Body (Skt., *nirmāṇa-kāya;* Ch., *ying-shen*). This theory can be traced back to Indian Buddhism and has been widely studied by scholars.[49] Generally speaking, "Dharma Body" denotes the essence of the Buddha, or the Buddha in and of Himself. "Bliss Body" denotes the body through which the Buddha enjoys the bliss resulting from enlightenment. "Transformation Body" refers to the body the Buddha assumes in cultivating and transforming sentient beings. Chih-i himself has his own understanding of the Dharma Body, the Transformation Body, and their relationship, as he remarks:

> In the [very] first moment that the Dharma Body as the origin is attained, the function of the Transformation Body is initiated right within the substance [of the Dharma Body].[50]

Chih-i speaks here of the Dharma Body and the Transformation Body in terms of *pen,* "origin" and *yung,* "function," respectively.[51] Elsewhere, he refers to the Dharma Body as *t'i* and to the Transformation Body as *yung.*[52] In Chinese, *pen* and *t'i* imply each other in meaning, and the combination of them, *pen-t'i,* is expressive of the ultimate Reality. Chih-i also states that the function of the Transformation Body is the manifestation of the Dharma Body, praising this function as inconceivable.[53] In view of this *yung-t'i* relationship between the Transformation Body and Dharma Body, and the identity of the Dharma Body and the Middle Way-Buddha Nature as described in section 1 above, we are certain that the function spoken of here is also the function of the Middle Way-Buddha Nature.

The functional nature in relation to the Transformation Body can be seen in the apparition of the Buddha or bodhisattva. That is, the Buddha and bodhisattvas, with the Dharma Body as their spiritual root, can assume different apparitions in order to save sentient beings. The apparitions assumed are in accord with the individual needs and circumstances of sentient beings. Indeed, the term *ying* in *ying-shen* signifies this point. Chih-i elaborates this issue in the following manner:

> If sentient beings should attain liberation by means of the [form of a] Buddha body, [the Buddha or bodhisattva] will assume the Buddha body to preach and distribute medicine to them. If they should attain liberation in the form of a bodhisattva, or pratyekabuddha, or śrāvaka, or the eight lower classes of life, such as god, dragon, etc., [the Buddha or bodhisattva] will assume the corresponding bodies.[54]

This passage clearly describes a soteriological transformation of sentient beings in the world, but in a mystical sense. The function revealed in the Transformation Body once again verifies Chih-i's emphasis regarding the world. This transformation is, to be sure, a vivid example of putting sentient beings into correct places with the perfect function.

4. The Truth in terms of the Mind

The functional nature of the Middle Way-Buddha Nature signifies the dynamism of Truth. That is, Truth itself can act, or initiate actions, in order to convert sentient beings. By this we mean that the personality who has attained the Truth acts or initiates actions; in Buddhism, this personality is the Buddha or bodhisattva. This conception of the Truth is quite different from what we usually think the Truth to be. We tend to conceive the Truth in terms of the Principle (Ch., *li*), which assumes permanence and universality. In other words, the Truth remains constantly as it is, without undergoing any change; it is universally applicable, whether it be in a logical, epistemological or metaphysical sense. We tend to ascribe an unchangeable and static nature to the Truth. It is hard to imagine that the Truth moves, much less that it functions and acts.

Chih-i's understanding of the Truth, which he terms "Middle Way-Buddha Nature," is rich in content. It is, on the one hand, the Middle Way, which is the Principle. This is evidenced in various compound terms composed of *chung-tao, chung* and *li,* which Chih-i articulates in his works. To give a few examples: *chung-tao li,*[55] *chung-li,*[56] *chung-tao chih li,*[57] *chung shih-li,*[58] *chung-tao i-shih chih li,*[59] *chung-tao fa-hsing chih li*[60] and others. The nature of the Principle assumed by the Middle Way is shown in its reference to the right state from which we are to see *dharmas:* the state of detachment from every extreme. The nature of the Principle spoken of in the context of this state is obviously static. Chih-i himself seems to be aware of the static nature of the Principle. In the delineation of the ten "such-likes"[61] or categories *(shih ju-shih)* of the *Fa-hua ching,* he ascribes three implications to "nature" *(hsing),* which is one of the categories. One of these implications is unchangeability *(pu-kai),* or motionlessness *(pu-tung hsing).* Another implication is that this category of nature is the nature of Reality *(shih-hsing),* which is identical to the nature of the Principle *(li-hsing).*[62] In this way, the Principle is associated with unchangeability and motionlessness, both of which signify nothing but static nature.

On the other hand, Chih-i approaches the Buddha Nature, which he identifies with the Middle Way, in terms of the Mind *(hsin).* This approach is from the standpoint of the Perfect Doctrine:

> If one contemplates the Mind to be the Buddha Nature and practises the Eightfold Noble Path perfectly, one is capable of writing the *sūtra* of the Middle Way immediately. With the understanding that all *dharmas* originate from the Mind, [then] the Mind is the Great Vehicle and the Mind is the Buddha Nature.[63]

We see here Chih-i's identification of the Buddha Nature with Mind in a practical and soteriological tone. That is, in the contemplation of the Mind as the Buddha Nature, one must practise the Eightfold Noble Path along the direction of the Perfect Doctrine. By doing so, one is able to attain enlightenment, an expression of which is "writing the *sūtra* of the Middle Way." Such an identification is also evidenced in the compound term "Buddha Nature-True Mind" *(fo-hsing cheng-hsin),* which Chih-i articulates in a discussion of the initiation of the Mind.[64]

It is the Mind that Chih-i associates with function and action. In his delineation of the ten categories, he states with regard to the two categories of force *(li)* and action *(tso):*

> Force as such denotes the force capable of functioning. This is like the bodyguard of the king who has numerous techniques. Because he is ill, the techniques are taken as missing. When the illness decreases, he

> is capable of functioning. The same is true with the Mind. It embraces various forces. Due to the disease of defilements, it cannot operate. To view it in its true nature, it embraces all forces. With regard to action, operation and construction are called "action." Apart from the Mind, there is nothing acted upon. Therefore we know that the Mind embraces all actions.[65]

In this passage, "force", "function", "operation" *(yün-wei),* "construction" *(chien-li)* and "action" are all raised in the context of the Mind and are expressive of a dynamic nature. The statement "apart from the Mind, there is nothing acted upon" should mean that, apart from the Mind, there is no action possible; apart from the Mind there is neither an object of action nor an object to be acted upon *(so-tso).* What Chih-i wants to emphasize is the Mind as the source of all actions. To speak of the object of action is nonsense outside of the context of actions which arise from the Mind. In fact, the statement in question reveals that Chih-i ascribes dynamism to the Mind exclusively. Because the Mind is identical to the Buddha Nature, which stands for the Truth, we therefore can speak of the functional and dynamic nature of the Truth.[66] This, indeed, complements our discussion in the above sections concerning the functional nature of the Middle Way-Buddha Nature.

5. The Middle Way-Buddha Nature embraces all *dharmas*

As has been pointed out previously, Chih-i criticizes, from the standpoint of the Perfect Doctrine, the Middle Way explicated in the Common Doctrine and the Mādhyamika as devoid of functions and not embracing all *dharmas.* In view of this criticism, the functional and all-embracing natures must have been attributed to the Middle Way-Buddha Nature as its characteristics. As a matter of fact, in the delineation of the five types of the Threefold Truth, in which such criticism is found, Chih-i frankly attributes the all-embracing nature to the Middle Way-Buddha Nature. He states:

> The former two types of the Twofold Truth are excluded, due to their failure to understand the [true] Middle Way. With the [true] Middle Way added to the five types of the Twofold Truth, we then have five types of the Threefold Truth. In respect to "the Gradual entering the Common," the aspect of "neither delusive nor non-delusive" is specified, and the Threefold Truth teaching is completed. [This means,]

> the delusive being conventional, and the non-delusive absolute, the "neither delusive nor non-delusive" is the Middle Way. The Middle Way explicated in the doctrine in question differs only from Emptiness. This Middle Way is devoid of functions and does not embrace various *dharmas*. In respect to the Threefold Truth of "the Perfect entering the Common," its Twofold Truth does not differ from that of the former, [i.e., "the Gradual entering the Common,"] However, it specifies the "neither delusive nor non-delusive" [Middle Way] which embraces all *dharmas* and is different from the former Middle Way [of "the Gradual entering the Common"]. In respect to the Threefold Truth of the Gradual Doctrine, it develops the conventional Truth into two Truths, [i.e., the Truth of Emptiness and that of Provisionality.] It takes the absolute Truth as the Middle Way, which is merely the Middle Way as the Principle. In respect to the Threefold Truth of "the Perfect entering the Gradual," the two Truths do not differ from the former [i.e., the Truths of Emptiness and Provisionality in the Gradual Doctrine]. But the absolute Middle Way is specified, which embraces the Buddhist *dharmas* fully. In respect to the Threefold Truth of the Perfect Doctrine, the Buddhist *dharmas* are embraced by not only the Middle Way but also by the absolute and conventional.[67]

With regard to this delineation, it should be noted that when Chih-i speaks of the Twofold Truth, he is referring to the Mādhyamika's (Nāgārjuna's in particular) absolute Truth of Emptiness and relative Truth, which is the provisionality of entities or *dharmas*. Chih-i is not satisfied with this Twofold Truth. Rather, he is in favor of the Threefold Truth, which includes the Middle Way as identical to the Buddha Nature. In this delineation, there are two points that deserve our attention:

a. The Middle Way in the context of the Threefold Truth of the Perfect Doctrine is spoken of in terms of embracing the Buddhist *dharmas*. This embracing nature is also ascribed to the Middle Way of other types of the Threefold Truth, in which the Perfect Doctrine is the guiding doctrine (the Threefold Truth of "the Perfect entering the Common" and that of "the Perfect entering the Gradual"). The term "Buddhist *dharmas*" *(fo-fa)* is sometimes replaced with "all *dharmas*" *(i-ch'ieh fa)* or "various *dharmas*" *(chu-fa)*. All of these terms refer to the entities in the empirical world. This term is different from "Buddhist Dharma," which corresponds to the same Chinese characters, i.e., *fo-fa;* the latter in Buddhism means Truth or Reality expressed in Buddhism. In Chih-i's works, *fo-fa* may mean entities.

It may also mean Truth or Reality. Which meaning it should carry depends on the context in which it is being discussed.

b. Chih-i does not mention the embracing nature when he raises the issue of the Middle Way in the context of the Threefold Truth of the Gradual Doctrine or the other type of the Threefold Truth in which the Gradual Doctrine is the guiding doctrine (the Threefold Truth of "the Gradual entering the Common"). Chih-i seems to be dissatisfied with the Middle Way of the Threefold Truth of the Gradual Doctrine, mentioning it in a regretful tone and pointing out that it is "merely the Middle Way as the Principle." Furthermore, in the descriptions of the Threefold Truth of "the Gradual entering the Common" and that of "the Perfect entering the Common," the Middle Way, as "neither delusive nor non-delusive," is mentioned in both cases. Chih-i points out, however, that the Middle Way in the latter case is "different from the one in the former case." These two points seem to suggest Chih-i's reluctance to ascribe the embracing nature to the Middle Way of the Gradual Doctrine, which is nevertheless identical to the Buddha Nature. Indeed, on one occasion when Chih-i discusses the Gradual Doctrine, he explicitly remarks that its Middle Way is a mere Principle *(tan-li)* that does not embrace various *dharmas*.[68]

Chih-i also states that the *tathāgatagarbha* contains all *dharmas*.[69] For him, the *tathāgatagarbha* is not different from the Buddha Nature[70] and the Truth *(shih-hsiang)*.[71]

6. The meaning of "embrace" in the passive voice

When Chih-i raises the issue of embracing *dharmas* of the Middle Way-Buddha Nature, he uses the terms *chü* and *pei* interchangeably. In the above quotation, for example, *pei* in *pu-pei chu-fa* and *chü* in *chü i-chieh fa* represent the same meaning: "embrace." Our present concern is, what does "embrace" mean in the assertion that the Middle Way-Buddha Nature embraces all *dharmas?* This is crucial to the understanding of the all-embracing nature of the Middle Way-Buddha Nature.

On the basis of our studies of the major texts, we have discovered no place in which Chih-i has explicitly and in detail explained what "embrace" means in this context. Its implications are not impossible to detect, however, and will be developed in the following discussions.

Chih-i asserts that liberation is attained in the realization of the

Middle Way-Buddha Nature, as pointed out in the beginning of this chapter. This is quite apparent to Buddhists advocating the doctrine of the Buddha Nature, which teaches that every sentient being is endowed with the Buddha Nature, and that enlightenment means the realization of this Buddha Nature.[72] Chih-i basically admits this doctrine, expressing the claim that every sentient being has the Buddha Nature on some occasions.[73] However, he does not confine the Buddha Nature to sentient beings, but broadens its dimension to cover the non-sentient. This is done by identifying the Buddha Nature with the Dharma Nature (Skt., *dharmatā, dharmatva;* Ch., *fa-hsing*), which means the true nature of *dharmas* or entities. He states straightforwardly: "Buddha Nature is Dharma Nature."[74] The expression "true nature of *dharmas*" signifies the character of inseparability from the *dharmas,* and thus the embracing of them. That is, the Dharma Nature embraces all *dharmas.* In view of the identification of the Dharma Nature with Buddha Nature, the latter also embraces all *dharmas.* It is in this context that we speak of the all-embracing nature of the Buddha Nature or Middle Way-Buddha Nature. We must not forget that the *dharmas* in question contain both sentient and non-sentient beings. Consequently, we can say that the Buddha Nature or Middle Way-Buddha Nature embraces not only sentient beings, but also non-sentient beings.

This all-embracing nature entails, in fact, that in the endeavor to attain enlightenment or liberation, one must realize not only the Middle Way-Buddha Nature, but also the *dharmas* (all sentient and non-sentient beings). If not, the characteristic of embracing the *dharmas* of the Middle Way-Buddha Nature will be of no importance. But what does such entailment mean?

Let us first discuss the case in which the *dharmas* denote sentient beings. In view of the assertion that all sentient beings possess the Buddha Nature, which makes them capable of attaining Buddhahood or liberation, realization of the Buddha Nature naturally contains the realization and liberation of sentient beings. In this context, the assertion that the Middle Way-Buddha Nature embraces all sentient beings actually means that this Nature is possessed as a potential by all sentient beings and that its realization will result in the liberation of the latter. Accordingly, "embrace" by itself in the active voice is transformed into the passive voice to mean "possessed by."

With regard to the case in which the *dharmas* denote non-sentient beings, we may make reference to Chih-i's well-known declaration from the perspective of the Perfect Doctrine:

> Even a single item of color or smell is the Middle Way. The *"dharma"* of the Middle Way embraces all *dharmas.*[75]

In the second half of this declaration, the expression *chung-tao chih fa* (literally, the *dharma* of the Middle Way) simply denotes *chung-tao* or the Middle Way itself. *Fa* in the expression does not have any substantial meaning; it is not the same as the *fa* in *chü i-ch'ieh fa* (embrace all *dharmas*), in which *fa* stands for entities in the phenomenal world.

This declaration can be approached in two different ways, in which "embrace" assumes different meanings. Speaking ontologically, the color or smell, as an existent, has its origin in the Middle Way because the Middle Way possesses all existents or *dharmas.* "Embrace" takes the active voice, meaning "possess." Speaking practically and soteriologically, however, the declaration involves quite another picture. Even a color or smell is expressive of the Middle Way. That is, the Middle Way can be revealed even in a common non-sentient being. What Chih-i wants to assert is not the origination of the color or smell from the Middle Way, but rather the unlimited pervasiveness of the Truth of the Middle Way. It is possessed by and therefore can be revealed in everything. It is in this context that Chih-i asserts that the Middle Way embraces all *dharmas.* "Embrace" takes the passive voice to mean "possessed by."

In Chih-i's major works, there is no sign that he is much interested in ontological issues. But his deep concern with practical and soteriological affairs is undeniable. In view of this concern, it is likely that "embrace" should be understood in the passive sense of "possessed by," and that the assertion that the Middle Way-Buddha Nature embraces all *dharmas* actually means that the Middle Way-Buddha Nature is possessed by all *dharmas.* Accordingly, the realization of the *dharmas* consists in the realization of the Middle Way-Buddha Nature or the Truth right within them. Chih-i himself understood the all-embracing nature of the Truth of the Middle Way in practical and soteriological terms: "If one understands that the various *dharmas* do not originate, one at once embraces all Buddhist *dharmas.*"[76] That the various *dharmas* do not originate signifies the insight of No-origination, which in turn indicates the transcendence of all extremes. As described previously, the transcendence of extremes denotes the realization of the Truth of the Middle Way, which will result in liberation. This insight can lead one to the soteriological goal and must be acquired in practice. Chih-i relates the issue of all-embracing nature to this insight. For him, the assertion that the Middle Way-Buddha Nature embraces all *dharmas* consists in the realization of the Middle Way not anywhere else but within the various *dharmas* themselves. This is possible only on the basis that the Middle Way-Buddha Nature is possessed by the *dharmas.*[77]

It is worthwhile to note that the idea of the non-sentient beings possessing the Buddha Nature *(wu-ch'ing yu-hsing)* appeared within the T'ien-t'ai tradition after Chih-i. Chan-jan (A.D. 711–782), an eminent T'ien-t'ai thinker, was a strong advocate of this idea.[78] There must be a close relationship between this idea and Chih-i's thought of the all-embracing nature of the Middle Way-Buddha Nature, both historically and philosophically. One of the major reasons is that the assertion that the Middle Way-Buddha Nature embraces all *dharmas* was taken to mean, as just has been argued, that this Nature is possessed by all *dharmas,* and consequently that the non-sentient beings possess the Buddha Nature because a part of the *dharmas* is non-sentient. This idea is a very straightforward and radical one. It is likely that the T'ien-t'ai followers, Chan-jan included, understood the term "embrace" in the assertion that the Middle Way-Buddha Nature embraces all *dharmas* in a passive manner, and their understanding of the assertion became one in which the Middle Way-Buddha Nature is possessed by the *dharmas.* In order to emphasize the unlimited pervasiveness of the Middle Way-Buddha Nature, they eventually worked out the radical idea in an active tone: even non-sentient beings possess the Buddha Nature. A detailed discussion of this issue is, however, out of the question here.[79]

7. "Embrace" in the active and methodological sense

Is "embrace" entirely passive in meaning? Can we say in some sense that the Middle Way-Buddha Nature does embrace the *dharmas,* which include both sentient and non-sentient beings? To speak in terms of compassion, the answer may be affirmative. As is commonly known to Mahāyāna Buddhists, compassion (Skt., *maitreya-karuṇa;* Ch., *tz'u-pei*) is an indispensable element in the practice of a bodhisattva, who is much concerned with the liberation of others.[80] Authentic compassion is all-embracing, rather than confined to a certain realm. That is, a true Buddhist should have compassion for both sentient and non-sentient beings. Having compassion for sentient beings is easy to understand, while having compassion for non-sentient beings seems unnatural in view of the latter's lack of feelings and consciousness. However, it is the non-sentient beings that constitute the vital conditions or circumstances of the sentient beings, which Chih-i calls the "pure Buddha Land." He once remarked in a regretful tone that if one abides in Emptiness, there will be no pure Buddha Land.[81] Consequently, if sentient beings are to be purified, non-sentient beings should be purified, too. It is in this sense that we may say that non-sentient beings are embraced by the Middle Way-Buddha Nature, or the latter embraces the former, in which "embrace" is in the active voice.

It is interesting to note that Chih-i divides compassion into three types in light of his theory of the Threefold Contemplation: the compassions related to the Contemplation of Emptiness, the Contemplation of the Provisional and the Contemplation of the Middle Way. Chih-i states that the former two compassions are shared by the bodhisattvas, whereas the latter compassion is confined to the *tathāgata* and is consequently called "*tathāgata* compassion" *(ju-lai tz'u-pei)*. Chih-i also states that this compassion shares the same substance with *shih-hsiang* or the Truth.[82] He says that the compassions related to the Contemplations of Emptiness and the Provisional have limits, while the *tathāgata* compassion is limitless and is the sea where various *dharmas* of the *tathāgata-garbha* assemble.[83] Although Chih-i does not elaborate this image, it is likely that the limitless nature of the *tathāgata* compassion consists in embracing both non-sentient and sentient beings by this compassion.

The all-embracing nature is also what determines *shih-hsiang* or the Truth to be titled *tathāgata-garbha,* i.e., the receptacle of all entities in Thusness. In enumerating the various names of the Truth, Chih-i remarks that because the Truth broadly embraces various *dharmas,* it is called *tathāgata-garbha.*[84] This Truth is, for Chih-i, nothing but the Middle Way-Buddha Nature.

The all-embracing nature of the Middle Way-Buddha Nature may be spoken of in methodological terms. That is, the Middle Way-Buddha Nature embraces all sorts of methods, which may be used for educational and soteriological purposes, for the liberation of sentient beings. How they are to be used must be in line with the individual needs of various sentient beings.

Chih-i remarks from the standpoint of the Perfect Doctrine that the Mind *(hsin)* of all sentient beings fully embraces "all doors toward the Truth" *(i-ch'ieh fa-men);* this means that the *tathāgata* (the Buddha) examines clearly the nature of this Mind and, on the basis of it, declares that there are countless doctrines and methods coming from the Mind.[85] Prior to this remark, Chih-i points out that, in the context of the Perfect Doctrine, all things come from the Mind, which is both the Great Vehicle (Mahāyāna) and the Buddha Nature.[86]

We observe two important points made by Chih-i in this context:

a. The Mind embraces all doors leading to the Truth.
b. The Mind is identical to the Buddha Nature.

The second point was already discussed above in section 4. We will therefore concentrate on the first point, which is simply expressive of the all-embracing nature of the Middle Way-Buddha Nature spoken of in methodological terms. On the basis of our study, we found no straightforward elaboration of this point in Chih-i's major works. However, its implication can be inferred by making reference to the concept of expedience *(fang-pien),* which entails the "door toward the Truth" *(fa-men)* in meaning, and *vice versa.* This expedience, in terms of its methodological nature, appears very often in Chih-i's works. It is particularly ascribed to the Buddha and bodhisattvas, as special weapons in their pursuit of transforming the world. For example, in the practice of the Contemplation of the Middle Way, Chih-i enumerates five items one must undergo, among which is the learning of the "great expedience" *(hsüeh ta-fang-pien).* With regard to this great expedience, he gives some concrete examples, including apparitions, analogies and discursions, and emphasizes that expedience is indispensable in benefitting others and in awakening them to the Truth. Indeed, the great expedience is, for Chih-i, a major way to express the *tathāgata*'s "great function without limits."[87]

In the voluminous WMCWS, Chih-i defines expedience or *fang-pien* in detail. He remarks:

> What is called *fang-pien* is for attaining the wisdom to the Truth. Therefore [we] need *fang-pien*. *Fang* is the partial method achieved by

> wisdom. *Pien* is the technique to make expedient use [of the method] skillfully. Making expedient use of the methods skillfully and benefitting others in accordance with the situations are therefore called *fang-pien.*[88]

Chih-i divides *fang-pien* into *fang* and *pien,* referring the former to the methods and the latter to the techniques that can use the methods skillfully. In Chinese, *fang* or *fang-fa* may mean a method, and *pien* or *pien-i* may signify an action based on one's initiative, or an action in response to what circumstances may require. In this action, the skill of using methods is involved. Chih-i's explanation of *fang-pien* in this way shows his delicacy in understanding and analysing Chinese terms. The goal of *fang-pien* or expedience—benefitting other people—remains, however, unchanged. It should be noted that, in the operation of *fa-men* or *fang-pien,* evil elements may be introduced or even taken as necessary. For example, in the conversion of a robber, the Buddha or bodhisattva himself may assume the apparition of a robber and perform evils with him in order to enhance the intimacy with the robber, which is most conducive to the robber's conversion.[89]

The proposition that the Mind embraces all doors toward the Truth is not often raised in Chih-i's major works. These doors toward the Truth can in fact be viewed as *dharmas* in a broader sense. We therefore think that the methodological implication of the all-embracing nature may be regarded as a complement to the implications explicated earlier concerning the meaning of "embrace."

8. Chih-i's Middle Way-Buddha Nature and Mādhyamika's Middle Way

With the understanding of Chih-i's conception of the Middle Way-Buddha Nature as derived from the above discussions, we now wish to respond to our second basic question concerning the difference between Chih-i's Middle Way-Buddha Nature and the Mādhyamika's Middle Way, focusing on five points.

First, Chih-i's Middle Way-Buddha Nature is an issue of *shih-hsiang,* or the Truth, and is the core of his whole system of thought. As seen from Chih-i's theory of the classification of the Buddhist doctrines, this Middle Way-Buddha Nature is his most crucial and important concept and is consequently the most emphasized doctrine. It is mentioned in many of Chih-i's important works, particularly in his commentaries on the *Vimalakīrti-nirdeśa-sūtra (Wei-mo ching),* i.e., the WMCLS and WMCWS. The Mādhyamika's Middle Way is only a complement to Emptiness, which is the Truth in the Mādhyamika system. As discussed in detail in Chapter II, this Middle Way reveals the transcendent nature of Emptiness. This nature is the transcendence of extremes, being and nothingness in particular. Although the Middle Way also is important, it is still subordinate to Emptiness; therefore, it does not attract the greatest attention from the Mādhyamikas. For the Mādhyamikas, it is the concept of Emptiness that characterizes their system, not the Middle Way.

Second, Chih-i's Middle Way-Buddha Nature, on the one hand, implicates the Mādhyamika's Middle Way, i.e., the transcendence of all extremes. On the other hand, it involves functional nature, which both Mādhyamika's Middle Way and Emptiness lack. Chih-i sees the Middle Way not merely as Principle, but also as the Mind. It is the Mind that is functional and capable of initiating actions. In Nāgārjuna's *Kārikā,* there is neither any mention of the nature of function nor any discussion of the relationship between the Mind, the Middle Way and Emptiness. As remarked previously, the function or functions are related straightforwardly to the transformation of the phenomenal world, which is the major religious concern of Mahāyāna Buddhism. The strength of a religion very much depends on whether or not its function or functions are emphasized; consequently, the functional nature is extremely significant in soteriological terms.

Third, Chih-i's Middle Way-Buddha Nature is attributed to the ever-abiding nature due to his identification of the Middle Way with the Dharma Body and Buddha Nature. Chih-i takes the Dharma Body and Buddha Nature, the former in particular, as an indestructible spiritual entity; the ever-abiding nature is also spoken of in this context. On the contrary, there is no mention of the Dharma Body and Buddha Nature in the *Kārikā,* much less an identification of the Middle Way with them. There is therefore no "ever-abiding nature" revealed in the *Kārikā.* Chih-i's criticism of Nāgārjuna, that his Twofold Truth is devoid of the "substance of the Middle Way,"[90] seems to reveal Chih-i's disagreement with Nāgārjuna's conception of the Truth. That is, Nāgārjuna's Truth, whether it be termed "Emptiness" or "Middle Way," is not established in terms of an indestructible spiritual substance or body, which Chih-i associates with the Dharma Body and Buddha Nature.

Fourth, with regard to the third characteristic of Chih-i's Middle Way-Buddha Nature—the "all-embracing nature"—there is no mention in the *Kārikā* that Emptiness or the Middle Way embraces all entities or *dharmas*. Nevertheless, the *Kārikā* does contain an idea in connection with the relationship between *nirvāṇa* and *saṃsāra,* the world of life and death. This idea can be, to a certain extent, regarded as similar to the first implication of "embrace" explicated previously, which basically advises that the Middle Way-Buddha Nature is the *dharmatā,* the "nature of *dharmas,*" that this Nature is possessed by the *dharmas,* and that it is to be realized and liberation attained within these *dharmas*. Therefore, this entails the inseparability of the *dharmas* from this Nature and its embracing of them. The idea in the *Kārikā*—that it is not possible that *nirvāṇa* is tenable apart from life and death[91]—is akin to this implication in view of the fact that the attainment of *nirvāṇa* results in the realization of the Truth, which is, for Nāgārjuna, Emptiness complemented by the Middle Way. It therefore seems possible to say that Emptiness or the Middle Way, as expounded in the *Kārikā,* embraces the entities or *dharmas* in the world of life and death.

This idea of Nāgārjuna is elaborated elsewhere in the *Kārikā:*

> *Saṃsāra* (i.e., the empirical life-death cycle) is nothing essentially different from *nirvāṇa. Nirvāṇa* is nothing essentially different from *saṃsāra.*[92]

> The limits (i.e., realm) of *nirvāṇa* are the limits of *saṃsāra.* Between the two, also, there is not the slightest difference whatsoever.[93]

These two verses advise that *nirvāṇa* and the world of life and death are not different from each other at all with respect to their *koṭi,* their "realm." In other words, the realm of *nirvāṇa* is just the realm of the world of life and death. It follows that *nirvāṇa* is realized nowhere but within the world of life and death. In replacing *nirvāṇa* and the world of life and death with Truth and the *dharmas,* respectively, we can say that Truth is realized nowhere but within the *dharmas*. This seems to imply that the Truth, whether it be Emptiness or the Middle Way, embraces the *dharmas*.

Despite this similarity of emphasis on the *dharmas* in Chih-i's thought and the *Kārikā,* we must cautiously remind ourselves that there is still a difference in the degree of emphasis. Chih-i explicitly states that the Middle Way-Buddha Nature embraces all *dharmas,* while Nāgārjuna remarks in a reservedly qualified manner that there is not the slightest difference between *nirvāṇa* and *saṃsāra.* It is clear that Chih-i adopts a more concrete and constructive attitude toward the world. With regard to the other two implications of the all-embracing nature—the implication associated with the compassion of the *tathāgatha* and the implication in its methodological references—there is no hint at all in the *Kārikā.*

Finally, Chih-i's Middle Way-Buddha Nature and Mādhyamika's Emptiness and Middle Way are bound together by the issue of Truth. Chih-i is well aware of this. How he criticizes Mādhyamika's Middle Way and establishes his own Middle Way-Buddha Nature is, undoubtedly, closely related to his conception of the Truth. The attribution of the three characteristics to the Middle Way-Buddha Nature clearly displays this conception: Truth is permanent, dynamic and all-embracing. This conception seems to be directed with an extremely positive and constructive attitude toward the empirical world. What Chih-i has in mind is that Truth must be established and realized in a close and concrete relationship with the empirical world. The functional and all-embracing natures of the Middle Way-Buddha Nature sufficiently give evidence to this point. Particularly, the concept of function is frequently emphasized in the FHHI and MHCK. The ever-abiding nature of the Middle Way-Buddha Nature also evidences this point, but in an indirect manner. That is, this nature renders the Middle Way-Buddha Nature in the status of *t'i,* or spiritual body, which is the substance or basis of all functions. From this vantage point this nature sustains and strengthens the functions exerted toward the empirical world.

It is in this sense that Chih-i criticizes the Middle Way of the Common Doctrine and Mādhyamika. His dissatisfaction is that this Middle Way does not have a concrete and constructive relationship with the empirical world, and is devoid of ever-abidingness and a functional nature. This criticism is, indeed, plausible and deserves our reflection, especially in view of the fact that this Middle Way merely signifies a state of transcending all extremes. This criticism is also applicable to the Mādhyamika concept of Emptiness, which, as explicated in the *Kārikā,* signifies the state of negating all false views and the state of negating the Self Nature, the state of non-substantiality.[94] This state is bound to be empty in content and futile in function. As signifying the Truth, it can merely be static. However, in view of the fourth point we made in this section and the idea of *t'i-fa* (the embodying of the entities of the Common Doctrine and Mādhyamika), Chih-i's criticism that this Middle Way does not embrace the *dharmas* may not fully do justice to the Common Doctrine and Mādhyamika (the latter in particular). Chih-i's interpretation seems slanted toward his system of thought, in which the all-embracing nature of the Truth (the Middle Way-Buddha Nature) is an important element. It seems that he distorts Nāgārjuna's *Kārikā* to serve his purpose of emphasizing this nature as pertaining exclusively to the Perfect Doctrine.

9. The Middle Way-Buddha Nature and other expressions of the Truth

Regarding our discussions of the Middle Way-Buddha Nature, one is apt to raise a question: Chih-i has used many expressions to describe the *shih-hsiang* or Truth; why should the Middle Way-Buddha Nature, which is only one of these expressions, be singled out and given particular attention? This is a significant question, and our response to it can enhance our understanding of Chih-i's notion of the Truth.

It is quite true that Chih-i has used many expressions or terms to describe the Truth. Some of them were inherited from the Buddhist schools or doctrines established before Chih-i, whereas others were his articulations. In the FHHI, chapter 8, he discusses *shih-hsiang* and enumerates many terms or phrases expressing its various aspects, including *shih-hsiang* itself, which denotes the indestructible Truth; Wondrous Existence *(miao-yu);* True, Good and Wondrous Form *(chen-shan-miao se);* Ultimate Emptiness *(pi-ching k'ung);* Suchness-Suchness *(ju-ju); nirvāṇa (nieh-p'an);* Empty Buddha Nature *(hsü-k'ung fo-hsing); Tathāgatagarbha (ju-lai tsang);* Middle and True Principle-Mind *(chung-shih li-hsin);* Middle Way *(chung-tao);* and Supreme Truth *(ti-i-i ti).*[95] Both the Middle Way and the Buddha Nature are taken as expressive of the Truth. It is therefore not difficult to understand why Chih-i identifies the Middle Way and the Buddha Nature and articulates a compound term, Middle Way-Buddha Nature or Buddha Nature-Middle Way, to emphasize this identification.

Our reasons for singling out the Middle Way-Buddha Nature and arguments for its significance in characterizing Chih-i's system of thought are as follows. First, as delineated above, the main issues in Chih-i's system are the conception of the Truth and its realization. Chih-i has a unique understanding of the Truth, particularly in comparison with the Mādhyamika. That is, the Truth is permanent, functional and all-embracing, possessing the three characteristics of ever-abidingness, meritorious function and embracing various *dharmas*. These characteristics are mainly explicated in the context of the Buddha Nature, with which Chih-i identifies the Middle Way. That the Middle Way signifies the Truth is beyond doubt. Consequently, it is manifest that the hyphenated "Middle Way-Buddha Nature" conveys the three characteristics of the Truth. The other terms or phrases enumerated above do not clearly convey these ideas.

Second, the compound term "Middle Way-Buddha Nature" carries an important practical message, which does not seem to be manifest in other terms or phrases expressing the Truth. This message, which is expressed in many of Chih-i's major works, the WMCWS in particular,[96] is that, in the endeavor for liberation, one sees or enters the Middle Way and then realizes the Buddha Nature. This practice of course does not mean that seeing the Middle Way and realization of the Buddha Nature are two steps—one after the other—in the endeavor for liberation, which would contradict the sudden manner Chih-i advocates as the way of attaining the Truth that he ascribes to the Perfect Doctrine. Rather, it means either that, in the realization of the Buddha Nature, the practice of the Middle Way is an important clue or item, or that the Buddha Nature is realized right in the practice and achievement of the Middle Way. The outcome is, to be sure, the attainment of the Truth. This orientation reveals different aspects of the Middle Way and Buddha Nature and enhances our understanding of the Truth in practical terms.

Third, among the three characteristics of the Truth, the meritorious function is most striking and is emphasized by Chih-i more than other characteristics. Chih-i spends many pages in the FHHI to deal with this function which deserves, indeed, our special attention because it is directly connected with the achievement of the Mahāyāna religious goal, the transformation of the phenomenal world. If this transformation is to take place, actions must be exerted upon the phenomenal world. These actions come, for Chih-i, from the functional nature of the Truth. But how can the Truth, which is usually taken as static, act or initiate actions? In this point, Chih-i shows his unique understanding of the Truth, as being not merely static, but also dynamic, thus rendering it capable of acting or initiating actions. Among the terms or phrases expressing the Truth, which one can fully account for this dynamism? Our answer is the Middle Way-Buddha Nature. As explicated in section 4, Chih-i understands the Buddha Nature in terms of the Mind, which can act in nature. In view of the identification of the Buddha Nature with the Middle Way, the Truth proper, we can speak of the dynamism of the Truth.

As a matter of fact, Chih-i has articulated a number of phrases in which a direct identification of the Middle Way as the Truth with the Mind is evidenced. These phrases include "Middle Way-True Mind,"[97] "Middle Way-Self Nature-Pure Mind"[98] and "Middle and True Principle-Mind," which was introduced above. Certainly these expressions are more straightforward than "Middle Way-Buddha Nature" in accounting for the dynamism of the Truth. However, no elaboration has been made on them, so we do not think they deserve special attention. In view of the above reasons and arguments, we singled out the Middle Way-Buddha Nature for discussion of the issue of the Truth or *shih-hsiang,* taking it to be the key concept in Chih-i's system of thought.

In this chapter, we have depicted the characteristics of the Middle Way-Buddha Nature or Truth. The Truth is not merely to be depicted, but also to be realized. This idea is particularly so for Chih-i, in view of his deep practical and soteriological concern. Indeed, the Truth can be more vividly and concretely understood in its realization, which is the topic of the next three chapters.

CHAPTER V

Four Alternatives in Mādhyamika and Chih-i

Having reviewed the key concepts, we must now ask: (a) What are Chih-i's philosophical methods as related to the realization of the Truth? and (b) How can they be related to Mādhyamika? With respect to the realization of the Truth, we find that Chih-i amply employs the methods of the Four Alternatives and their negative, the conception of identification, and the epistemology of the Threefold Contemplation. These, as Chih-i's philosophical methods, all have their origin in the Mādhyamika. However, in utilizing Mādhyamika thinking, Chih-i does not hesitate to modify and establish his own type of philosophizing, particularly in the cases of the Threefold Contemplation and identification.

The nature of the Four Alternatives of the Mādhyamikas, in Nāgārjuna's work in particular, has been studied by many modern scholars, including R. H. Robinson, Y. Kajiyama, K. V. Ramanan, R. Pandeya, S. S. Chakravarti and myself.[1] We shall make reference to these studies in explaining the nature of the Four Alternatives.

1. Contradictions of the Four Alternatives and the association with the Truth

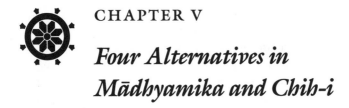

The Four Alternatives (Skt., *catuṣkoṭi;* Ch., *ssu-chü*), or tetralemma, is an important form of thinking in Mādhyamika philosophy and is also employed in the *Kārikā.* As suggested in the name, it normally consists of four alternatives or statements, including an affirmation, a negation, a synthesis of both affirmation and negation, and a transcendence of both affirmation and negation. These four forms are meant to exhaust the ways in which we may relate to something. In the present work, the "Four Alternatives" in capital letters will refer to the form of thinking while the "four alternatives" in lowercase letters will refer to the four statements in this form of thinking. A typical example of the Four Alternatives, which is also often mentioned by scholars, is shown in the *Kārikā* as follows:

> Everything is suchness *(tathyam),* not suchness, both suchness and not suchness, and neither suchness nor not suchness. This is the Buddha's teaching.[2]

This verse includes four alternatives:

1. Everything is suchness.
2. Everything is not suchness.
3. Everything is both suchness and not suchness.[3]
4. Everything is neither suchness nor not suchness.

These statements can be taken as four propositions that can be easily symbolized, respectively, as follows:

1. P
2. $\sim P$
3. $P.\sim P$
4. $\sim P.\sim\sim P$

P implies the affirmation of suchness, P the negation, $P.\sim P$ the synthesis of both, and $\sim P.\sim\sim P$ represents the transcendence of both. Apparently, these four alternatives are full of contradictions. The first one, P, and the second one, $\sim P$, contradict each other. The third one, $P.\sim P$, is a combination of the first and second and opposes the law of non-contradiction in Aristotelean logic. In the fourth alternative, $\sim P.\sim\sim P$, $\sim\sim P$ can be turned into P through the principle of double negation. Thus, the alternative is rendered as $\sim P.P$, or $P.\sim P$, which is simply the third alternative. Therefore, the fourth one is also self-contradictory.

Despite the contradictions, the Four Alternatives is taken as the apprehension of the Truth, as is evidenced by the Sanskrit expression *buddha-anuśāsana (buddhānuśāsana),* i.e., the instruction of the Buddha, which is the understanding and realization of the Truth. Kumārajīva's translation, *chu-fo fa,* the *Dharma* of the Buddhas, is also expressive of this claim. The corresponding expression in the verse in question, quoted in the TCTL, even pinpoints the Truth of the *dharmas (chu-fa chih shih-hsiang)* as the target of the employment of the Four Alternatives.

The thinking of the Four Alternatives also appears in another verse in the *Kārikā:*

> The Buddhas have provisionally employed the term *ātman* and instructed on the true idea of *anātman*. They have also taught that any (abstract) entity as *ātman* or *anātman* does not exist.[4]

This verse lacks the third alternative, but this lack should not affect the structure or nature of the Four Alternatives. The verse deals with the problem of self. The affirmation of self *(ātman)* and negation of it *(anātman)* are linked together. Kumārajīva's Chinese translation is:

> The Buddhas sometimes talk about self, sometimes non-self. In the Truth of the *dharmas,* there is no self nor non-self.[5]

Here, self is affirmed, negated, and both self and non-self are transcended in the form of the Four Alternatives. The association of the Four Alternatives, and the fourth alternative in particular, with the Truth of the *dharmas* is also mentioned.

In the TCTL, a verse that reveals the Four Alternatives is quoted:

1. The *dharmas* are [in the nature of] non-origination and non-extinction,
2. not [in the nature of] non-origination and non-extinction,
3. both [in the nature of] non-origination and non-extinction, and not [in the nature of] non-origination and non-extinction,
4. neither [in the nature of] non-origination and non-extinction, nor not [in the nature of] non-origination and non-extinction.[6]

The TCTL also remarks that this verse is related to deep penetration into the Truth of the *dharmas.*[7] Although the subject matter of the verse (i.e., the nature of non-origination and non-extinction) is a very complicated one, the Four Alternatives' fourfold structure in the verse is conspicuous and its association with the realization of the Truth is emphasized.

We now have a problem. The Four Alternatives is occupied with contradictions, yet it is associated with the Truth and is obviously taken by the Mādhyamikas as conducive to the realization of the Truth in methodological terms, at least as the way in which the Truth is expressed. How can this be so?

2. Educational implication of the Four Alternatives

In dealing with this problem, let us first re-examine the Four Alternatives. The first alternative, P, and the second one, $\sim P$, contradict each other. The third one, $P.\sim P$, brings the previous two together and is thus nothing but a repetition of the contradiction between them. The fourth one, $\sim P.\sim\sim P$, can be reduced to the third one and is therefore a repetition of this contradiction as well. In this sense, both the third and fourth alternatives do not suggest anything new, and the first and second alternatives would be sufficient. But this should not be so. It is four alternatives that are proposed, not two. The third and fourth alternatives must have their own roles to play and cannot be replaced by the previous ones. The crucial point is, we think, that we should not see the four alternatives logically or formally. Rather, we should pay attention to the content of each alternative and the occasion on which the related alternative is proposed. In this respect, we may consider two possibilities. First, different alternatives are employed to respond to various sentient beings with diverse talents in particular circumstances in the teaching of the Truth. In this employment, any subject matter may be picked up to fit the individual condition. Second, different alternatives are employed to classify the diverse understandings of the Truth or other subject matters of sentient beings. The first possibility reveals the educational implication of the Four Alternatives, while the second possibility reveals its role as a tool for classification.

Some outstanding commentators of the *Kārikā,* such as Piṅgala, Candrakīrti and Bhāvaviveka have explicated the Four Alternatives in educational and classifying terms. These explications were brought to our attention by such modern scholars as Robinson and Kajiyama. In this section, we will discuss the educational implication.

Robinson remarks that the Four Alternatives can be used as a pedagogical device. In his *Early Mādhyamika in India and China,* he quotes Piṅgala's comments on the typical verse 18:8 of the Four

Alternatives, in which suchness (*tathyam,* but Robinson renders it "real") is picked up as the subject matter. Piṅgala's comments in Robinson's translation are as follows:

> As for "everything is real," when you analyze the real-nature of the *dharmas*, [you find that] they all enter the absolute truth, are all equal, are all of one mark, that is, they are markless. It is just like the different colors and different tastes of all the streams which become one color and one taste when they enter the great ocean.As for "everything is unreal," when the *dharmas* have not entered the real-mark, they are contemplated analytically one by one, and they are all [seen to] have nothing real in them. They only exist because of the combination of many conditions.As for "everything is both real and unreal," there are three classes of living beings—superior, medium, and inferior. The superior contemplate the marks of the *dharmas* as "not real and not unreal." The medium contemplate the marks of the *dharmas* as "all both real and unreal." The inferior, because their powers of knowledge are shallow, look on the marks of the *dharmas* as "partly real and partly unreal." Because *nirvāṇa*, and the [other] unconditioned *dharmas* are imperishable, they look on them as real. Because *saṃsāra* and the conditioned *dharmas* are counterfeit, they look on them as unreal.As for "[everything] is not real and not unreal," [the Buddhas] declared "not real and not unreal" in order to refute "both real and unreal."[8]

Prior to these comments, Piṅgala specified that the Four Alternatives are expressed by the Buddhas to transform sentient beings, and that the Buddhas are in possession of countless expedient devices.[9] Piṅgala, apparently, takes the Four Alternatives to be an effective device in teaching sentient beings the Truth of the *dharmas* or entities, with each alternative responding to a particular situation.

Robinson also introduces Candrakīrti's comments on the Four Alternatives in stanza 18:8 commented on by piṅgala, remarking that Candrakīrti's interpretation is slightly different from Piṅgala's:

> [Candrakīrti] considers the tetralemma as an expedient device *(upāya)* that the Buddha uses in giving progressively higher instruction to the different grades of living beings. First the Buddha speaks of phenomena as if they were real, in order to lead beings to venerate his omniscience. Next, he teaches that phenomena are unreal, because they undergo modifications, and what is real does not undergo modifications. Thirdly, he teaches some hearers that phenomena are both real

> and unreal—real from the point of view of worldlings, but unreal from the viewpoint of the saints. To those who are practically free from passions and wrong views, he declares that phenomena are neither real nor unreal, in the same way that one denies that the son of a barren woman is white or that he is black.[10]

As seen from the quotations, both Piṅgala and Candrakīrti's interpretations of the Four Alternatives are quite clear, and the educational implication of the Four Alternatives is also beyond doubt. For instance, in Candrakīrti's interpretation, the first alternative advises that phenomena or the empirical entities are real. It affirms the entities in order to initiate and enhance the faith in the Buddha and Buddhism of the hearer, who is probably a novice in the religion. The understanding of the entities as such is, of course, superficial. In the second alternative, the nature of Dependent Origination of the entities is touched upon. The reality of the entities is negated because of their being subject to changes that result from Dependent Origination. In order to avoid the hearer's tendency toward an annihilative understanding of these entities, the third alternative suggests that the entities are both real and unreal. That is, they are real from the worldly viewpoint, but unreal from the supreme viewpoint, that of the saints. At this stage, a more sophisticated understanding of the entities is involved. Entities cannot be approached in a merely affirmative or negative manner, so in order to obtain a fuller understanding of the entities, a synthetic viewpoint must be adopted. Practically speaking, however, this stage is not to be resorted to because, in practice, there is no position to maintain, including this synthetic viewpoint. Attachment to any definite viewpoint, whether it be affirmative, negative or synthetic, is bound to limit and lose one's freedom that is essential to the attainment of liberation. This idea justifies the rejection of both the reality and unreality of the entities in the fourth and final alternative.

Another verse of the Four Alternatives, in which the self is picked up as the subject matter, also shows the educational implication.[11] In his delineation of this verse, Bhāvaviveka remarks that the Buddhas instructed sentient beings about the provisional self in light of the continuity of the mind and its mental states, such as love and hate. When sentient beings attached themselves to the self and took it as having permanent substantiality, which tended to initiate perversions and sufferings, the Buddhas preached the doctrine of non-self.

In order to awaken those having deep faith in the *Dharma* to the supreme Truth of Emptiness (i.e., the nature of being devoid of Self Nature), the Buddhas simply refrained from explicating self and non-self.[12] In other words, the Buddhas employed the first, second and fourth alternatives to educate sentient beings, respectively, corresponding to their individual conditions.

The educational implication of the Four Alternatives can be spoken of in two roles. First, each alternative can be taken as expressive of the understanding of the entities or the Truth from a particular angle in conformity with the hearer's individual conditions. There will generally be up to four angles for four different hearers or groups of hearers. (Sometimes three when one alternative is missing). It is not necessary for these angles to have any logical or practical relationship to each other. What is important is that the alternative employed can educate the hearer and enhance his understanding of the Truth. The interpretations of Piṅgala, Candrakīrti and Bhāvaviveka reveal this role, yet they tend to put the four angles and alternatives in an ascending order and regard the latter ones as more pertinent to higher or more mature understanding of the Truth.

Second, the four alternatives and angles can be placed in a progressive and ascending order and the hearer is educated to understand the Truth on a gradual and progressive basis. In this case, there is only one hearer or group of hearers, and the four alternatives are introduced one after the other. Education is a progressive process; one cannot be educated to attain perfect understanding of the Truth all of a sudden. Consequently, the latter alternatives can be introduced only when the former are fully digested and absorbed.

In view of the progressive and ascending order of the four alternatives in the understanding of the Truth from a lower stage to a higher, the Four Alternatives, as a thought device, may be construed as dialectical. An alternative in the form of affirmation or thesis (i.e., the first alternative), tends to see the Truth from a relative and partial angle. So does the second alternative, but in the form of negation or antithesis. An alternative in the form of synthesis of both affirmation and negation (i.e., the third alternative), can rectify the relativity and partiality of the first and second alternatives, but it is apt to be attached to psychologically. Such attachment can be overcome by an alternative in the form of the transcendence of both affirmation and negation (i.e., the fourth alternative). We have pointed out in Chapter II that the authentic Truth should be absolute and undifferentiated in nature. There is little doubt that the latter two alternatives pertain more to this nature than the former two. If dialectics are understood as a thought process in which the level of Truth is elevated through negation, antithesis or transcendence, we can roughly say that the Four Alternatives is a form of dialectic.

This dialectical character is also admitted by Robinson, who states that the alternatives form an ascending series in which each alternative, except the first, is a counteragent to the one before it. He concludes that this is a dialectical progression, each alternative negating and cancelling its predecessor, and that the whole argument moves forward to the negation of the fourth alternative, which is supposed to dispose of all "views."[13] Here, "the negation of the fourth alternative" does not denote "the negation" of the fourth alternative; rather, it refers to "the fourth alternative" whose function is negation, i.e., the negation of its predecessors. In his explication of the fourth alternative in terms of disposing of all views, Robinson tends to associate this alternative with attainment of the highest Truth, which is free from all relative and partial views. This hermeneutic is echoed by Kajiyama, who suggests that the previous three alternatives can be taken as reflecting an expedient purpose, while the fourth alternative reveals the highest Truth and cannot be refuted. He concludes that the Four Alternatives is dialectical.[14]

3. Classification role of the Four Alternatives

Robinson emphasizes the educational implication of the Four Alternatives without, however, mentioning its role as a method of classifying different teachings. Kajiyama is aware of the latter, in addition to the former. He states:

> The Four Alternatives, on the one hand, reveals the different understandings of people having different talents and dispositions towards the same object. On the other hand, it represents the gradual and progressive instructions directed to students of different grades.[15]

The revelation of people's different understandings is, indeed, based on a classification of these understandings. Regretfully, however, Kajiyama does not extend any further elaboration in this respect. This classification of different understandings suggests the classifying role of the Four Alternatives, which is important in the sense that it can be closely related to Chih-i's classification of Budhist doctrines. In view of this connection, we will study the classifying function in detail.

The typical verse 18:8 of the Four Alternatives, in which suchness or reality is picked up as the subject matter, is expounded by Bhāvaviveka in classifying terms. In his *Po-je-teng lun-shih,* he comments on this verse in the following way:

> The objects such as internal and external organs and forms, etc., are taken as non-perversive from the viewpoint of worldly and provisional Truth. Therefore, everything is real. From the viewpoint of the supreme meaning, however, the internal and external organs, etc. originate from causes and are produced from delusion, without any substantiality. This nature is different from what they appear to be [i.e., the real entities they seem to be]. Therefore, everything is unreal. In view of the mutual dependence of the two Truths, [everything is] both real and unreal. When the practitioner attains the fruit [of enlightenment], he discerns the authentic nature of all entities without discriminations. He does not see [the difference of] reality and unreality. This is why we say that everything is neither real nor unreal.[16]

Bhāvaviveka's point is clear. The very same thing—the empirical entities that we encounter in this actual world—can be understood from different viewpoints expressed by the different alternatives. The outcome is different understandings of the same thing. The first alternative advises that entities are real in the light of common sense. The second alternative advises that, in light of the doctrine of Dependent Origination or Emptiness, entities are devoid of substantiality or Self Nature and therefore unreal. Common sense and Emptiness represent two different viewpoints dependent on or relative to each other. In order to avoid attachment to either viewpoint, the third alternative synthesizes both of them and advises that the entities are both real and unreal. Nevertheless, "reality" and "unreality" represent two understandings based on the discrimination of entities, which has no place to stand in the experience of enlightenment. When one is enlightened, one does not maintain any discrimination, including that of reality and unreality. It is in this context that the fourth alternative advises that the entities are neither real nor unreal.

In this way, the Four Alternatives form a classifying scheme in which different understandings of the same thing can be classified as affirmative, negative, synthetic and transcendent, corresponding to their related alternatives. Each of the understandings may be held to be true in light of a specific viewpoint. Interestingly, the viewpoints or angles related to the four alternatives are also in an ascending order with regard to the understanding of the entities.

We see, then, that the Four Alternatives can have both educational and classifying roles. One may ask if there is any relationship between these two. Our understanding is that the classifying function can be closely related to the educational role in the sense that it is the basis of the latter. An instructor has to be familiar with the various possible understandings of a certain subject matter and be able to classify them in logical and practical order before he can select a suitable one with which to instruct. Effective education of sentient beings *via* the Four Alternatives depends on an appropriate application of the classification of the various understandings in terms of the Four Alternatives.

4. The negative of the Four Alternatives and its revelation of the Truth

The Four Alternatives consists of two forms in Mādhyamika: the affirmative and the negative. So far we have been dealing with the affirmative one. We will now turn to the negative form as seen in the following typical verse, which is often quoted and employed by Chih-i and other T'ien-t'ai thinkers:

> At nowhere and at no time can entities ever exist by originating out of themselves, from others, from both (self-other), or from the lack of causes.[17]

This verse refutes four statements: that entities exist by self-origination; that entities exist by other-origination; that entities exist by self-other origination; that entities exist by the lack of causes. If self-origination is taken as the subject matter, then the statement that entities exist by self-origination is composed of an affirmation. The statement that entities exist by other-origination denotes that they do not exist by self-origination, which is a negation. The third statement, that entities exist by self-other origination, is a synthesis of self-origination and other-origination. As for the statement that entities exist by the lack of causes, because causes are confined to self-causes and other-causes, it simply means that entities exist by neither-self-nor-other origination. This statement is composed of a transcendence of both self-origination and other-origination. In view of the fact that affirmation, negation, synthesis and transcendence are entailed in the four statements, respectively, these statements can be taken to be in the form of the Four Alternatives, or as the affirmative form of the Four Alternatives. Piṅgala also speaks of these four statements in terms of the Four Alternatives in his commentary of the *Kārikā*.[18] The refutation of these four statements indicates the negative of the Four Alternatives.

What is the purpose of using the negative of the Four Alternatives? Piṅgala comments as follows:

> What is called "non-self-origination" means that entities cannot originate from their own substantiality. [Their origination] must depend on the causes. . . . If the self is untenable then the other is also untenable. Why? Because [the existence of] the other is dependent upon [the existence of] the self. If [the entity] does not originate from the self, it cannot originate from the other either. As regards self-other origination, it involves two faults: self-origination and other-origination. If entities can originate from lack of causes, this would mean [that they are] permanent. This is not the case. If there are no causes, there will be no effects.[19]

Piṅgala speaks of the origination of entities in terms of causality or relational conditions, which do not include self, other and the other alternatives. That is, entities originate from a combination of causes. But, then, what do "self, other, ..." mean when we say that entities cannot exist by originating "out of themselves, others, ..." or that entities cannot undergo self-origination, other-origination, ... ? In response, Piṅgala states:

> There is no Self Nature in the causes. Because there is no Self Nature, therefore self-origination is impossible. Because there is no Self Nature, therefore there also is no Other Nature. Why? Because [the existence of] Other Nature is dependent upon [the existence of] Self Nature. Other Nature to the "other" is also Self Nature.[20]

It is specified that self, other and the other alternatives are spoken of on the level of Self Nature, which actually does not exist at all.

"Because there is no Self Nature, therefore self-origination is impossible." That is, entities are devoid of Self Nature; therefore, they cannot originate from themselves. Because "other" is related to "self," there is no Other Nature and entities cannot originate from "others," either. Therfore, Piṅgala refutes the idea of Self Nature and Other Nature and that of self-origination, other-origination, and self-other origination. As for origination without causes, it violates the principle of causality and is also to be refuted. Piṅgala concludes that the origination of entities is untenable from self, other, both, and neither, as expressed by the four alternatives, respectively. Therefore, he arrives at the Truth of No-origination *(pu-sheng).*[21]

The major concern of the verse in question is, according to Piṅgala, to reveal the Truth of No-origination in the sense that entities cannot originate from self, other or both, which are spoken of in terms of Self Nature, or from a lack of causes either. This argument is made by employing the negative of the Four Alternatives. Does No-origination, then, imply that there is no origination of entities at all? The answer is by all means negative. The Truth is that entities originate from causes or Dependent Origination; they are in the nature of Emptiness. Consequently, entities are devoid of Self Nature. In No-origination, what is refuted is the origination of entities from the standpoint of Self Nature, not the origination of entities from the standpoint of Dependent Origination or Emptiness. Our understanding as such is echoed by Kalupahana, who, in expounding Nāgārjuna's position in question, remarks:

> When Nāgārjuna said, "The self nature of an existent is not evident in the causal condition, etc." (I.3), he was not rejecting or denying conditions, but only self nature *(svabhāva)* that some philosophers were positing in the condition *(pratyaya)* in order to account for the arising of the effect.[22]

Conditions, here, are the basis of Dependent Origination. The empirical world can originate merely from dependence on these conditions. The concept of conditionality logically rejects the supposition of Self Nature, which is self-sufficient.

In view of the fact that No-origination signifies the refutation of origination spoken about in the context of the discussion of Self Nature, which itself is vehemently rejected in the doctrine of Emptiness, we may infer that No-origination can be closely associated with Emptiness. In fact, No-origination can be taken as a form to negate

Self Nature and is therefore expressive of Emptiness. We should not forget that Nāgārjuna understands Emptiness mainly in terms of the negation of Self Nature. The negative of the Four Alternatives, in demonstrating No-origination, can also be taken as a device to negate Self Nature.

We may also infer that the negative of the Four Alternatives, by which No-origination is revealed, can be closely associated with the revelation of Emptiness. This association is strengthened by Nāgārjuna's understanding of Emptiness in terms of the relinquishing of false veiws. This understanding has been detailed in Chapter II above. Nāgārjuna's point is that all views based on concepts that are attached to as extremes can split the Truth of Emptiness from its wholeness and absoluteness. Nāgārjuna shows that concepts taken as extremes are actually partial and relative, and therefore are contrary to the undifferentiated and absolute nature of the Truth. Therefore, these views are false and need to be relinquished in the revelation of Emptiness.

It is also inferred that all extremes should be refuted. Any one of the forms of the four alternatives—whether it be an affirmation, a negation, a synthesis or a transcendence—is apt to be taken as an extreme. When this happens, it has to be refuted. Therefore, the negative of the Four Alternatives is proposed in the revelation of Emptiness. Self-origination, other-origination and self-other origination are all false views based on the extreme nature of self, other and self-other respectively. The extremity is formed in the ascription to the self and other of Self Nature, which is a mere fabrication. Origination from a lack of causes is, of course, also a false view or extreme that violates the principle of causality. The negative of the Four Alternatives is, in fact, a vivid model in which the refutation of false views is demonstrated.

At this point, a doubt may arise. It is not difficult to understand that the previous three alternatives are to be refuted, for they tend to create problems of attachment. That is, in the first alternative, the affirmative is conducive to an attachment to the affirmation of something. In the second alternative, the negation is conducive to an attachment to the negative of something. In the third alternative, the synthesis is conducive to an attachment to both the affirmative and negative aspects of something. However, it is somewhat unnatural that the fourth alternative, which reveals the state of transcendence of extremes, should be refuted as well. Here, we must remind ourselves of the warning from the Mādhyamikas that Emptiness is not to be adhered to, or that Emptiness is to be emptied. This is because Emptiness, as the negation or transcendence of Self Nature and false views, itself may in turn be attached to. The same is true with the transcendent implication in the fourth alternative. The refutation of this alternative means that even the transcendent state should not be attached to. Attachment to a transcendent state will by all means cause false views.

From the above discussions, we come to an understanding that the major concern of the negative of the Four Alternatives is the refutation of Self Nature and false views. As Nāgārjuna understands Emptiness and its revelation in terms of this refutation, it seems safe to construe the negative of the Four Alternatives as a straightforward device through which Emptiness is revealed.

To go further, the refutation of the four forms in the negative of the Four Alternatives reflects the overcoming of the limitation of concepts. This overcoming is the power of the negative of the Four Alternatives and is closely related to the revelation of the Truth. To demonstrate this point, let us study two verses in the *Kārikā.*

> It cannot be said that the Blessed One exists after *nirodha* (i.e., release from worldly desires). Nor can it be said that He does not exist after *nirodha,* or both, or neither.[23]

> It cannot be said that the Blessed One even exists in the present living process. Nor can it be said that He does not exist in the present living process, or both, or neither.[24]

The message communicated here is that the categories or concepts of "exist" (is), "not exist" (is not), "both-exist-and-not-exist" (both-is-and-is-not) and "neither-exist-nor-not-exist" (neither-is-nor-is-not) cannot be ascribed to the Blessed One, whether He is released from worldly desires or is in the present living process. Piṅgala does not comment on these two verses. Our understanding is that "exist" and "not exist" linguistically indicate two opposite states of something taken as an item in this empirical and relative world. So also do "both-exist-and-not-exist" and "neither-exist-nor-not-exist," which are used to depict the world. Such categories or concepts have serious limitations in two senses. First, the relationship between the concepts and the states they imply is conventional. In our use of language, whatever concept corresponds to any particular object, state or act is decided conventionally. To relate concepts to the world so that the latter can be established is a conventional process. Second, the concepts themselves are relative and dependent, as far as their meanings are concerned. "Exist" is relative to and dependent upon "not exist," and *vice versa*. There is no concept that can claim absolute and independent meaning about the world. Therefore, the world, as treated in this manner, is conventional and relative; the concepts to comprehend the world can exist only in a conventional and relative sense. Conventionality and relativity are the limitation of concepts. In view of this limitation, concepts cannot transmit the Truth, which is ultimate and absolute in nature. They can transmit only what is conventional and relative. False views often come from improper use of concepts, taking them as expressive of the Truth. Accordingly, in order to realize the Truth as such, the conventionality and relativity of the concepts must be transcended or overcome through a refutation of the four forms in the negative of the Four Alternatives.

With regard to the refutation of concepts or categories in the negative of the Four Alternatives, Sprung tends to share this same understanding. He remarks:

> The *catuṣkoṭi* exhausts the ways in which the verb "to be" may be employed in assertions: one may affirm the "is" of something, or affirm the "is not" or "both-is-and-is-not," or "neither-is-nor-is-not." In all four ways language is being used ontologically; the verb "is," in whatever variation, implies the being or non-being of what the assertion is about. Nāgārjuna and Candrakīrti repudiate all of the four alternatives. They repudiate the ontological implication of the verb "to be."[25]

"In all four ways language is being used ontologically" means here that language, whose major elements are concepts, as used in the Four Alternatives, is taken as corresponding to the Truth of the world and entities; it is therefore able to transmit the Truth. This is an improper understanding of language and must be repudiated. The "ontological implication" in Sprung's remarks is for us the potential to transmit the Truth of the world and entities. Language or concepts, whether they be expressed in the Four Alternatives or whatever form, cannot claim this implication or potential because of their provisional and relative character.

The negative of the Four Alternatives appears quite often in the *Kārikā*.[26] It is also mentioned in the TCTL:

> The meaning of ultimate Emptiness is devoid of definite forms and should not be clung to. Awakening cannot be achieved by means of communication and interpretation. It cannot be termed being, or nothing, or both, or neither.[27]

This quotation explicitly informs the reader that the ultimate Emptiness or Truth transcends the Four Alternatives. The negative of the Four Alternatives is also seen in the TCTL elsewhere, though indirectly.[28]

5. From Mādhyamika to Chih-i

With reference to the issue of the Four Alternatives, it is important to note that in the Mādhyamika this issue consists of two forms: the affirmative form of the Four Alternatives and its negative, as delineated above. Both of these forms are, in fact, not creations of the Mādhyamikas, but have their origin in Primitive Buddhism.[29] There the Four Alternatives is taken as expressive of four extremes, while the negative of the Four Alternatives is favored as expressive of the Middle Way, the state of release from these extremes. Nāgārjuna does not make a clear-cut contrast between the Four Alternatives and its negative; rather, he tends to speak of both forms in positive terms and regard them as conducive to the revelation of the Truth. That is, the affirmative form of the Four Alternatives is educational in leading the hearers to recognize the various aspects of the Truth in accordance with their individual conditions, or in leading them to recognize the Truth on a gradual basis from the lowest stage to the highest. This idea has already been elaborated in our previous discussions. As for the negative form of the Four Alternatives, Nāgārjuna sees it as a straightforward device through which to reveal the Truth. In the operation of this device, the four forms of affirmation, negation, synthesis and transcendence represented by the four alternatives, respectively, are refuted simultaneously. The Truth is revealed straightforwardly in this simultaneous refutation. In view of the fact that there is no sign that Nāgārjuna downplays or negates the affirmative form of the Four Alternatives in favor of the negative form, we are reluctant to term the latter the "negation of the Four Alternatives." Rather, we refer to it as the "negative of the Four

Alternatives" in the sense that it is the negative form of the Four Alternatives. There is, for Nāgārjuna, no distinctive contrast between the Four Alternatives and its negative. We must bear this in mind before coming to a comparison of Chih-i and Nāgārjuna on the issue of the Four Alternatives.

The issue of the Four Alternatives receives full and specific treatment in Chih-i's system. He frequently quotes in his major works two typical verses in the *Kārikā* that reveal the Four Alternatives and its negative.[30] There is no doubt that Chih-i inherits the Four Alternatives and its negative from Nāgārjuna, and that he was the great thinker in Chinese Buddhism who adopted and elaborated on these methods.[31]

Chih-i's employment of Nāgārjuna's methods is a big topic, which would in itself require a whole book to deal with because it is found scattered throughout Chih-i's major works and is articulated in considerable detail. What deserves our attention most is that Chih-i employs these methods on different occasions, touching on a variety of concepts and issues. Before delineating this employment, we wish to make the following statistical and literary observations and reflections on these instances.

a. Of the Four Alternatives and its negative, the former appears much less in the *Kārikā;* it is mentioned merely twice. (Cf. notes 2 and 5.) With regard to the frequency of employing these two methods, Chih-i does not have one dominate over the other. Each method enjoys approximately the same opportunity of employment. The Four Alternatives is found mostly in the SCI and FHHI,[32] while its negative appears most frequently in the MHCK.[33]

b. With regard to the Four Alternatives, Kumārajīva translates the predicates of the four alternatives, which appear in the typical verse in the *Kārikā* (cf. section 1 above and note 2), as real, unreal, both real and unreal, and neither real nor unreal, respectively. Chih-i sometimes holds to this translation, but at other times he renders the predicates as "being," "emptiness," . . . . He has also felt free to turn "being," "emptiness," . . . . into "being," "nothingness," . . . .[34] Plainly speaking, the difference is only for literary variety, but lacks any conceptual difference.

c. In the *Kārikā,* the Four Alternatives is typically presented in the process of referring to "suchness" (cf. section 1 above and note 2), while its negative appears in reference to "origination" (cf. section 4 above and note 17). In principle, reference to suchness, origination or whatever does not affect the nature of these two methods. The difference is merely for literary variety because, whichever subject matter is taken, the outcome of the logical symbolization remains unchanged. For instance, the Four Alternatives composed of suchness, not suchness, both and neither, and the Four Alternatives composed of self-origination, other-origination, both and neither, are equally symbolized as P,∼P, P.∼P, ∼P.∼∼P. Chih-i is aware of this point. Therefore, in the employment of the Four Alternatives and its negative, he refers to suchness, origination and other subject matter interchangeably.

d. In practice, however, the implications of the employment of the two methods cannot be found merely in the outcome of their logical symbolization. These implications are often related to the subject matter picked up in the presentation of the methods. For instance, the frequent reference made to ignorance and the delusive mind shows a practical concern for working on these subjects in revealing or attaining the Truth. This is particularly true in Chih-i's employment of the methods. On the basis of the interchangeability of the subjects, he does not hesitate to pick up those which are more relevant to his practical and soteriological purposes. This point will be discussed more in due course.

6. Chih-i's treatment of the Four Alternatives

The issue of the Four Alternatives treated by Nāgārjuna has been widely studied by scholars. However, the same issue treated by Chih-i has not yet attracted much attention from them. The study that follows therefore reflects very much our own conclusions regarding the related matters.

With regard to the method of the Four Alternatives, Chih-i seems much more concerned about how to use it than what it denotes. There is, however, an occasion in the WMCLS in which the issue of denotation is indirectly addressed. After quoting a typical verse from the TCTL (cf. note 3) and indicating that this verse is also used in the *Kārikā,* Chih-i remarks:

> Therefore we know that the Buddhas taught the *Dharma* in terms of these four doors. The real denotes the *Dharmatā,* as the authentic Principle, and [the category of] being is used as the door. As regards the

> unreal, the ultimate Emptiness is taken as the door. As regards both the real and unreal, it denotes the identity of ignorance and wisdom, and the identity of wisdom and the ultimate Emptiness, as mentioned earlier. This is the door of both the real and unreal. As regards neither the real and unreal, it denotes the double negation of Emptiness and being. This is the door of the Middle Way, which is neither Emptiness nor being. These four doors are for those who wish to attain the Way. They will be enlightened immediately upon hearing this.[35]

Chih-i chooses here a typical verse from the *Kārikā* as an example to express his own view of the Four Alternatives. On the one hand, he speaks of the Four Alternatives in terms of four doors characterized by being, Emptiness, both being and Emptiness, and neither being nor Emptiness. On the other, he relates the Four Alternatives to four epistemological view points we may have about the world or entities: the real, the unreal, both the real and unreal, and neither the real nor unreal. He uses such terms and relationships as "*Dharmatā*," "Emptiness" and the "identity of ignorance and wisdom" to expound these view points. These terms and relationships are very much characterized by practical and soteriological motifs. In Chih-i's thought, the identity of ignorance and wisdom, in particular, suggests an extremely important manner, in which the Truth is to be attained. This relationship will be dealt with in great detail in Chapter VII below. In view of this connection, the four view points are highly relevant to the realization of the Truth. They can be taken as representing four approaches to the Truth or four levels of the Truth, accounting for the corresponding apprehension of the four levels of Truth through the four doors.

Chih-i's employment of the Four Alternatives is based on the idea described above, and is therefore an issue of realizing the Truth. This employment is called the "penetration of the Way *via* four doors" *(ssu-men ju-tao)*,[36] or the "penetration of the Principle *via* four doors" *(ssu-men ju-li)*.[37] There are various ways through which to approach the Buddhist Truth that can be, for Chih-i, summarized into four basic patterns which he calls the "four doors." He calls these doors "the door of being," "the door of Emptiness," "the door of both being and Emptiness" and "the door of neither being nor Emptiness."[38] We have pointed out earlier that Chih-i's theory of the classification of Buddhist doctrines is the backbone of his system, and the employment of the Four Alternatives here is undertaken from the same perspective. Chih-i remarks that the four doors are explicated in each of the four Doctrines, and that each of these four doors is conducive to penetration into the Truth. However, for expedient purposes, the *sūtras* and *śāstras* usually emphasize and use one door in relation to the realization of the Truth expounded in each of the four Doctrines. That is, the Tripiṭaka Doctrine emphasizes and uses the door of being, the Common Doctrine the door of Emptiness, the Gradual Doctrine the door of both being and Emptiness, and the Perfect Doctrine the door of neither being nor Emptiness.[39] Obviously, Chih-i is seeking from the *sūtras* and *śāstras* as authorities justification for his association of the four doors with the four Doctrines in a corresponding and ascending order. We are not concerned with the endeavor to seek justification from Buddhist authorities, but we observe that such an association is strikingly in conformity with Chih-i's understanding of the four Doctrines. That is, the four doors are differentiated into two groups, one containing the door of "being" and the door of "Emptiness," the other containing the door of "both being and Emptiness" and the door of "neither being nor Emptiness." This differentiation is made on the basis that the Truth advocated in the Tripiṭaka Doctrine and Common Doctrine is one-sided *(p'ien)*. Hence, these two Doctrines are associated respectively with the door of being and the door of Emptiness, each of which Chih-i tends to regard as one-sided. On the contrary, the Truth advocated in the Gradual Doctrine and Perfect Doctrine, which Chih-i specifies as the Middle Way-Buddha Nature, is perfect *(yüan)*. Therefore, these two Doctrines are associated with the door of "both being and Emptiness" and the door of "neither being nor Emptiness," respectively.[40] In view of this association, it seems that "both being and Emptiness" and "neither being nor Emptiness" can be related to the concept of "perfect." Chih-i does not elaborate this point, but "both being and Emptiness" and "neither being nor Emptiness" are, nevertheless, certainly not one-sided. In Chinese, what is not one-sided is adequate and will tend to be perfect. With regard to the difference within each of the two groups, Chih-i contrasts the manners of the Tripiṭaka Doctrine and Common Doctrine, by which the Truth is to be attained, as inferior and skillful, respectively; he typifies their doors as the "side door" *(p'ien-men)* and "main door" *(cheng-men)*. He also contrasts the doors of the Gradual Doctrine and Perfect Doctrine as "side door" and "main door," respectively.[41]

Chih-i's classification of Buddhist doctrines is articulated in an ascending order. The final Doctrine (the Perfect Doctrine) is for Chih-i the highest one. In view of the parallel relation between the four doors and the four Doctrines, it is logical to infer that the four doors are also arranged in an ascending order. As a matter of fact, Chih-i has noted this point:

> The people functioning in the three realms [of desire, form and non-form] see these realms as differentiation. The śrāvakas and pratyekabuddhas see these realms as Suchness. The bodhisattvas see these realms as both Suchness and differentiation. The Buddha sees these realms as neither Suchness nor differentiation, and illuminates both Suchness and differentiation as well. Here, we take what the Buddha sees to be the correct substance of Truth.[42]

Chih-i speaks here of the Truth in terms of four levels and presents these four levels of Truth in the form of the Four Alternatives. The four doors corresponding to the four levels of Truth are also implied, although Chih-i replaces being and Emptiness with differentiation and Suchness, respectively. The ascending character of the four alternatives and four doors can be seen through the ascending order of the people in the realms of desire, form and non-form, the śrāvakas and pratyekabuddhas, the bodhisattvas and the Buddha, who approach the Truth through different doors. This ascending process terminates in the Buddha, who, going beyond others, attains the correct substance of Truth *(shih-hsiang cheng-t'i)*. This Truth, for Chih-i, is superior to the Truth attained by others. Correspondingly, the door to the correct substance of Truth, which is clearly established on the basis of the fourth alternative, is superior to the other doors. This also shows Chih-i's ascription of superiority to the fourth alternative with regard to the attainment of the Truth.

7. The Four Alternatives as an analogical device

Now we wish to reflect on Chih-i's Four Alternatives in light of Nāgārjuna's, the latter having educational and classifying implications. Let us start with a question: What is the most striking feature in Chih-i's employment of the Four Alternatives? The answer is obvious, that is, he uses the Four Alternatives to analogize four different doors to express four different aspects of the Truth, all in the light of his classification of Buddhist doctrines. To be specific, the first alternative is used as an analogy to the door of being in order to express the Truth advocated by the Tripiṭaka Doctrine. The second alternative is used as an analogy to the door of Emptiness in order to express the Truth advocated by the Common Doctrine. The third alternative is an analogy to the door of both being and Emptiness in order to express the Truth advocated by the Gradual Doctrine. Finally, the fourth alternative is an analogy to the door of neither being nor Emptiness in order to express the Truth advocated by the Perfect Doctrine. The hearers are taught with the specific door that is most pertinent to their individual conditions (their interests, concerns, talent, etc.). Chih-i remarks explicitly:

> [The four doors] are all different expressions responding to individual talents.[43]

Accordingly, the hearers are led to recognize the different aspects of the Truth. However, in view of the fact that the four doors, like the four Doctrines, are in an ascending order, each hearer will finally be taught with the door of neither being nor Emptiness; in this way, the hearer will be led to the Truth advocated by the Perfect Doctrine, i.e., the correct substance of Truth. In this sense, the Four Alternatives is taken as a device in which analogies are made for educational and soteriological purposes, and in this educational implication, Chih-i and Nāgārjuna can be brought together.

Here, one may raise two questions. First, why should the analogy be articulated in this manner? Is there any logical basis for such an articulation? In other words, why should the first alternative be used to analogize the door of being, the second the door of Emptiness, and so forth? Second, why should the door of being be associated with the Tripiṭaka Doctrine, the door of Emptiness the Common Doctrine, and so forth? Is there any doctrinal or practical ground for such association?

In response to the first question, our understanding is that the articulation of the analogy has to do with the four logical forms composing the four alternatives (affirmation, negation, synthesis and transcendence). The affirmation in the first alternative tends to reveal the affirmative or phenomenal aspect of the Truth, which is spoken of in the understanding of the world and entities. Thus, the analogy of the first alternative is expressed appropriately in the door of being. The negation in the second alternative tends to reveal the negative or non-*substantial* aspect of the Truth, so in this case, the analogy of the second alternative is best expressed by the door of Emptiness. The synthesis in the third alternative combines both aspects of the Truth. Correspondingly, the analogy of the third alternative is pointed out clearly in the door of both being and Emptiness. The transcendence in the fourth alternative reflects the state of transcending both aspects, so the analogy of the fourth alternative is described appropriately as the door of neither being nor Emptiness. Each analogy articulated has, indeed, a logical basis.

With regard to the second question, Chih-i himself does not explicitly account for this kind of association. This issue is, however, not difficult to deal with in light of his classification of Buddhist doctrines as delineated in Chapter III, above. Chih-i holds that the Tripiṭaka Doctrine emphasizes the phenomenal aspect of entities and tends to see them as something real. Its association with the door of being seems natural. The Common Doctrine emphasizes the non-substantial or empty nature of entities, leading to its association with the door of Emptiness. The Gradual Doctrine advocates the gradual procedure in the realization of the Truth of entities, in which one must experience different levels of understanding of the Truth, from the lowest to the highest. These different levels are presented by being and Emptiness, so the association of the Gradual Doctrine with the door of both being and Emptiness is proper. Finally, the Perfect Doctrine advocates the sudden manner of the realization of the Truth of entities, in which all differentiations, including those of being and Emptiness, must be transcended and overcome suddenly. Here lies the basis for the association of the Perfect Doctrine with the door of neither being nor Emptiness. In this sense, the association of the four doors and the four Doctrines also has doctrinal and practical bases.

Let us return to a comparison of Chih-i and Nāgārjuna. Chih-i's Four Alternatives as an analogical device is based on his classification of Buddhist doctrines. As can be seen from the above delineation, by parallelling the four alternatives with the four Doctrines, he refers each alternative to a specific Doctrine. As each Doctrine has its own favored type of Truth, each alternative is therefore associated with, or regarded as the door to, a specific type of Truth. It should be noted particularly that this fourfold scheme does not imply the splitting up of the Truth. Rather, it implies that the Truth can be approached through different dimensions or doors. Chih-i himself has also pointed this out:

> The Truth cannot be [ascribed even with the numeral of] one; how can it be [ascribed with the numeral of] four? We should know that "four" denotes the [four] doors to the Truth.[44]

Chih-i's point is that what can be spoken of in terms of numerals is countable and relative in nature, and that the Truth is absolute in nature and goes beyond the realm of countability. It cannot be counted even with the numeral of one, much less those larger than one. If it is the one, it is the one in an absolute sense: the absolute One. The "four" or four doors simply imply various understandings of the Truth. Consequently, Chih-i's employment of the Four Alternatives in the form of an analogy can be taken as a constructive scheme in the development of Buddhist thought in terms of synthesizing different Buddhist doctrines and leading one to a more comprehensive understanding of the Buddhist Truth. In addition, from the analogy articulated in the light of his classification of Buddhist doctrines, Chih-i skillfully uses the Four Alternatives to expound and advertise this classification. The first alternative expresses the Tripiṭaka Doctrine; the second alternative the Common Doctrine, and so on. With regard to Nāgārjuna, the situation is different. He does not parallel the four alternatives with specific Buddhist doctrines and does not seem to even have a clear and strong idea of the classification of Buddhist doctrines. However, we should not forget that his Four Alternatives has a classifying implication, which is helpful in classifying different understandings of the same thing. It is not impossible to develop a classification scheme of various Buddhist doctrines on the basis of this classifying implication of the Four Alternatives. In view of the close relationship between Chih-i and Nāgārjuna, it is likely that the former's classification of Buddhist doctrines was influenced by this classifying implication. We are not in a position here to explore this possibility, but we are sure, at least, that this classifying implication is entailed in Chih-i's treatment of the Four Alternatives as an analogical device, because the paralleling of the four alternatives (or doors) with the four Doctrines presupposes a classifying scheme of various Buddhist doctrines.

The method of the Four Alternatives is, for both Chih-i and Nāgārjuna, educational in leading sentient beings to learn the different aspects of the Truth, leading finally to the correct substance of Truth. Chih-i's analogy of the four alternatives to the four doors on the basis of his classification of Buddhist doctrines is a positive and constructive development of the method in the sense that it helps us understand the abundant contents of the Buddhist Truth. However, there is an important point to which we must turn our attention. The use of the Four Alternatives as an analogical device is limited. That is, the analogy is articulated provisionally and conventionally and is undertaken through relative concepts or names, such as "being" or "Emptiness." This renders the Four Alternatives in a relative manner. Moreover, in the analogy, the Truth is not demonstrated straightforwardly, but by a medium to which it is analogised. The analogy cannot lead one to encounter the Truth face to face. It is in this sense of limitation that Chih-i views the Four Alternatives with a reserved, qualified attitude, calling it "conceivable."

"Conceivable" *(ssu, ssu-i)* is spoken of in contrast to the "inconceivable" *(pu-ssu, pu ssu-i).* In Chih-i's terminology, the conceivable refers to what can be described by names and consequently is relative in nature, while the inconceivable refers to that which cannot be described by names and consequently is absolute. It is also possible to see the conceivable as pertaining to the realm of speculation, and the inconceivable as beyond this realm. Chih-i contrasts the conceivable and inconceivable in relation to the Four Alternatives:

> [What is] named in terms of the Four Alternatives pertains to the origination of causality and dependence, and is therefore conceivable and speakable. . . . [The absolute cessation and contemplation] is beyond dependence and relativity, and so is not what is made. It cannot be conceived in terms of the Four Alternatives. Therefore it is inexpressible in language and not an object of cognition.[45]

Chih-i is plainly associating the Four Alternatives here with causality and relativity, which he regards as in the nature of what is originated; he thinks that what is originated is conceivable and speakable. It is in this context that he cautiously evaluates the method of the Four Alternatives. That is, the conduciveness of this method to the understanding of the Truth can be admitted, as long as this understanding is confined to the conceivable and relative.[46] This means simply that the Four Alternatives can merely lead us to attain the relative Truth. It has nothing to do with the absolute Truth, which is inconceivable in character and must be attained through another method. To go further, Chih-i is aware of the danger of attachment to the Four Alternatives and warns us against this attachment. His point is that the categories used in the Four Alternatives (being, nothingness, etc.) cannot be asserted determinately, otherwise one is bound to become committed to ignorant views.[47] This point seems to imply that these categories should not in any way be associated with the determinate Self Nature, the attachment to which is the cause of all false views.

8. Chih-i's treatment of the negative of the Four Alternatives

Now we come to a discussion of the negative of the Four Alternatives in Chih-i's system. As in the case of the Four Alternatives, Chih-i is more interested in the use of the negative of the Four Alternatives than in giving a clear definition of this method. On one occasion, however, he makes the following remarks:

> As things do not undergo self-origination, how can there be knowledge of the self as its object? As there is no other-origination, how can there be knowledge of mutual dependence as its object? As there is no self-other-origination, how can there be knowledge of the major and subsidiary causes as its objects? As there is no non-causal-origination, how can there be knowledge of the natural [origination] as its object? If one clings to these four views [of self-origination, other-origination, self-other-origination and non-causal-origination], various kinds of ignorance and defilement will arise, but then, how can these be called knowledge? Now, with the [understanding of] no-origination, etc., we eradicate the [clinging to] fourfold Self Nature. When [the clinging to] Self Nature is eradicated, there will be no dependence [on the Self Nature], neither will there be any *karma,* or suffering, etc. With a pure Mind in the constant state of non-dichotomy, one is able to manifest *Prajñā* [wisdom].[48]

In this remark, the so-called "knowledge of the self as its object" *(tzu-ching chih),* as well as other similar phrases, do not constitute true knowledge. They are spoken of in the context of clinging to Self Nature. That is, "knowledge of the self as its object" denotes the knowledge whose object is the self, which is taken as having its own Self Nature. "Knowledge of mutual dependence as its object" *(hsiang-yu-ching chih)* denotes the knowledge whose object is an "other" upon which something depends in its origination. This "other" is taken as having Self Nature.[49] The other two alternatives follow similar conclusions arising from the views of self-origination, other-origination, etc., which are also spoken of in terms of Self Nature. Consequently, they lead to the fourfold Self Nature responding to the four sorts of origination. Chih-i seems to think that these views represented by the Four Alternatives are false due to their clinging to Self Nature, which is nothing but a conceptual fabrication. He suggests that we should eradicate the fourfold ways of clinging to Self Nature with the correct understanding of non-self-origination, etc., which is expressive of No-origination. The eradication of clinging to Self Nature will result in the non-dichotomous state of the mind, the "pure Mind." This pure Mind can initiate the *Prajñā* wisdom, which is, for all Buddhists, the very wisdom with which the Truth can be realized.

Chih-i's point is that if the Four Alternatives, represented by self-origination, etc., is clung to and associated with Self Nature, false views are bound to arise. He also seems to conceive that the clinging to Self Nature is what makes the mind dichotomous and prevents *Prajñā* wisdom from being manifested. Therefore, one should refute the Four Alternatives and renounce any speculation regarding Self Nature. In doing so, one is able to reveal the authentic nature of knowledge, namely, *Prajñā,* and see the Truth. Here, Chih-i seems to relate the Four Alternatives to the clinging of Self Nature and the dichotomous tendency of the mind, both of which only obstruct one's apprehension of the non-substantial and non-dichotomous Truth. This is, we believe, the sense in which Chih-i refuted the Four Alternatives and emphasized its negative, implying that the Truth is to be attained in the negation of Self Nature and the rejection of dichotomous or false views. Nāgārjuna also held to this implication. Consequently, with regard to the issue of the negative of the Four Alternatives, Chih-i and Nāgārjuna basically shared the same conception.

Chih-i employs the negative of the Four Alternatives on many occasions and makes reference to a variety of subjects, such as ignorance, Suchness, dreams, various *dharmas* and the delusive mind. Of these various subjects, the delusive mind is mentioned most. In view of the limited space in the present work, it is impossible to describe in detail all of Chih-i's references. We can only concentrate here on an example, in which the manner and basic concern of Chih-i's employment of this method can be seen. The example reads:

> To behold this mind of desire, [one may ask] if it originates from the organ, or the object, or both, or neither. If it originates from the organ, it would have originated by itself before encountering the object. If it originates from the object, [then there will be a difficulty, namely,] the object is another thing from the self, how can it be related to me? If it originates from the organ and object together, then two minds should have arisen [one from the organ and the other from the object]. Yet it is impossible to originate without a cause. To trace the desire in terms of the Four Alternatives, [we find that] the desire does not have a place to come from. . . . Ultimately it is empty and quiescent.[50]

The mind of desire is a delusive mind. Chih-i endeavors to employ the Four Alternatives here to trace the origination of this delusive nature, but the endeavor fails because each of the four alternatives cannot avoid a difficulty. Here, some explanation is needed concerning the form of the Four Alternatives in this example, especially with regard to the second alternative. The origination of the organ (organ-origination) is taken as the affirmation in the first alternative. This is all right. In the second alternative, however, Chih-i picks up the object and tries to form a negation in terms of object-origination. This sounds problematic because the object is not an opposite of the organ, and object-origination cannot be taken in the form of a negation in contrast with organ-origination as an affirmation. To speak in terms of symbolization, if organ-origination is symbolized as "p," object-origination cannot be symbolized as "$\sim$p." This identifies the difficulty of taking origination of the object (or "object-origination") as the second alternative, which is based on a negation. In this case, our understanding is that we should see the issue in a looser and more flexible sense. We need not adhere too much to the logical form of negation because Chih-i is not interested in logic; he is more concerned with the practical and soteriological. In the affirmation of organ-origination, the organ is posited as the subject matter. Anything that is not the organ, i.e., "not-organ," can be taken loosely as its opposite. This gives rise to "not-organ" origination as the negation of organ-origination. In the present example, the object represents whatever is not the organ. Accordingly, object-origination is expressive of not-organ origination and is thus the negation of organ-origination. In this sense, the second alternative can be worked out in conjunction with the former alternative in accordance with the normal relationships among the four alternatives.

This passage also illustrates two other points concerning the negative of the Four Alternatives. First, the delusive mind cannot come from anywhere; there is no background to which the origination of the delusive mind can resort. Second, the nature of the delusive mind is fundamentally empty. With regard to the first point, it is natural for one to relate the origination of something to a cause, whether it be self, other, both, or neither. In the example at hand, the organ stands for the self-cause, while the object stands for the other-cause. Indeed, these aspects of self, other, both, and neither exhaust all the logical causal natures (causes) one can conceive. Chih-i would not object to the tendency to seek a cause to account for the origination of something, so far as this origination is regarded as a phenomenon in empirical and relative terms. He also remarks that the origination of the mind must depend on major and subsidiary causes.[51] In fact, the category of origination is what we use to describe entities coming into being prior to our sensation, as well as ideas that appear in our thought. Origination is, in this sense, no more than a conventional device and thus has a relative nature. Apart from this sense, origination has no meaning. But people tend to attribute to the concept of origination an ultimacy and to envision that, outside the realm of relativity, there is something in the nature of "origination;" this then promotes problems of self-origination, other-origination, self-other-origination, or non-causal-origination, all of which have absolute status and could exist by themselves. Such attribution and perception are nothing but issues based on our conceptual fabrication and unavoidably initiate false views. It is such attribution and perception that Chih-i objects to, and the negative of the Four Alternatives expresses this objection. In relation to this point, Chih-i states:

> What is called delusion is the origination of the mind. This origination is [in reality] devoid of self-nature, other-nature, self-other-nature and non-causal-nature. When the origination takes place, it does not come from self, other, both and neither.[52]

Chih-i mentions four natures that exhaust all natures that can be conceived. These four natures can be associated with the four logical forms (affirmation, negation, synthesis and transcendence) in the four alternatives. To be specific, origination from self-nature is in the form of affirmation. Origination from other-nature denotes the origination from not-self-nature and therefore is in the form of negation. Origination from self-other-nature is a synthesis of the previous two. Finally, origination from non-causal-nature denotes a transcendence of this synthesis. Thus the four natures correspond to the four alternatives, and in view of this correspondence, the negation of the four natures is demonstrated in the negative of the Four Alternatives. The four natures are, indeed, equally expressive of Self Nature or *svabhāva* in the absolute sense. What Chih-i is doing here is to employ the negative of the Four Alternatives to bring to our attention the fact that the origination of the mind (or whatever else) in whatever form (i.e., self-origination, other-origination, etc.) is really devoid of Self Nature or any definite ground or status of existence. This teaching is the Truth of No-origination with which Nāgārjuna was deeply concerned.

Chih-i's second point, that the nature of the delusive mind is fundamentally empty, is logically entailed in the first point. If the origination of an entity does not have Self Nature, then there will be no origination in the absolute sense. It follows that the entity, which originates in the relative sense, will not originate in the absolute sense at all. That is, it is devoid of the absolute Self Nature and is therefore empty.

From Chih-i's arguments as shown above—namely, that both origination and whatever originates are devoid of Self Nature and are therefore in the nature of Emptiness—it is clear that the concern guiding Chih-i's employment of the negative of the Four Alternatives is the realization of the Truth: the Truth of No-origination that is absolute in nature. This No-origination is just another expression of Emptiness. This is a straightforward realization of the absolute Truth, in which no analogy is undertaken. We have shown in section 4 that both Nāgārjuna and Piṅgala also share this understanding of No-origination. As explicated in Chapter IV above, Chih-i basically speaks of the Truth in terms of the Middle Way-Buddha Nature, which embraces the meaning of Emptiness. In most cases in which the negative of the Four Alternatives is used to reveal the Truth, Chih-i seldom specifies the Middle Way-Buddha Nature. There is one occasion, however, on which Chih-i refers to the Truth revealed through this method as Emptiness, Provisionality and the Middle Way. That is, he employs this method in a threefold process *(san-fan)* and concludes that, through this threefold process, one can penetrate into the meaning of Emptiness, Provisionality and the Middle

Way.[53] Emptiness, Provisionality and the Middle Way are, for Chih-i, expressive of various aspects of the Truth of Middle Way-Buddha Nature. This will be discussed in the following chapter.

9. Chih-i's negative of the Four Alternatives from a practical and soteriological perspective

We now wish to reflect on Chih-i's negative of the Four Alternatives in light of Nāgārjuna's. Our study so far has demonstrated that both Chih-i and Nāgārjuna admit without the slightest reservation that the negative of the Four Alternatives is conducive to a straightforward revelation of the Truth in the absolute sense. In the *Kuan-hsin lun,* a small work written shortly before his death, Chih-i remarks that the verse in the *Kārikā* in which the negative of the Four Alternatives is found (see section 4 and note 17) is meant to interpret the doctrine of No-origination.[54] This No-origination is the first of the Eight Negations or the so-called "Eight-Nos" *(pa-pu),* which appears in the beginning verse of the *Kārikā.*[55] This verse of Eight-Nos transmits the most profound Buddhist message by means of the negation of eight categories (origination, extinction, destruction, permanence, etc.). The message is that the absolute Truth transcends all extremes based on relativity and thus cannot be ascribed with categories, which are relative in nature. This teaching brings about the doctrine of No-origination, No-extinction, No-destruction, No-permanence, etc. Chih-i's remark plainly shows his view that the negative of the Four Alternatives aims at attaining the absolute Truth of No-origination, which is, as pointed out previously, expressive of Emptiness. It also shows his close relation to Nāgārjuna on this issue. Chih-i ascribes special importance to No-origination and thinks that all chapters in the *Kārikā* are expressive of No-origination, as has been discussed earlier.[56] Indeed, in Chih-i's eyes, No-origination represents the absolute Truth expounded in the *Kārikā,* presented by means of the negative of the Four Alternatives. In the understanding and employment of the negative of the Four Alternatives, Chih-i's views are basically in conformity with Nāgārjuna's. In this regard, we can certainly state that Chih-i inherits Nāgārjuna's thought.

There is, however, a significant difference between the two great thinkers with regard to the employment of the negative of the Four Alternatives. Nāgārjuna usually makes reference to general matters, as he is not much concerned about specifying a particular subject matter, as is evidenced in the typical verse on No-origination mentioned above, as well as in others. In this typical verse, the subject matter to be ascribed with the nature of No-origination is *bhāvāḥ,* which denotes entities or *dharmas* in general. With respect to this point, Chih-i is quite different and precise. On many occasions he specifies the subject matter as the mind, or more appropriately, the delusive mind. He often argues, by means of the negative of the Four Alternatives, that the delusive mind does not originate from itself, other, both, or neither. By this means he comes to the conclusion that the delusive mind is in the nature of No-origination, or is not to be gained in the ultimate sense.[57] Theoretically speaking, whatever is taken as the subject matter does not affect the role of the Four Alternatives, which is to awaken people to the Truth through the realization of the nature of No-origination. The Truth is No-origination and can be demonstrated in anything. In practice, however, in the endeavor to awaken to the Truth of No-origination, it is always better to pick up an intimate or particular subject matter to start with, than to stray into the midst of external and indefinite things. The delusive mind rises out of our own existence and is consequently an intimate subject matter to work upon. Once we realize the nature of No-origination of this mind by means of the negative of the Four Alternatives, we will tend to restrain ourselves from giving rise to any delusive motives, and this delusive mind will gradually be kept under control. Chih-i himself is certainly aware of the practical importance of the specification of this delusive mind. In the MHCK, he classifies the subjects for cessation and contemplation into ten categories, among which the leading one is composed of the five aggregates (Skt., *skandha;* Ch., *yin*), the eighteen realms (Skt., *dhātu;* Ch., *chieh*) and the twelve entrances (Skt., *āyatana;* Ch., *ju*).[58] Within this category, Chih-i picks up the aggregate of consciousness (Skt., *vijñāna-skandha;* Ch., *shih-yin*), and advises us to concentrate on it in the practice of contemplation because it is intimate to each of us. This aggregate of consciousness is nothing but the mind, the root of defilements. He states:

> The mind is the root of defilements, and is described as such. If one wants to contemplate and observe [the defilements], one must tackle their root. This is like the acupuncture treatment, in which one must find out the acupoint. Now, we should leave the *chang* [i.e., the dis-

> tant] and pick up the *ch'e* [i.e., the less distant], leave the *ch'e* and pick up the *ts'un* [i.e., the least distant]. Let us put aside the four aggregates of form, etc., but contemplate the aggregate of consciousness alone. The aggregate of consciousness is the mind.[59]

Chih-i's point is obviously that, after the nature of No-origination of the intimate delusive mind is realized, the realization of the nature of No-origination can easily incorporate distant things in general. This is indeed a commendable procedure to follow from the practical point of view.[60]

To go further, the specification of the mind in the realization of the nature of No-origination signifies the No-origination of the mind. This is an extremely important practice in the soteriological sense. The No-origination of the mind should not be taken in the annihilative sense to mean the extirpation of the mind. As will be delineated in Chapter VII, the mind embraces both the pure and impure (for instance, Dharma Nature and ignorance) in any single moment and is delusive. In the practice of the No-origination of the mind, one is concerned about overcoming the impure and revealing the pure in the mind. The outcome is that the delusive mind is transformed into the pure Mind, which is the basis of enlightenment and liberation. In this sense, the negative of the Four Alternatives, through which the No-origination of the mind is revealed, is highly soteriological.

To emphasize the soteriological significance of the negative of the Four Alternatives, Chih-i even goes so far as to specify the subject matter as liberation itself in the employment of the method. He states:

> [The liberation] does not originate from self-liberation, therefore it is not named in terms of the self-nature. It does not originate from other-liberation, therefore it is not named in terms of other-nature. It does not originate from self-other, therefore it is not named in terms of self-other-nature. It does not originate from neither-self-other, viz., the non-causal, therefore it is not named in terms of non-causal-nature. . . . The liberation does not depend on the four extremes for origination.[61]

The paradigm is quite similar here to the one used to refute the origination of the mind[62] and is patterned on the negative of the Four Alternatives. Chih-i's argument is that the origination of liberation cannot be related to any form of Self Nature—whether it be self, other, self-other, or non-causal—and that liberation has nothing to do with Self Nature. It is in this sense that he advises soteriologically that liberation does not arise from the four extremes, which obviously denote the four alternatives associated with Self Nature.

The delusive mind and liberation as the soteriological goal tend to form two opposite poles to each other. It is apparent that the origination of the former should be refuted. It is, however, somewhat unnatural that the origination of the latter should likewise be refuted. In employing the method of the negative of the Four Alternatives, Chih-i does not distinguish between them, which may cause confusion. Our understanding is that the goal of Chih-i's method is the refutation of the origination of anything or any event ascribed with Self Nature, including even liberation as the result of enlightenment. This refutation has, of course, to do with the realization of the Truth. In this respect, Chih-i is quite in line with Nāgārjuna. That Chih-i picks up liberation as the subject matter in the argument of No-origination should not be taken as his objection to initiating liberation; he simply holds that liberation does not take place in any association with Self Nature. The advice that liberation does not arise from the four extremes tends to mean that liberation is possible in the transcendence of the four extremes. This advice demonstrates a deep concern for liberation, rather than an objection or indifference to it.

Nevertheless, a problem still remains. The Truth for Nāgārjuna is Emptiness, which he understands mainly in terms of the negation of Self Nature. The purpose of the negative of the Four Alternatives is the refutation of Self Nature. Accordingly, the method corresponds and is quite conducive to the realization of the Truth. It appears, then, that this method is a sufficient one. Chih-i's case, however, is different. The Truth for him is the Middle Way-Buddha Nature, which, as described in some detail in Chapter IV above, has very abundant contents, including Emptiness. The negative of the Four Alternatives does not fully correspond to the realization of this Truth, so it is an insufficient method. It is in this sense that Chih-i must rely on other methods, which will be discussed shortly.

CHAPTER VI

Epistemic-soteriological Character of the Threefold Contemplation

Between the Four Alternatives and its negative, Chih-i considers the latter to be the authentic philosophical method leading to the realization of the Truth. He would not, however, be satisfied with this method since it only eliminates falsehood but does not positively reveal the Truth. The negative of the Four Alternatives is merely a method based on negating relative categories which are often falsely attributed to the absolute Truth. Origination, for example, is an important category attributed to the Truth of entities in an absolute sense, whether it be self-origination, other-origination, both or neither. It is thought in the Mādhyamika that none of these four sorts of origination pertain to the absolute Truth, and that they must be negated to pave the way for the revelation of the absolute Truth. This method of negation represents the way to reveal the Truth in a negative manner: to tell what the Truth is not. It can never positively reveal what the Truth is.

The Mādhyamika Emptiness and Middle Way—which are taken as the negation of Self Nature and false views, and the transcendence of extremes, respectively—are just what this method is suitable to reveal. The nature of non-origination, non-extinction, etc., is quite in line with the negative character of this method. In view of this character, it is understandable that Nāgārjuna uses the negative of the Four Alternatives so frequently in the *Kārikā*. Chih-i's case is different. Although he does not ignore the negative and transcedent aspects of the Truth, he is certainly more concerned about the positive and constructive relationship between the Truth and worldly entities and affairs. From the functional and all-embracing nature that he ascribes to the Middle Way-Buddha Nature, he is undoubtedly of the opinion that the Truth cannot be spoken of and fully understood without making reference to this empirical world. The

Truth is, for Chih-i, comprehensive in content, covering both negative and positive, transcendent and worldly aspects. It is both Emptiness and No-emptiness and cannot be fully realized until both aspects are accounted for. This purpose cannot be served by the negative of the Four Alternatives, which merely accounts for the negative. The Threefold Contemplation is proposed precisely in the context of serving this purpose.

The Threefold Contemplation *(san-kuan)* is composed of the Contemplation of Emptiness *(k'ung-kuan),* Contemplation of the Provisional *(chia-kuan),* and Contemplation of the Middle Way *(chung-kuan).* We will explain the translation of *kuan* as "contemplation" later. As a philosophical method of revealing the Truth, the Threefold Contemplation is different from the negative of the Four Alternatives in the sense that the latter merely copes with the nature of No-origination or the empty nature of the object; the Threefold Contemplation, on the other hand, copes with both the empty nature and the provisional or worldly nature of the object as well as the synthesis of these two natures. Chih-i claims that this Threefold Contemplation has its origin in the Mādhyamika. To be more specific, it can be traced in Nāgārjuna's concepts of Emptiness, Provisional Name and Middle Way.[1] As a matter of fact, the Threefold Contemplation does have a close relationship with the Mādhyamika concepts of Emptiness, Provisional Name and Middle Way. In view of this, we must first examine the meaning of these three concepts in the Mādhyamika context before studying the character of the Threefold Contemplation. As Emptiness and the Middle Way have been dealt with in Chapters II and III above, we will now focus on the Provisional Name here.

1. Provisional Name in Nāgārjuna's context

Provisional Name (Skt., *prajñapti;* Ch. *chia-ming*) appears in the *Kārikā* twice. It is mentioned in the verse of the Threefold Truth (cf. note 1 of the present chapter) together with Emptiness and the Middle Way. In this verse, Nāgārjuna reminds us of the provisionality of Emptiness, or the fact that Emptiness is a Provisional Name. His point seems to be that Emptiness is provisionally established to denote the Truth; Emptiness as a name or concept does not convey anything ultimate. (Cf. Chapter II.7 above.) Nāgārjuna here does not take a positive view of provisionality or the Provisional Name.

Provisional Name is also mentioned in the following verse:

> Nothing could be asserted to be *śūnya, aśūnya,* both *śūnya* and *aśūnya,* and neither *śūnya* nor *aśūnya.* They are asserted only for the purpose of provisional understanding.[2]

In this verse, Nāgārjuna negates the Four Alternatives composed of Emptiness *(śūnya),* Non-emptiness *(aśūnya),* both Emptiness and Non-emptiness, and neither Emptiness nor Non-emptiness, and treats this form of thinking as being of provisional character. In the previous chapter, we have analyzed the fact that Nāgārjuna speaks of the Four Alternatives in educational, classifying and therefore expedient terms. The provisional character of the Four Alternatives here may be related to this context. What Nāgārjuna wants to say is that the Four Alternatives does not pertain to anything absolute and ultimate. Consequently, from the negative of the Four Alternatives and the reduction of the Four Alternatives to provisionality, Nāgārjuna's reluctance to take a positive view of the Provisional Name is also inferred.

Provisional Name in Sanskrit, *prajñapti,* means "appointment," "agreement," and "engagement."[3] Generally speaking, it denotes some sort of mental articulation, in which a name is appointed to represent certain worldly entities, which are in the nature of dependent or relational origination. From the standpoint of the ultimate Truth, all entities are devoid of Self Nature and are therefore empty. However, these entities all originate from combinations of conditions or factors and consequently assume their existence in space and time as appearances or phenomena. In response, we provisionally appoint names to denote and distinguish these entities, and the Provisional Name comes into being. Provisionality here pinpoints the character of appointing names. "Provisional" in Chinese, *chia,* means "borrowed" or "instrumental" and is therefore without absolute reference.

With regard to the meaning of the Provisional Name, *prajñapti,* Sprung states:

> I understand a *prajñapti* to be a non-cognitive, guiding term which serves to suggest appropriate ways of coping with the putative realities on which it rests for its meaning and to which it lends meaning. "Person" rests on the putative reality of psycho-physical traits, and "char-

> iot" presupposes wheels, axle, and so on. There is, in truth, no entity "person" and none "chariot" named by these words.[4]

That there is in Truth no entity "person" and no "chariot" named by these words means that there are no such entities as person and chariot which have an independent Self Nature. "Person" is a Provisional Name that we appoint to denote the assemblage of certain psycho-physical traits, and the assemblage does not refer to anything that has its own Self Nature and can exist independently.

In the *Kārikā,* no explicit meaning of Provisional Name is given. Nāgārjuna might have thought that such meaning as described here was commonly known already, so there was no need to explain it. Or perhaps he simply did not emphasize the Provisional Name. The latter conjecture is supported by the fact that the Provisional Name is not mentioned at all in his other important work, the *Vigrahavyāvartanī.*

In penetrating deeper into the Provisional Name, however, the issue becomes more complicated. Naming an entity is different from the entity itself. The former is a mental manipulation, which is conceptual in nature, while the latter refers to the empirical and worldly existence. Provisional Name here is spoken of in the context of the former, rather than the latter. In other words, Provisional Name primarily refers to the act in which something is provisionally named, rather than to the object that is named. This act is, in fact, an act of naming, with the purpose to distinguish something from others. As naming is undertaken with names or concepts, such as "chariot," "table," etc., this act is clearly conceptual. Moreover, names and concepts pertain to the realm of language, and naming is expressive of the function of language. It follows that this act is an act of utilizing language. It should also be noted that, because an act of naming is to name something on a provisional or conventional basis, this act would naturally infer the provisionality or conventionality of the name. Provisional Name may therefore also denote this nature of provisionality and conventionality.

Regarding the Provisional Name as an act of naming entails a concern for the conceptual, while to construe it in the sense of an object to be named entails a concern for the empirical and worldly. This distinction is extremely important, especially in terms of determining one's attitude toward the empirical world. In the case of Nāgārjuna, when he declares Emptiness to be a Provisional Name, he is pinpointing the provisionality of Emptiness as a name or concept. That is, in reality there is no name or concept, including "Emptiness," that can represent the ultimate without restriction. "Emptiness" is nothing but an articulated name or concept with which to denote the ultimate Truth. Provisional Name here obviously refers to the act of articulating names or concepts. With this conceptual articulation, the message of the provisionality of Emptiness as a name is also inferred. And when Nāgārjuna connects the Four Alternatives with a provisional understanding or the Provisional Name, he is reducing the Four Alternatives to an operation of language, whose main content is names and concepts. Provisional Name is thus also taken here as an act of using names and concepts. As seen from the *Kārikā,* Nāgārjuna undoubtedly construes the Provisional Name in the sense of an act of naming or utilizing language. Indeed, the Sanskrit term, *prajñapti,* is expressive of an act. Matilal delineates the Provisional Name in terms of dependent designation. This dependent designation is, according to him, the act of designating something like a chariot, which is dependent on other things, such as the set of wheels and the axle. He points out that all our designations are "synthetic" in operation, in which we synthesize various elements into something in order to designate them.[5] The act of designating something is exactly what we understand Nāgārjuna's Provisional Name to be, i.e., the act of naming.

2. Provisional Name in the context of the *Ta-chih-tu lun* (TCTL)

In the TCTL, the Provisional Name assumes the denotation as seen in the *Kārikā,* but it also goes further. On some occasions, the Provisional Name is used as a verb:

> The five aggregates assemble. [The assemblage] is provisionally named "sentient being."[6]

> Because of the transcendence of the two extremes, [the state] is provisionally named "Middle Way."[7]

> The various factors assemble, and so [the state] is provisionally named "old age."[8]

On the first occasion, the Provisional Name conveys a thought process in which the name "sentient being" is provisionally worked out. On the second occasion, the name "Middle Way" is provisionally introduced to denote the state of the transcendence of extremes. We can therefore assert that the Middle Way is a Provisional Name. This assertion is akin to the assertion that Emptiness is a Provisional Name, in the sense that both the Middle Way and Emptiness are names provisionally worked out to denote the ultimate. On the final occasion, "old age" is provisionally named to depict the state of a person caused by the assemblage of various factors. On these three occasions, it is beyond doubt that the Provisional Name is treated as an act of naming.

The author of the TCTL does not, however, see the Provisional Name as merely an act of naming. He tends to ascribe to the Provisional Name some substantive bearing by associating it with objects or entities. For example, he says:

> The common people, because of their erroneous views, regard [what is made] as being. The wise do not cling to the form of what is made, understanding that it is merely a Provisional name.[9]

The Provisional Name here is directed to entities as phenomena, such as a chariot, house, body, etc. Because these things are causally originated, or, as mentioned in the text, made *(yu-wei)* by causes, there are indeed no entities that have Self Nature and that can exist independently. What the Provisional Name denotes is the assemblage of causes, without which nothing can maintain existence. For example, the assemblage of the head, legs, stomach, vertebrae, and so on, is provisionally named "corporal body."[10] The Provisional Name denotes the assemblage of these causes, not the "entity" in itself.

This tendency of associating Provisional Name with objects is strengthened in the articulation of two terms: "provisional name-being" *(chia-ming yu)* and "provisional name-form" *(chia-ming hsiang)*. In these terms, the subjects are being *(yu)* and form *(hsiang)*, but they are established on the basis of the Provisional Name or provisionality. With regard to provisional name-being, the TCTL states:

> The provisional name-being is like the curd, which is composed of four factors, i.e., color, smell, taste and touch. When these causal factors combine together, there is provisionally the name "curd." The being of the curd is not of the same sort as that of its causal factors. It is unreal and yet it is not unreal in the sense as the hare's horn, or the hair of the tortoise.[11]

The provisional name-being is therefore a kind of being between the real and the unreal. This kind of being is based on a combination of causal factors; it is apparent that this kind of being denotes the combination itself, which appears as entities. The provisional name-form refers in the TCTL to such things as chariot, house, forest, etc.[12] As both provisional name-being and provisional name-form denote entities as objects, the Provisional Name is also brought close to the objects.

On another occasion, the Provisional Name is identified with things and given considerable emphasis. The TCTL states:

> [Subhūti] delineates the ultimate Truth of various entities without eradicating the Provisional Names. . . . The bodhisattva recognizes that all entities are Provisional Names, and consequently one should learn to acquire the [wisdom of] *prajñāpāramitā*. Why? Because all entities have nothing but Provisional Names, and they all follow the [wisdom] *prajñāpāramitā* [which recognizes] the characteristic of ultimate Emptiness.[13]

The idea of delineating the ultimate Truth of various entities without eradicating the Provisional Name originally comes from the *Prajñāpāramitā-sūtra.*[14] This is just another expression of the idea of realizing Emptiness right in the embodiment of the entities *(t'i-fa ju-k'ung),* with which Chih-i characterizes the Common Doctrine. Mādhyamika and the Prajñāpāramitā thought belong, in Chih-i's view, to the Common Doctrine. The Provisional Name in this context obviously denotes the realm of entities, and the ultimate Truth in question is by all means Emptiness. What is conveyed here is the inseparability of the realization of the absolute from the relative empirical entities, leading to the importance of these entities in soteriological aspects. The Provisional Name is construed in the sense of an object or objects.

3. Provisional Name in Chih-i's context

So far we have discussed the concepts of Emptiness, Provisional Name and Middle Way in the Mādhyamika's context. We will now proceed to see how Chih-i understands them. As Emptiness and the Middle Way have been dealt with in Chapter III, in what follows we will focus on the Provisional Name.

With regard to the meaning of the Provisional Name, some important changes can be witnessed in Chih-i's system. First, the term "Provisional Name," or *chia-ming,* is in most cases reduced to "the Provisional," or *chia.* This deletion of the term "Name," or *ming,* does not simply signify a change in terminology. Rather, it signifies a shift in denotation from a stress on the nominal aspect to that of the substantive aspect, based on a greater concern about the substantive and worldly than the nominal and conceptual. In our terminology, the stress placed on the nominal aspect reveals the tendency to take the Provisional Name as an act of naming, while the emphasis made on the substantive aspect reveals the tendency to construe the Provisional Name in the sense of an object.

Second, Chih-i does speak of Emptiness, Provisional Name and the Middle Way in terms of objects *(ching).* In delineating the operation of the Threefold Contemplation, he remarks:

> To contemplate an object with the contemplation, the object would be tripled. To initiate the contemplation with the object, the contemplation would be tripled. . . . To contemplate the three [objects] as one and to initiate the one [single contemplation] into three is inconceivable.[15]

The contemplation denotes the Threefold Contemplation, while the triple object denotes the three aspects of the object: Emptiness, the Provisional and the Middle Way. The triple object is also mentioned elsewhere:

> The three sorts of wisdom formed by the Threefold Contemplation in one single Mind apprehend the triple object that is inconceivable.[16]

For Chih-i, Emptiness and the Middle Way are manifestly not real objects; "objects" *(ching)* ascribed to them should not be taken seriously. Only the Provisional can be construed as an object in the proper sense, i.e. the substantive entity or the world of substantive entities. This Provisional is detailed elsewhere:

> With regard to the Provisional to be contemplated, there are two sorts of Provisional, which contain all entities [or *dharmas*]. The first is the Provisional of love, and the second is the Provisional of [false] views.[17]

Chih-i attempts here to classify the Provisional. However, this classification is not our concern at the moment; our concern is that the Provisional contains all entities or *dharmas (i-ch'ieh fa)* and thus is another expression for the world of *dharmas*. It is beyond doubt that the Provisional *(chia)* in Chih-i's context is basically construed in the sense of objects, referring to the substantive world, which is empirical and relative in nature. It is beneficial to relate this understanding to the issue of *ch'u-chia* and *ju-chia* discussed in Chapter IV above. *Chia,* or the Provisional, is expressive of the empirical world of *dharmas,* which includes both sentient and non-sentient entities.

It should be noted that when the substantive *dharmas* or the world of substantive *dharmas* are spoken of in terms of the Provisional, they are in the nature of relational or dependent origination. They are non-substantial and consequently empty; they are provisional and not ultimate. Chih-i is fully aware of the nature of their provisionality, but he does not assume a pessimistic viewpoint. Rather, he tends to think that this provisionality is just what makes the *dharmas* and the world as they are. It is due to its provisionality that the world is subject to change and transformation, which is initiated by the function of the Middle Way-Buddha Nature. We can also say that it is only in the Provisional that the functional nature of the Middle Way-Buddha Nature can secure its manifestation. It is in this sense that Chih-i emphasizes and is concerned about the Provisional and its provisionality.

It should be added as well that although Chih-i substantiates the Provisional Name and ascribes to it the sense of an object, he does not forget its original meaning as an act of naming. For example, in the exposition of the Contemplation of entering into the Provisional from Emptiness, which will be described in detail soon, Chih-i remarks that the illusive is provisionally named "worldly Truth" *(shih-ti)*.[18] The Provisional Name, here, is taken to mean the act of naming. Chih-i also defines the Provisional as the "provisional appointment of what is null in nature."[19] He also employs the expression of the "provisional name-being,"[20] which did not appear in the *Kārikā,* but appeared in the TCTL and seemed to relate the Provisional Name to the sense of an object. Nevertheless, the discussion elaborating the sense of the act of naming is very seldom found in Chih-i's works and thus will not be discussed here. There is certainly a transition in the denotation of the Provisional Name from the *Kārikā* to Chih-i *via* the TCTL. This transition is a shift from an emphasis on the nominal and conceptual to an emphasis on the substantive and worldly. It seems clear that Nāgārjuna is more concerned about the former and Chih-i, the latter.

4. The epistemic-soteriological character of contemplation

Having clarified the denotations of Emptiness, Provisional Name and the Middle Way in the Mādhyamika context as well as Chih-i's understanding of these three concepts, we now come to a discussion of Chih-i's method of the Threefold Contemplation. Chih-i gives contemplation a general definition as follows:

> The Dharma Sphere being penetrated and illumined, [everything] being magnificiently bright, this is called "contemplation."[21]

> The quiescence of the Dharma Nature is called "cessation," while being quiescent but constantly illuminating is "contemplation."[22]

It is obvious here that the contemplation in question is predominantly epistemological in character. This character is also deeply practical and soteriological. What is contemplated is not an object as a phenomenon, but the Truth itself, or more appropriately, the ultimate Truth, *shih-hsiang.* What is achieved in the contemplation is not confined to objective knowledge about the relative empirical world. Rather, the major concern is the realization of the Truth in a broad sense. Through contemplation as such, the Truth can be properly understood and realized.

Chih-i explicates contemplation elsewhere in terms of "contemplate to attain" *(kuan-ta)* and "contemplate to penetrate" *(kuan-ch'uan).* "Contemplate to attain" is proposed in the sense of attaining the Truth and the original pure nature of sentient beings, while "contemplate to penetrate" is mentioned in the sense of overcoming all kinds of defilement and eventually penetrating into the Absolute without obstruction.[23] What deserves our attention most in this matter is that contemplation concerns not merely the realization of the Truth, but also the realization of our pure nature. This pure nature refers to our Buddha Nature, which is, for Chih-i, also the Mind. This equivalence is not surprising at all, if we remind ourselves of Chih-i's unique conception of the Truth in terms of the Middle Way-Buddha Nature, which is both the Way or Truth, and our Buddha Nature or Mind. People may tend to think that the way or Truth is objective and our Buddha Nature or Mind is subjective, but this object-subject duality does not exist in Chih-i's system of thought. It is overcome in the synthesis and identification of the Middle Way and Buddha Nature in the Middle Way-Buddha Nature, which is the authentic and ultimate Truth for Chih-i.

Another point deserving our attention is that the contemplation in question assumes a strong dynamic sense and a close association with the empirical existence of *dharmas*. In the above quotation, Chih-i characterizes contemplation as "being quiescent but constantly illuminating" *(chi erh ch'ang-chao),* in contrast with the mere quiescent denotation of cessation, conveying the sense that the contemplation is established on an ever-dynamic and ever-functional ground. In contemplation as such, what is contemplated is the Truth, i.e., the Middle Way-Buddha Nature. This Truth is not some "Truth" in a transcendent and consequently isolated sense; rather, it has an all-embracing nature and is therefore the very Truth of the *dharmas:* the Truth of the empirical world. The contemplation is undertaken in a close association with the empirical *dharmas,* towards which the dynamism is directed. The dynamic sense and empirical association in this kind of contemplation are also reflected in Chih-i's criticism of the Tripiṭaka Doctrine advocated by the Hīnayānists:

> Although the cessation and contemplation [of the śrāvaka and pratyekabuddha] lead to the liberation from the life-death cycle, they are dull as they enter Emptiness by the destruction of matter. This Emptiness can be named "cessation," as well as "neither cessation nor noncessation." However, it cannot be named "contemplation." Why? Because this involves the destruction of the body and the annihilation of the wisdom, therefore it is not named "contemplation."[24]

Chih-i is accusing the Hīnayānists here of being nihilistic. In the pursuit of attainment of the Truth (i.e., Emptiness), they commit two mistakes. First, in order to attain Emptiness, they destroy matter, which denotes the empirical realm of *dharmas*. The destruction of matter is undertaken by its disintegration as detailed in Chapter III above. Consequently, the Truth is contemplated without any association with the empirical world. Second, Chih-i states that the Hīnayānists destroy the body and annihilate wisdom. This criticism is reminiscent of the permanent nature of the Middle Way-Buddha Nature expounded in Chapter IV above. Chih-i's point seems to be that the Hīnayānists do not establish the permanent Buddha Nature, which is identical to the Mind, as the spiritual ground in the pursuit of enlightenment. The Mind is, in fact, the source of all sorts of wisdom. For this reason, when the practitioner perishes physically, the Hīnayānists believe there is nothing of the individual left behind; consequently, there is no way to speak of function or dynamism of any sort. In view of this lack of empirical association and dynamism in the Hīnayānists' contemplation, Chih-i does not regard this contemplation as authentic. It therefore can be inferred that the contemplation Chih-i has in mind assumes a strong dynamic sense and a close association with the empirical world. This will be expounded in full when we discuss Chih-i's Threefold Contemplation in forthcoming sections. This conception of the contemplation is exactly in line with the permanent, functional and all-embracing nature of the Middle Way-Buddha Nature, and Chih-i's Threefold Contemplation is in fact worked out in the perspective of this Middle Way-Buddha Nature.

At this point it is necessary to discuss the translation of the two terms *chih* and *kuan,* the latter in particular. In many Chinese Buddhist schools, *chih* and *kuan* were taken as two important practices in the attainment of the Truth. What we are concerned about here is their denotations in Chih-i's system. Chih-i understands *chih* in terms of the quiescence of the *Dharmatā,* which signifies the termination of all sorts of perversions and attachments obstructing us from seeing the true nature of the *dharmas*. It consequently can be rendered as "cessation," which refers to the cessation of these perversions and attachments.

With regard to *kuan,* the interpretive problem is more complicated. Scholars have made many suggestions. For instance, Hurvitz renders it as "view,"[25] Tamaki as "observation,"[26] W. T. de Bary as "insight,"[27] and Chung-yuan Chang as "contemplation."[28] Chang renders Chih-i's *san kuan* as "Threefold Contemplation."[29] The rendition of *kuan* as "view" or "observation" is feasible, but the problem is that both view and observation are too common and are hardly reminiscent of the attainment of the Truth. It is unnatural to speak of viewing or observing the Truth in a soteriological sense. "Insight" and "contemplation" are better renderings in the sense that they are more pertinent to the attainment of a soteriological goal. Chih-i defines *kuan* as "being quiescent but constantly illuminating." He seems to emphasize the aspect of the constant illumination of *kuan,* which involves a deeply functional and dynamic sense. Of "insight" and "contemplation," the latter seems to transmit the implication of dynamism more straightforwardly. Therefore, we have translated *kuan* as "contemplation" and *san-kuan* as the "Threefold Contemplation."

5. The epistemic-soteriological character of the Threefold Contemplation

In Chih-i's system, the specific method of contemplation through which the Truth is seen is the Threefold Contemplation. This Threefold Contemplation is, as described above, epistemic-soteriological in character; this is specified in the following way:

> What is illumined is the Threefold Truth; what is initiated is the Threefold Contemplation; [what results from] the accomplishment of the Contemplation is the Threefold Wisdom.[30]

The issues of the Threefold Truth *(san-ti)* and Threefold Wisdom *(san-chih)* are raised in the context of the Threefold Contemplation. The Threefold Truth can be regarded here as corresponding to the cognized object, the Threefold Contemplation to the cognition, and the Threefold Wisdom to the cognizing subject. The epistemological structure of the Threefold Contemplation is very clear. The concern here is not only with the knowledge about the empirical world, but also with enlightenment in a soteriological sense. The term "threefold" in the so called "Threefold Truth," "Threefold Contemplation" and "Threefold Wisdom" refers unanimously to Emptiness, the Provisional and the Middle Way. The Threefold Truth is composed of the Truth of Emptiness *(k'ung-ti),* the Truth of the Provisional *(chia-ti)* and the Truth of the Middle Way *(chung-ti).* The composition of the Threefold Contemplation has been accounted for in the opening remarks of this chapter. With regard to the Threefold Wisdom, more explanation is needed here. The components of this wisdom are on many occasions enumerated as *i-ch'ieh chih, tao-chung chih* and *i-ch'ieh-chung chih.*[31] *I-ch'ieh chih* is associated with Emptiness, *tao-chung chih* with the Provisional, and *i-ch'ieh-chung chih* with the Middle Way. That is, they are the wisdoms to illumine Emptiness, the Provisional and the Middle Way, respectively. For Chih-i, (1) Emptiness denotes the empty and therefore universal nature of *dharmas,* (2) the Provisional denotes the empirical world in the nature of variety and particularity, and (3) the implication of the Middle Way includes the synthesis of Emptiness and the Provisional. Accordingly, it seems safe to construe (1) *i-ch'ieh chih* to be the wisdom of universality, (2) *tao-chung chih* to be the wisdom of particularity, and (3) *i-ch'ieh-chung chih* to be the wisdom of both universality and particularity. We can also formulate a rough picture of the epistemology of the Threefold Contemplation: in the Contemplation of Emptiness, the wisdom of universality illumines Emptiness; in the Contemplation of the Provisional, the wisdom of particularity illumines the Provisional; and in the Contemplation of the Middle Way, the wisdom of both universality and particularity illumines the Middle Way.

Still, we must take a further step in order to obtain a more subtle and precise epistemic-soteriological picture of the Threefold Contemplation. In the MHCK, Chih-i states:

> The contemplation consists of three kinds. [The first,] "entering into Emptiness from the Provisional" *(ts'ung-chia ju-k'ung)* is called "Contemplation of the Twofold Truth" *(erh-ti kuan).* [The second,] "entering into the Provisional from Emptiness" *(ts'ung-k'ung ju-chia)* is called "Equal Contemplation" *(p'ing-teng kuan).* These two Contemplations are ways of expedience. They lead to the Middle Way and simultaneously illumine the two Truths [of Emptiness and the Provisional]. Every intention dying out, one spontaneously flows into the sea of all-embracing wisdom *(sarvajñā).* This is called the "Contemplation of the Middle Way-Supreme Truth" *(chung-tao ti-i-i-ti kuan).*[32]

Chih-i discusses the Threefold Contemplation here in more specific terms. The three Contemplations of Emptiness, the Provisional and

Middle Way, which comprise the Threefold Contemplation, are not taken in an isolated context. Rather, the Contemplations of Emptiness and the Provisional entail each other, and the Contemplation of the Middle Way synthesizes the other two.

The Contemplation of Emptiness is specifically taken as the Contemplation of the Twofold Truth. It takes place along the direction "from the Provisional to Emptiness," with Emptiness as its focus. The Contemplation of the Provisional is specifically taken as the Equal Contemplation, which takes place along the direction "from Emptiness to the Provisional," with the Provisional as its focus. With regard to the titles "twofold-truth" and "equal," Chih-i's explanation is that "twofold-truth" refers to the combination of two aspects (i.e., Emptiness and the Provisional) in the act of contemplating Emptiness. In other words, the Provisional is what Emptiness is based on, and it is through the Provisional that Emptiness can be expressed. It follows that the Provisional is the expressing, and Emptiness the expressed. The Contemplation of the Twofold Truth is made possible through the combination of these two aspects.[33] "Equal" in the term "Equal Contemplation" can be accounted for by dividing the Contemplation into two steps: "(coming) from Emptiness" and "entering into the Provisional." The practitioner, after realizing Emptiness, does not abide in the transcendent state of Emptiness because he knows that this is not yet the ultimate Truth. He retreats from Emptiness and enters into the Provisional (i.e., the world of provisionality), devoting himself to helping others. This is "(coming) from Emptiness." In helping others, he offers different remedies according to their individual needs. This is "entering into the Provisional." The so-called "equal" is contrasted with the "unequal" of the Contemplation of the Twofold Truth because, in the Contemplation of the Twofold Truth, one negates the Self Nature of the Provisional and regards the Provisional as empty. In this action one negates the Provisional with Emptiness. One does not, however, turn back to negate Emptiness with the Provisional. In the Equal Contemplation, in which one negates the attachment to Emptiness and turns back to the Provisional, one negates Emptiness with the Provisional. Emptiness and the Provisional are equally made use of and each negated once. Therefore, this Contemplation is called "Equal Contemplation."[34]

Now we come to the Contemplation of the Middle Way, or that of the Middle Way-Supreme Truth. The above quotation from the

MHCK refers to this Contemplation merely as "simultaneously illumining the two Truths of Emptiness and the Provisional." The passage then continues with more descriptions of this Contemplation:

> In the former Contemplation (i.e., the Contemplation of the Twofold Truth), one contemplates the Emptiness of the Provisional, which is equivalent to emptying *saṃsāra.* In the latter Contemplation (i.e., the Equal Contemplation), one contemplates the Emptiness of Emptiness, which is equivalent to emptying *nirvāṇa.* [In the Contemplation of the Middle Way-Supreme Truth,] one simultaneously negates the two extremes [of *saṃsāra* and *nirvāṇa*], and this negation is called "double-emptiness contemplation." It is the expedient way, by which one is able to realize the Middle Way. Therefore we state that when every intention dies out, one flows into the sea of all-embracing wisdom. Moreover, the former Contemplation uses Emptiness, and the latter Contemplation the Provisional; this is the expedient way for simultaneous preservation of both. Therefore when one enters into the Middle Way, one can simultaneously illumine the two Truths.[35]

Some interpretation is needed here. In the Contemplation of the Twofold Truth, one contemplates the negation of the Self Nature of the empirical world, which the Buddhist often expresses in terms of *saṃsāra* or the life-death cycle. This is the Emptiness of the Provisional, or the negation of the Provisional. In the Equal Contemplation, one contemplates the negation of the Self Nature of Emptiness. This is the Emptiness of Emptiness, or the negation of Emptiness. These two negations, if held separately, are bound to be extremes, which are not pertinent to the perfect state. To attain the perfect state, they have to be synthesized to form a twofold negation *(shuang che),* a simultaneous negation of both Emptiness and the Provisional. This expresses the state of the Middle Way. However, the pictures of the Contemplation of the Twofold Truth and Equal Contemplation can be looked at from another angle. That is, on the one hand, the Contemplation of the Twofold Truth negates the Provisional with Emptiness which can be construed as an affirmation of Emptiness. On the other hand, the Equal Contemplation negates Emptiness with Emptiness which logically implies a return to the Provisional, or an affirmation of the Provisional. Therefore, as a result of this synthesis, we come to the affirmation or illumination of both Emptiness and the Provisional. This is, in fact, a twofold affirmation or illumination *(shuang-chao)* of Emptiness and the Provisional, thus expressing the state of the Middle Way. It is consequently seen that in the Contemplation of the Middle Way, one not only negates and transcends both Emptiness and the Provisional, acquiring a state of transcendence and non-duality, but also synthesizes both Emptiness and the Provisional. This synthesis may entail a positive and constructive attitude toward the empirical world by means of a non-dual mind. In this Contemplation, the sense of function is also obvious, in view of the role one plays in the affirmation of the Provisional, or "entering into the Provisional" *(ju-chia)*. This role is, as mentioned above, to help others by offering different remedies according to their individual needs.[36]

6. How is the Threefold Contemplation possible?

Having completed above separate discussions of the three Contemplations of Emptiness, the Provisional and the Middle Way, we must now note that these three Contemplations actually form a threefold contemplation. That is, in practice, the three Contemplations are undertaken not separately and gradually, but simultaneously and suddenly, as if there is only one contemplation. This simultaneity and suddenness of the three Contemplations is expressed in the so-called "Threefold Contemplation in one single Mind" *(i-hsin san-kuan)*. With regard to this expression, Chih-i states:

> As regards [the idea that] one *dharma* is all *dharmas*, which means the *dharma* originated from causes and conditions, this is the Provisional Name and [is pertinent to] the Contemplation of the Provisional. If one thinks that all *dharmas* are one *dharma*, I would declare that it is Emptiness. [This is pertinent to] the Contemplation of Emptiness. If it is non-one and non-all, it is [pertinent to] the Contemplation of the Middle Way. Focusing on Emptiness, [one realizes that] everything is Emptiness, and no Provisionality and Middle Way are available, which are not Emptiness. All are synthesized in the Contemplation of Emptiness. Focusing on the Provisional, [one realizes that] everything is Provisionality, and no Emptiness and Middle Way are available that are not Provisionality. All are synthesized in the Contemplation of the Provisional. Focusing on the Middle Way, [one realizes that] everything is the Middle Way, and no Emptiness and Provisionality are available that are not the Middle Way. All are synthesized in the Contemplation of the Middle Way. [Those three Contemplations] are the

> inconceivable Threefold Contemplation in one single Mind explicated in the *Chung-lun.*[37]

A similar description also appears elsewhere,[38] in which Chih-i adds:

> If we merely pick up one Contemplation [of either Emptiness, the Provisional or the Middle Way] as the name [of the three Contemplations], the understanding mind would penetrate into all.

Chih-i speaks here of Emptiness and the Provisional in terms of one *dharma (i-fa)* and all *dharmas (i-ch'ieh fa),* respectively. "One *dharma*" denotes the universal empty nature of all *dharmas,* viz., Emptiness. "All *dharmas*" denotes the variety of empirical existence and consequently the Provisional. The identification of the one *dharma* and all *dharmas* signifies that Chih-i does not isolate Emptiness and the Provisional from each other, but sees them as entailing each other in meaning. One cannot be properly understood without making reference to the other. This relation between Emptiness and the Provisional is reminiscent of the relation between Emptiness and Dependent Origination expounded in the *Kārikā.* The second half of the first quotation above is particularly significant, in the sense that it divulges Chih-i's harmonious understanding of the Contemplations of the three aspects of Emptiness, the Provisional and the Middle Way. This understanding involves the fact that the Contemplation of one of the three aspects necessarily embraces the other two. It follows that the Contemplation of Emptiness, the Provisional or the Middle Way is at the same time the Contemplation of Emptiness, the Provisional and the Middle Way as a unified totality. The difference among the separate Contemplations is merely a difference of emphasis. That is, the Contemplation of Emptiness emphasizes Emptiness, and so on. In view of the simultaneous apprehension of Emptiness, the Provisional and the Middle Way, this sort of contemplation is called the "Threefold Contemplation". And, in view of its being completed suddenly rather than gradually, it is called the "Threefold Contemplation in one single Mind."

Ultimately speaking, there are in fact no such things as these three Contemplations because the Contemplation—whether of Emptiness, the Provisional, or the Middle Way—is in content a contemplation of these three aspects all together. There is one contemplation only, in which Emptiness, the Provisional and the Middle Way are realized simultaneously. It is exactly in this context that Chih-i proposes his well-known phrase, *chi-k'ung chi-chia chi-chung,* which means that there is no temporal interval in the realization of Emptiness, the Provisional and the Middle Way. *Chi* in this phrase signifies the simultaneity, or the negation of any temporal interval. Chih-i states:

> The three Truths are completely embraced in the one single Mind only. To distinguish their features, they can be depicted one after the other. With regard to the true principle, however, they are all only within the one single Mind. Emptiness, the Provisional and the Middle Way are realized all of a sudden, as if three characteristics are revealed in one single moment.[39]

The three Truths denote Emptiness, the Provisional and the Middle Way. What attracts us most, here, is the simultaneous realization of these Truths. It is due to this simultaneity that the three Truths can be termed the "Threefold Truth," which signifies the inseparability of the Truths. It is exactly this simultaneity that the above phrase pinpoints; Chih-i has, indeed, laid great emphasis on this simultaneity.[40] The idea that the three Truths are completely embraced in the one single Mind only also deserves our attention. It serves as a complement to the above phrase, proclaiming the simultaneous realization of the three Truths to be purely a matter of the Mind itself.

In our experience of knowing things, we can know only one object at a time if we wish to know it clearly. If two objects, e.g., an orange and an apple, are to be known at the same time, confusion is bound to arise and distinctive images of both objects will be impossible. Two objects can be distinctively known merely through a step-by-step manner. It is impossible to know two objects simultaneously, much less more than two. Here then is a crucial question: How is the Threefold Contemplation possible, in which Emptiness, the Provisional, and the Middle Way are contemplated by one single Mind simultaneously? This question is crucial because the phrase is closely associated with absolutely authentic Truth, the attainment of which is the true concern of the *sūtra,* i.e., enlightenment.[41] The Threefold Contemplation is what Chih-i sees to be the way to attain the absolute Truth. It is even more important than the negative of the Four Alternatives in the sense that it provides a positive way to attain the Truth, while the latter provides only a negative way.

To our disappointment, however, Chih-i does not positively address this important question in his major works. Instead, he contrasts the theory of the three Contemplations explicated in the Perfect Doctrine with that explicated in the Gradual Doctrine, declaring that the latter favors the gradual manner in carrying out the three Contemplations, while the former advocates the sudden manner.[42] He also depicts the epistemic context of the Threefold Contemplation in such beautiful and admirable expressions as the "non-expedient and non-ultimate, non-superior and non-inferior, non-anterior and non-posterior, non-juxtaposed and non-separate, non-large and non-small,"[43] and states that in such Contemplation the wisdom is the object and the object is the wisdom, both penetrating each other without any obstruction.[44] These descriptions are paradoxical to common sense. They divulge the fact that relative categories—such as expedient and ultimate, superior and inferior, etc.—are not applicable to the Threefold Contemplation; they also demonstrate that the epistemic context of the Threefold Contemplation is different from the epistemic context based on a subject-object dichotomy. The problem of how Emptiness, the Provisional, and the Middle Way, as three different aspects, can be contemplated simultaneously remains untouched. Likewise, this problem has not been pinpointed and seriously dealt with by modern scholars.

Tamura picks up the issue of the Threefold Contemplation in one single Mind. He states:

> The common people clung to the secular Provisional, without knowing that the Provisional is Emptiness. Therefore Emptiness was asserted. The Hīnayānist śrāvakas and pratyekabuddhas clung to Emptiness and forgot to leave for the Provisional. Therefore the Provisional was asserted. The Mahāyānist bodhisattvas came and descended to the Provisional. But the Mahāyānists also had a danger. They penetrated too much into the Provisional and consequently forgot Emptiness. . . . Thereupon the Middle [Way] was asserted, so that Emptiness should not be forgotten in the midst of the Provisional. Ultimately, or as a result, the epistemology of the coherence and mutual identity of Emptiness, the Provisional, and the Middle [Way] (perfect and sudden cessation and contemplation, Threefold Contemplation in one single Mind) was formed.[45]

This description is, as Tamura himself puts it, a historical retrospection of how the Threefold Contemplation came into being in the

Buddhist context. It tells from a practical and educational point of view why the Threefold Contemplation is needed. We believe that Chih-i would have agreed with Tamura in this regard, but Tamura's description does not pinpoint the problem we have raised here, which is concerned with the possibility of the Threefold Contemplation as such.

7. The Middle Way-Buddha Nature in the Threefold Contemplation

Here we will attempt, largely through references to Chih-i's conceptions, to tackle the problem mentioned above: the possibility of the Threefold Contemplation in a single Mind. The key to the solution of this problem is, we think, the Middle Way-Buddha Nature, which is for Chih-i the authentic Truth, *shih-hsiang*. Our observation is that what is contemplated in the Threefold Contemplation must be the authentic Truth, i.e., the Middle Way-Buddha Nature: Emptiness, the Provisional and the Middle Way are nothing but the three aspects of this Middle Way-Buddha Nature.

We have discussed the three characteristics of the Middle Way-Buddha Nature in Chapter IV above. These three characteristics—permanence, dynamism and the all-embracing nature—are proposed in contrast to the Emptiness advocated by the Tripiṭaka Doctrine and Common Doctrine (which is severely criticised by Chih-i). These features by no means exhaust all the characteristics of the Middle Way-Buddha Nature. Chih-i certainly would not object to the ascription of Emptiness (i.e., non-substantiality) to the Middle Way-Buddha Nature as an attribute. What he would vehemently object to is the ascription of mere Emptiness to the Truth. Indeed, he has declared:

> The Contemplation of Emptiness is commonly shared by the Hīnayāna, Mahāyāna, One-sided Doctrine and Perfect Doctrine.[46]

This means that Emptiness is a common concept acceptable to all Buddhist schools and doctrines. On this basis, we have good reason to believe that the Middle Way-Buddha Nature, which represents the Truth in the Perfect Doctrine, contains the implication of Emptiness.

The fact that the Provisional is contained in the Middle Way-Buddha Nature is obvious in view of the all-embracing nature of the latter. It has been made clear that Chih-i substantiates the Provisional and takes it as expressive of the empirical world of *dharmas,* which are exactly what the all-embracing nature pinpoints. The Provisional and all-embracing nature are indeed closely related to each other. The Middle Way-Buddha Nature contains, undoubtedly, the implication of the Middle Way in the Contemplation of the Middle Way. This implication is, as the expressions *shuang-che* and *shuang-chao* suggest, that both Emptiness and the Provisional are to be negated yet affirmed. *Shuang-che* is double negation of Emptiness and the Provisional, and *shuang-chao* is double affirmation of Emptiness and the Provisional.[47]

Therefore, Emptiness, the Provisional, and the Middle Way are the three aspects of the Middle Way-Buddha Nature. What, then, do we mean when we say that Emptiness, the Provisional, and the Middle Way are contemplated in a single Mind? The meaning involves the fact that both natures of Emptiness and the Provisional (i.e., the non-substantiality and provisionality of the *dharmas*) are apprehended in the realization of the Middle Way-Buddha Nature without attachment to either nature. In this kind of contemplation, what we are concerned about, basically, is not the separate aspects of Emptiness, the Provisional, and the Middle Way, but rather the Middle Way-Buddha Nature as a totality embracing these aspects. In such a context, what is worked on is not any particular member or members, but a singular unified nature of contemplation.

This understanding of the Threefold Contemplation—which reduces Emptiness, the Provisional, and the Middle Way to the Middle Way-Buddha Nature—seems reasonable. But there still remains an important issue: in the epistemic situation of the Threefold Contemplation, the main concern is not to cognize anything in a dichotomous subject-object relationship (whether it be the Middle Way-Buddha Nature, or whatever), but to be involved in an *event* with a profound soteriological purpose. Chih-i is aware of this point. As a matter of fact, he justifies this sense of the event by means of interpreting the Threefold Contemplation in terms of the transformation of the empirical world. In the WMCLS, he states:

> First, [the Contemplation of] entering into Emptiness from the Provisional aims at the destruction of *dharmas* and overcoming them. Then, [the Contemplation of] entering into the Provisional from Emptiness

> aims at the establishment of *dharmas* and embracing them. The authentic Contemplation of the Middle Way aims at teaching and transforming sentient beings, [which then attain] the wisdom of penetrating the Ultimate. Penentrating the Ultimate is called the long-abidingness of *dharmas;* and the long-abidingness of *dharmas* infers the permanence of the Dharma Body.[48]

> [What is called the] long-abidingness of *dharmas* means to lead [sentient beings] to realize the Buddha Nature and so to abide in the *Mahā-nirvāṇa.*[49]

These are extremely significant and inspiring descriptions of the Threefold Contemplation. It is plainly revealed here that the Threefold Contemplation has an ultimate concern, i.e., the establishment of *dharmas* and transformation of sentient beings. The establishment and transformation are events in which the three characteristics of the Middle Way-Buddha Nature all assume their proper meanings, as shown in the following elaborations.

In the Threefold Contemplation, the role of the Contemplation of Emptiness is to destroy and overcome the *dharmas.* This tends to denote the negation of the empirical world. However, the Emptiness in question is not mere Emptiness. Rather, it is Emptiness associated with the Provisional, as suggested in the expression "entering into Emptiness from the Provisional." In this context, the negation of the empirical world is not entirely nihilistic, and what is to be destroyed are not the *dharmas* themselves, but, as Chih-i says elsewhere, overcoming them in terms of destroying the attachment to *dharmas.*[50] The role of the Contemplation of the Provisional is to establish and embrace the *dharmas.* It is manifestly evident that the establishment of *dharmas* and embracing them carry a soteriological sense; cultivating sentient beings and leading them to enlightenment is their main concern. Chih-i also refers the establishment and embracing of *dharmas* to persuade others to endeavor for the attainment of the Buddha Body,[51] which also means the attainment of Buddhahood. Here, the affirmation of the *dharmas* or empirical world is evidenced; this empirical world is, for Chih-i, what the Provisional signifies. Likewise, this Provisional is not the mere Provisional, but the Provisional associated with Emptiness, as suggested in the expression "entering into the Provisional from Emptiness." Having this association with Emptiness, the affirmation of the empirical world can be held in the awareness that this world is non-substantial after all, and the attachment to it should consequently not happen.

With regard to the Contemplation of the Middle Way, Chih-i speaks of its role in terms of the teaching and transforming of sentient beings so they will attain the wisdom of penetrating the Ultimate. This role may embrace a very profund religious meaning. The Ultimate *(shih),* which denotes the ultimate Truth *(shih-hsiang),* or simply the Truth, is very much associated with the empirical world. This is seen from Chih-i's identification of the penetration of the Truth with the long-abidingness of *dharmas (fa chiu-chu),* which obviously pinpoints the affirmation and preservation of the empirical world. Here, Chih-i's deep worldly concern is manifested. Nevertheless, we need to ask, what does the identification of the penetration of the Truth with the long-abidingness of *dharmas* mean? From the association of the long-abidingness of *dharmas* with the permanent Dharma Body *(dharmakāya)* and Buddha Nature *(buddhatā),* it seems that the Dharma Body and Buddha Nature are what support and strengthen the *dharmas* or the empirical world. As the Dharma Body and Buddha Nature assume permanence, the empirical world also inherits this permanence. For Chih-i, the Dharma Body and Buddha Nature are identical with each other, and are nothing but the Middle Way-Buddha Nature. This Middle Way-Buddha Nature is exactly what *shih* (or the Truth) denotes. The realization of this Middle Way-Buddha Nature also embraces the realization of the empirical world and renders the latter into permanent nature, leading to an identification of the penetration of the Truth with the long-abidingness of *dharmas.*

The Threefold Contemplation is actually concerned with the transformation of perception of the empirical world in the realization of the Middle Way-Buddha Nature. This transformation entails a deep sense of the affirmation and preservation of the empirical world and closely conforms to the all-embracing nature of the Middle Way-Buddha Nature. This nature can be fully developed and realized only in the transformation of perception of the empirical world into a focus on the sentient part of the *dharmas.* This is evidenced in Chih-i's explication of the authentic Contemplation of the Middle Way in terms of teaching and transforming sentient beings and enabling them to attain the wisdom of penetrating the Ultimate. This authentic Contemplation of the Middle Way *(chung-tao cheng kuan)* is, no doubt, more emphasized than the Contemplations of Emptiness and the Provisional.

With regard to the transformation or establishment of non-sentient *dharmas,* Chih-i does not elaborate. In our opinion, Chih-i is writing only in a hyperbolic sense, rather than a substantial or actual sense. That is, it signifies that the transformation is all-covering. If the transformation is to be carried out by the bodhisattva, since the bodhisattva's compassion is all-covering, it covers not only sentient beings, but also the non-sentient. In the work of transformation, endeavors undertaken are due to the functional nature of the Middle Way-Buddha Nature. The statement that the bodhisattva puts sentient beings into correct places with the perfect function expounded in Chapter IV above, vividly evidences the operation of this nature. The permanent and persistent significance of this kind of transformation also comes from the permanent nature of the Middle Way-Buddha Nature. Indeed, the three characteristics of the Middle Way-Buddha Nature all reveal their significance in the transformation of the empirical world, focusing on sentient beings in particular.

In light of the above study, we are in a better position to respond to the difficult question: how is the Threefold Contemplation possible? First, the establishment of the empirical world of *dharmas* is not separable from the destruction of attachment to this empirical world. This process does not happen sequentially, but both take place simultaneously. Once attachment is destroyed, the empirical world is established. The empirical world is established right at the moment of the destruction of the attachment; there is no temporal interval whatsoever. They are not two events, but one. Therefore, the Contemplation of Emptiness and the Contemplation of the Provisional are, in essence, two aspects of one Contemplation. The main concern of this one Contemplation can be concluded to be the establishment of the empirical world. Again, we must point out that the establishment of the empirical world or *dharmas (li-fa)* should be understood in a specified sense. That is, the empirical world is established in the sense that sentient beings, or human beings in particular, undertake a correct attitude toward it. We should emphasize the importance of the empirical world as the place (and the only place) where enlightenment is attainable. Yet we should not be attached to the empirical world as something that has Self Nature or substantiality. Although Chih-i himself does not explicitly spell this sense out, it can be inferred from his emphasis on the all-embracing nature of the Middle Way-Buddha Nature.

Second, the teaching and attainment of the wisdom of penetrating the Truth on the part of sentient beings take place at the same time as the establishment of the empirical world. They are, likewise, not consecutive events, but one event with different aspects. Consequently, we can understand that the former two Contemplations and the Contemplation of the Middle Way are but one Contemplation, which is the Threefold Contemplation. In this Threefold Contemplation, the empirical world is transformed in the realization of the Middle Way-Buddha Nature, and the Middle Way-Buddha Nature is realized in the transformation of the empirical world. This is, for Chih-i, the experience of enlightenment. In this context, the Threefold Contemplation can be better construed as the Contemplation of the Middle Way-Buddha Nature, where "contemplation" is taken not only in the cognitive sense, but also in a practical and soteriological sense. The latter sense is even more important in view of Chih-i's deep practical and soteriological concern. Accordingly, Emptiness, the Provisional and the Middle Way are not treated separately, but are unified in the Middle Way-Buddha Nature; the Threefold Contemplation concerns nothing but the realization of this Middle Way-Buddha Nature. As this realization is one single event, there is no difficulty in coping with Emptiness, the Provisional, and the Middle Way in temporal dimensions. Consequently, there is no such problem as the possibility of the Threefold Contemplation.

8. The Threefold Contemplation and the verse of the Threefold Truth

We pointed out in the first note of this chapter that Chih-i explicitly relates his Threefold Contemplation to the verse of the Threefold Truth in the *Kārikā*. In some places, he takes his phrase of *chi-k'ung chi-chia chi-chung* to be the predicate of the things of causal origination, tending to ascribe this phrase to the *Kārikā*.[52] He also construes the Emptiness delineated in the verse of the Threefold Truth as expressive of the transcendent Truth, the Provisional Name as expressive of the conventional Truth, and the Middle Way as expressive of the Middle Way-Supreme Truth, concluding that this verse expounds Mahāyānism and explicates the doctrine of the Threefold Truth.[53] Chih-i even goes so far as to interpret the Emptiness delineated in the verse of the Threefold Truth in terms of destroying and overcoming attatchment to the *dharmas;* the Provisional Name in terms of establishing and embracing the *dharmas;* the Middle Way in terms of teaching and transforming sentient beings and securing the long-abidingness of the *dharmas*.[54] Chih-i clearly acknowledges an extremely close relationship between his Threefold Contemplation and the verse of the Threefold Truth, but is this really the case from a doctrinal perspective? Let us wind up our long discussion in this chapter by examining this issue carefully.

It is true that Chih-i lays deep stress on the verse of the Threefold Truth, as evidenced by the frequent quotation of this verse in his major works.[55] It is also true that the three concepts in the verse—Emptiness, Provisional Name, and the Middle Way—have considerable bearing on the formation of the Threefold Contemplation, in the sense that the meanings of these three concepts are, by and large, inherited by the Threefold Contemplation. This is particularly true with Emptiness. Chih-i's understanding of Emptiness in terms of destroying and overcoming the *dharmas* (which, as pointed out previously, actually pinpoints the attachment to the *dharmas*) is very much in line with Nāgārjuna's conception of Emptiness, which is the negation of Self Nature and false views. Both Chih-i and Nāgārjuna emphasize the practical and soteriological significance of this concept.

This similarity is nevertheless outweighed by the difference. A close relationship between the Threefold Contemplation and the verse of the Threefold Truth can hardly be endorsed. First, although there are Mādhyamika traces in the Threefold Contemplation, Chih-i's own elaborations are overwhelming. In Mādhyamika, Emptiness stands for the Truth and tends to be an independent concept, by which we mean primary and fundamental. That is, as expressive of the Truth, Emptiness can stand by itself without associating with anything else. Emptiness in the Threefold Contemplation is quite different. The Contemplation of Emptiness is more appropriately termed by Chih-i as the "Contemplation of entering into Emptiness from the Provisional." Emptiness in this context is not mere Emptiness, but Emptiness with the Provisional as its background. It is spoken of in the context of a process in which both Emptiness and the Provisional are involved, rather than in the context of mere Emptiness. Such Emptiness is inseparable from the Provisional. Mere Emptiness is one-sided and transcendent, and therefore cannot stand for the perfect Truth. Emptiness backed by the Provisional is an Emptiness with close connections to the empirical, and is consequently more embracing. For Chih-i, Emptiness does not seem to stand for the Truth by itself. Rather, it is an aspect of the Truth: the Middle Way-Buddha Nature. So is the Provisional. Both Emptiness and the Provisional are subordinate to the Middle Way-Buddha Nature. In this sense, Emptiness does not tend to be an independent and fundamental concept. The Provisional Name in the *Kārikā* (as studied in section 1) denotes the act of naming, while the Provisional in Chih-i's system is substantiated and taken as referring to either an object or the empirical world. The difference is beyond controversy. With regard to the Middle Way, we have shown clearly in Chapters I, II and III that Nāgārjuna's Middle Way denotes the state of the transcendence of extremes, while Chih-i's Middle Way is substantiated in the dimension of the Buddha Nature. The former is subordinate to the Truth of Emptiness, while the latter is taken to be the authentic Truth itself, i.e., the Middle Way-Buddha Nature. With regard to these three concepts, Chih-i makes distinguishable modifications and elaborations, which would have been hardly imagined by Nāgārjuna and his Mādhyamika followers.

Second, in the Threefold Contemplation, what is to be contemplated is the Threefold Truth, which is a combination of the Truths of Emptiness, the Provisional, and the Middle Way. What Chih-i terms as "transcendent Truth" and "conventional Truth"[56] are the Truth of Emptiness and the Truth of the Provisional, respectively. The important point, to which we should pay full attention, is that the articulation of the Threefold Truth is based on the supposition that Emptiness, the Provisional, and the Middle Way stand in parallel positions, so each is independent of the others. Only out of such a supposition can one work out the Truths of Emptiness, the Provisional, and the Middle Way and sum them up into a Threefold Truth. Such a supposition, however, is not held by Nāgārjuna at all. In the Sanskrit original of the verse of the Threefold Truth, the concepts of Emptiness, the Provisional, and the Middle Way are not placed in parallel positions. Rather, they are brought together to reveal the denotation of Emptiness in a more subtle manner: Emptiness is the Middle Way because of its provisionality. It is clear that the major issue is Emptiness, and that the Provisional Name and the Middle Way are complementary in helping cope with this issue.[57] To be more specific, Nāgārjuna regards Emptiness as the Truth. He does not take the Middle Way to be the Truth independent of the Truth of Emptiness, not at least in the sense that Emptiness is the

Truth. The Middle Way is, in the *Kārikā,* subordinate to the Truth of Emptiness. As for the Provisional Name, we have shown earlier that, in the *Kārikā,* it mainly denotes the act of naming and does not attract much attention. There is a long way to go to elevate such a Provisional Name to the Truth of the Provisional, in which the whole empirical world is encompassed, and which is so much emphasized by Chih-i. There is, indeed no sign that Nāgārjuna sees Emptiness, the Provisional Name and the Middle Way to be three Truths. To title the verse in question "the verse of the Threefold Truth" is inappropriate and misleading. It is therefore unlikely that an interpretation of this verse in terms of the Threefold Truth is justifiable.[58]

In the Threefold Truth verse, or even the entire *Kārikā,* there is clearly no indication that Nāgārjuna has the conception of Three Truths, or the Threefold Truth, much less the thought of *chi-k'ung chi-chia chi-chung.* Nāgārjuna, however, has the conception of Two Truths, or the Twofold Truth, which will be touched upon in the forthcoming chapter.[59]

CHAPTER VII

Practical Significance of Identification

In the realization of the Truth, we are unavoidably confronted with a question: In what manner is the Truth to be realized? This question can be formulated more straightforwardly as follows:

1. Should we realize the Truth in an isolated context, apart from this spatio-temporal world, as if the Truth itself has nothing to do with our empirical circumstances whatsoever? Or, should we realize the Truth in association with our empirical circumstances?
2. If the answer to the latter question is affirmative, how close, then, should the association of the Truth be to our empirical circumstances?

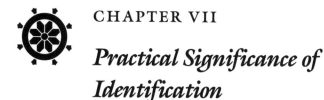

We will see later that both Chih-i and the Mādhyamika respond affirmatively to the position that the Truth should be realized in a close association with the empirical world. They speak of such association in terms of identification or non-difference. Nāgārjuna claims that the life-death cycle and *nirvāṇa* are not different from each other; consequently, they are identical to each other. This identity occurs in a reserved sense, as will be delineated soon. Chih-i adopts a very radical attitude, declaring that defilements are themselves enlightenment, and that the life-death cycle is itself *nirvāṇa.*[1] The life-death cycle pertains here to the empirical world, and *nirvāṇa* and enlightenment are the result of realizing the Truth. It is in this sense that we will discuss the identification of the Truth with the empirical world.[2] As *nirvāṇa,* enlightenment, liberation, and realization of the Truth are unanimously understood in the sense of a soteriological goal sought by sentient beings, we will not, except in special cases, distinguish them in our discussion of this issue of identification. Nāgārjuna generally uses *nirvāṇa* to express this goal, while Chih-i uses the term "liberation" (Skt., *mokṣa;* Ch., *chieh-t'o*). There is essentially no difference between these two terms.

This identification suggests a method in which to realize the Truth. "Method" here is taken in a broad sense. It means a correct practical relationship of identification between the Truth and the empirical world. It may also signify an appropriate manner: the Truth should be realized in the light of its close connection to the empirical world.[3]

It should be noted, however, that Chih-i holds a somewhat different viewpoint toward this identification from that of Nāgārjuna and the Mādhyamikas, besides sharing some common understanding with the latter. In this issue of identification, he is also critical of the Common Doctrine, which includes Mādhyamika. To obtain a clear picture as to how Chih-i can be related to and differentiated from the Mādhyamika in this issue, let us first examine Nāgārjuna's position regarding the practical significance of his identification.

1. The identification of *nirvāṇa* and the life-death cycle

In the *Kārikā,* Nāgārjuna explicitly declares the non-difference between *nirvāṇa* and *saṃsāra,* or the life-death cycle:

> *Saṃsāra* is nothing essentially different from *nirvāṇa. Nirvāṇa* is nothing essentially different from *saṃsāra.*
>
> The limits *(koṭi)* of *nirvāṇa* are the limits of *saṃsara.* Between the two, also, there is not the slightest difference whatsoever.[4]

It should be cautiously noted that with regard to the relationship between *nirvāṇa* and *saṃsāra,* Nāgārjuna uses "non-difference" rather than "identity." He does not spell out "identity." Our understanding is that the denotation of identity can be inferred logically from "non-difference." However, there is a difference in tone between identity and non-difference, which signifies different degrees or attitudes in affirming the identity of *nirvāṇa* and *saṃsāra.* To be specific, to say that *nirvāṇa* is *saṃsāra* signifies a straightforward and resolute affirmation of the identity of *nirvāṇa* and *saṃsāra.* But to say that *nirvāṇa* is not different from *saṃsāra* reveals an affirmation of the identity in a reserved sense. This reserved sense will be vividly seen when we come to the contrast between Chih-i and Nāgārjuna's attitudes toward the empirical world in the realization of the Truth.

We must bear this reserved sense in mind when we speak of Nāgārjuna's identification of *nirvāṇa* and *saṃsāra*.

In the two verses quoted above, *nirvāṇa* refers to the uncommon enlightened life, which is achieved in the realization of the Truth of Emptiness, while *saṃsāra* or the life-death cycle refers to common everyday life lived in this empirical world. In this sense, the identification of *nirvāṇa* and the life-death cycle is another expression of the identification of the Truth and the empirical world. As is commonly maintained by Buddhists, including Nāgārjuna himself, *nirvāṇa* is pure in nature, and the life-death cycle impure, so it is appropriate to ask in what sense they can be identified with each other. The Sanskrit word *koṭi,* which appears in the first half of the second verse, suggests that they are identified in their limit or realm. That is, *nirvāṇa* and the life-death cycle share the same realm: the realm of one is exactly that of the other. What Nāgārjuna means here is that *nirvāṇa* is attained nowhere else than within the life-death cycle. The realm in which *nirvāṇa* can be established is that of the life-death cycle, or simply the life-death cycle itself. There is, therefore, a practical implication in this identification of *nirvāṇa* and the life-death cycle: the Truth is to be realized right in the life-death cycle and not elsewhere. Nāgārjuna also warns that it is not possible for *nirvāṇa* to exist apart from the world of life and death.[5]

It should be noted here that the statement that *nirvāṇa* and the life-death cycle share the same realm should be taken in a purely practical and soteriological sense. *Nirvāṇa* is to be attained in the life-death cycle; the realm is the realm of the life-death cycle. *Nirvāṇa* is not a place; therefore, it cannot have a realm of its own, but it can have a realm where it is to be attained. This realm is the realm of the life-death cycle, or simply the life-death cycle.

In light of the contrast that *nirvāṇa* is pure and the life-death cycle impure, Nāgārjuna tends to construe them as the outcome of different lives lived differently. A person who clings to and is for this reason manipulated by his surroundings will remain in the life-death cycle, while one who does not cling will attain *nirvāṇa*. This distinction between *nirvāṇa* and the life-death cycle is testified to in the following verse:

> The status of the birth-death cycle is due to existential grasping (of the *skandhas*) and relational condition (of the being). That which is non-grasping and non-relational is taught as *nirvāṇa*.[6]

Therefore, whether a person lives in the life-death cycle or in *nirvāṇa* depends on whether he is manipulated by causes or conditions *(pratītya)* or is free from them. Whatever the outcome, one has to remain closely associated with this actual, empirical world. *Nirvāṇa* must be, and yet can only be, achieved on the ground of this empirical world, which is the only possible realm where *nirvāṇa* can assume actual meaning. This empirical world is simply the life-death cycle, in which the liberation of sentient beings—human beings in particular—is emphasized. It is in this context that Nāgārjuna does not distinguish between *nirvāṇa* and the life-death cycle.

With reference to the three verses quoted in this section, T. R. V. Murti remarks:

> There is no difference whatever between *nirvāṇa* and *saṃsāra;* Noumenon and phenomena are not two separate sets of entities, nor are they two states of the same thing. The absolute is the only real; it is the reality of *saṃsāra,* which is sustained by false construction *(kalpanā).*[7]

Murti tends to categorize *nirvāṇa* and the life-death cycle here as the noumena and phenomena, respectively, and regards them as referring to the same set of things, which denotes what one faces in the empirical world. Murti's remarks also pinpoint the same realm shared by *nirvāṇa* and the life-death cycle. This realm is precisely the realm occupied by the set of things. In addition, with regard to the relationship held by Nāgārjuna between *nirvāṇa* and the life-death cycle, Sprung remarks that *nirvāṇa* has no other ontic range *(koṭi)* than that of the life-death cycle.[8] This ontic range denotes nothing but the realm of actual empirical things. Sprung undoubtedly also regards *nirvāṇa* and the life-death cycle as having the same realm.

2. Identification of Emptiness and form

With regard to the identification of *nirvāṇa* and the life-death cycle, or the unworldly and worldly, there is a similar idea in which Emptiness and form *(rūpa),* extending even to the whole realm of aggregates *(skandha),* are identified with each other. This idea complements the identification of *nirvāṇa* and the life-death cycle. It is not found in the *Kārikā,* but is seen in the TCTL in various places.

As a matter of fact, this idea originally appeared in the Prajñāpāramitā literature, whose thought is extensively expounded in the TCTL. The *Heart Sūtra,* for instance, states:

> Form is emptiness and the very emptiness is form; emptiness does not differ from form, form does not differ from emptiness; whatever is form, that is emptiness, whatever is emptiness, that is form, the same is true of feelings, perceptions, impulses and consciousness.[9]

Here, form and Emptiness are identified with each other. We have no intention to study this identification in detail.[10] What we want to point out is that, in the statement that form is Emptiness, Emptiness is used as a predicate to explain form: form is non-substantial and empty. There is imbedded here an epistemological concern on the part of form. In the statement that Emptiness is form, in which form is used as a predicate to explain Emptiness, the situation is different. Emptiness, which means the state of non-substantiality, does not need form to explain it epistemologically. It is consequently difficult to talk about the epistemological concern involved with Emptiness. We think that the concern is practical. That is, the statement that Emptiness is form means that Emptiness should be understood and realized in form. If our hermeneutics make sense, it is possible that the identification of Emptiness and form is also one in realm. The realm of Emptiness is the realm of form. Although Emptiness is not a place and therefore cannot have a realm of its own, it has a realm in which it is to be realized. This realm is nothing other than that of form. Therefore, Emptiness shares the same realm with form and is identical to form from a practical point of view. The affirmation "Whatever is form, that is Emptiness, whatever is Emptiness, that is form" means that Emptiness and form refer to the same thing. This meaning may be approached in different ways. It nevertheless entails the practical implication that Emptiness has to be realized in reference to whatever is within the realm of form. In this sense, we may say that Emptiness shares the same realm with form and that they are identical to each other.[11]

Form stands for the five aggregates—form, feelings *(vedanā),* perceptions *(saṃjñā),* impulses *(saṃskāra)* and consciousness *(vijñāna)*—which are the elements comprising human existence. Human existence is in the nature of Dependent Origination and is not essentially different from the empirical world. Therefore, form tends to stand for the empirical world as well. Accordingly, it seems possible to say that Emptiness shares the same realm with and is identical to the empirical world in a practical sense. That is, Emptiness is to be realized in the empirical world.

If the above understanding is correct, it is possible to relate the identification of Emptiness and form to that of *nirvāṇa* and the life-death cycle, construing them as different ways of expressing the immanent character of the realization of the Truth. That is, the Truth must be realized in the empirical world. Indeed, these two identifications can be "identified" with each other in the sense of equally expressing this immanent character. In view of Nāgārjuna's intimate connection with Prajñāpāramitā thought, we believe that he inherited the latter's view and went on to identify the unworldly with the worldly, maintaining the need to realize the unworldly within the worldly.

As a matter of fact, the author of the TCTL does relate the identification of Emptiness and form to that of *nirvāṇa* and the world or the life-death cycle. He states:

> The Buddha told Subhūti, "Form is Emptiness, and Emptiness is form . . . ." Emptiness is *nirvāṇa,* and *nirvāṇa* is Emptiness. It is also stated in the *Kārikā:* "*Nirvāṇa* is not different from the world, and the world is not different from *nirvāṇa.* The realm of *nirvāṇa* and that of the world are the same, without the slightest difference."[12]

Here, the author of the TCTL not only relates the identification of Emptiness and form to that of *nirvāṇa* and the world or the life-death cycle, but also identifies Emptiness and *nirvāṇa* with each other. He obviously regards both identifications as conveying the same message, which contains the practical implication that *nirvāṇa* or Emptiness must be attained in the empirical world.

3. The importance of ordinary practices

Nāgārjuna's identification of *nirvāṇa* and the life-death cycle shows his affirmative response to our first question proposed at the beginning of this chapter. This response is that we should realize the Truth in a close association with the empirical world. *Nirvāṇa,* the Truth, must be attained and is attainable only in the empirical world. This point is important but still quite formal. How close should the association be? Speaking specifically, in the empirical world in which we live, we communicate with each other through language; we perform such practices as educating our children and looking after the sick. Here, language and practices affect us deeply in our daily life. Can they be related to the realization of the Truth?

It is with these considerations that our second question is concerned; they should be accounted for in the issue of identification. To deal with this question, we must first examine Nāgārjuna's theory of the Twofold Truth. To examine this theory, let us start by quoting the related verses in the *Kārikā:*

> The teaching of the *Dharma* by the various Buddhas is based on the two truths; namely, the relative (worldly) truth and the absolute (supreme) truth.[13]

> Those who do not know the distinction between the two truths cannot understand the profound nature of the Buddha's teaching.[14]

It is shown here that the Twofold Truth is composed of the worldly Truth (Skt., *lokasaṃvṛti-satya;* Ch., *shih-su ti*) and the supreme Truth (Skt., *paramārtha-satya;* Ch., *ti-i-i ti*). In the *Kārikā,* Nāgārjuna does not explicitly mention what the two Truths denote; he merely emphasizes the need to distinguish between them in understanding the Buddha's profound teaching. As a matter of fact, the issue of these two Truths has been studied extensively by modern scholars, whose works are quite well known and are accessible to students of Buddhism.[15] It is beyond doubt that the supreme Truth signifies here the Truth of Emptiness, which is absolute in nature. But what does the worldly Truth signify? The Sanskrit term *saṃvṛti,* which is the key to the understanding of this Truth, is ambiguous in meaning. It may mean language itself. It may also mean what is expressed by means of language. In this respect, Matilal states:

> Whatever is expressed in our speech behavior along with the speech behavior itself constitutes the realm of *saṃvṛti,* the "conventional," the "practical."[16]

Matilal understands *saṃvṛti* in terms of speech behavior, which is based on language and what it expresses. Language functions conventionally and relatively; what it expresses is also conventional and relative. Accordingly, *saṃvṛti* concerns what is conventional and relative, which can be nothing but things and behavior in the empirical world. It seems safe, therefore, to construe the worldly Truth as roughly signifying the Truth or knowledge of the empirical world. The term "Truth" (Skt., *satya;* Ch., *ti*) is in fact not a good expression, as it is commonly associated with a sense of absoluteness. Nāgārjuna advises that we should distinguish between the supreme Truth and the worldly Truth. Such a distinction has to be based on the distinction between the supreme and the worldly, between Emptiness and the empirical world.

Because of limited space in the present work, we cannot study the theory of Nāgārjuna's Twofold Truth in detail. Our concern here is to examine how this theory can be significantly related to the association of the realization of the Truth with the empirical world. In this respect, the distinction between Emptiness and the empirical world is not constructive. A clue, however, lies in the verse just following the two quoted above. This verse, an elaboration of the previous ones, reads:

> Without relying on everyday common practices (i.e., relative truths), the absolute cannot be expressed. Without approaching the absolute truth, *nirvāṇa* cannot be attained.[17]

The same verse also appears in the *Vigrahavyāvartanī.*[18] Nāgārjuna speaks here of the worldly Truth in terms of *vyavahāra,* which means actions or ordinary practices undertaken in our ordinary daily life. These practices certainly include such items as educating children and looking after the sick. Pingala focuses on the operation of speech or language, stressing its worldliness and conventionality.[19] Kajiyama points out that in Mādhyamika philosophy, *vyavahāra* is synonymous with *saṃvṛti.*[20] *Saṃvṛti,* as noted above, may mean language. Language is undoubtedly an important element in rendering ordinary practices possible; it is itself a practice prevailing in our daily life. It therefore seems possible to take *vyavahāra* as signifying ordinary practices, with an emphasis on language and its behavior. In the verse above, Nāgārjuna articulates a hierachy with regard to the attainment of *nirvāṇa:* a person expresses the supreme Truth through ordinary practices and attains *nirvāṇa* through the supreme Truth. He strongly asserts that the supreme Truth cannot be expressed *(deśyate)* without relying on ordinary practices. In other words, the supreme Truth can merely be expressed through ordinary practices.

We must pay the greatest attention here to this assertion. Let us re-examine its Sanskrit original:

> *vyavahāramanāśritya paramārtho na deśyate.*

Inada's translation—"without relying on everyday common practices, the absolute truth cannot be expressed"—is adequate. So is Ui's.[21] Both of them render the Sanskrit verbs (*āśritya* in continuative form and *deśyate* in the passive voice) as "relying" and "to be expressed," respectively. Kalupahana renders *āśritya* as "relying" and *deśyate* as "taught," translating the statement in question as: "Without relying upon convention, the ultimate fruit is not taught."[22] The rendition of *deśyate* as "taught" is more correct grammatically and literally. The difference is, however, not serious. These scholars tend to see ordinary practices or conventions as instrumental to the expression of the supreme Truth. That is, ordinary practices function as a means for us to get to know the supreme Truth.

Murti has a similar understanding. He speaks of the supreme Truth in terms of the end or goal and *saṃvṛti* in terms of the means. He sees *saṃvṛti* as the ladder or the jumping board that enables us to reach our objective: the supreme Truth.[23] By *saṃvṛti* he denotes what is conventionally believed in common parlance.[24] This denotation is akin to what we mean by *vyavahāra,* i.e., the practices in the empirical world. For Murti, the conventional or empirical is indispensable in the revelation of the supreme Truth.

Still, we may go even further. In Nāgārjuna's Sanskrit assertion, *ā-śri* (the root of *āśritya*) may signify "affix," "adhere," "rest on" or "inhabit," besides the denotations of "relying on" and "depending on."[25] This additional denotation links the *paramārtha* and *vyavahāra* in a stronger sense. The supreme Truth must be expressed not merely through relying on ordinary practices, but also right in ordinary practices themselves. Apart from ordinary practices, the supreme Truth cannot be expressed. There is a subtle and significant difference between relying on ordinary practices to express the supreme Truth and expressing the supreme Truth in ordinary practices themselves. In the former case, ordinary practices still tend to be instrumental and consequently external to the act of expressing the supreme Truth. In the latter case, ordinary practices become a part of expressing the supreme Truth. There is no instrumental and external sense to the issue at all. Theoretically speaking, ordinary practices in the instrumental sense may be dispensed with when the supreme Truth is expressed. Ordinary practices, if they are a part of expressing the supreme Truth, can never be dispensed with.

Second, the passive *deśyate* may denote "being expressed." It may also denote "being demonstrated" or "being realized" in a stronger sense of action. Kumārajīva renders *deśyate* as "(being) attained" *(te),* apparently favoring the latter option.[26] Therefore, the issue with regard to the supreme Truth is not merely its expression, but also its realization or attainment.

In view of these interpretations, Nāgārjuna's statement can assume more of a practical and soteriological implication. That is, one should not merely express the supreme Truth through relying on ordinary practices, but should also attain the supreme Truth right in these practices. Ordinary practices can never be dispensed with. They can be undertaken only in the empirical world, so the empirical world should never be forsaken. This practical and soteriological implication is also in line with Nāgārjuna's identification of *nirvāṇa* and the life-death cycle, which insists that *nirvāṇa* shares the same realm with the life-death cycle and can be attained only in this realm. In this respect, Kalupahana also comments:

> Freedom *(nirvāṇa)* would not be absolute freedom that has nothing to do with human life. It is no more than the absence of certain constraints (such as greed, hatred, and confusion) in the life of a human being.[27]

4. Extirpation of defilements

When we talk about the realization of the Truth or the achievement of liberation, we admit that we are common people and live in the life-death cycle, which is full of suffering. Why is this so? All Buddhists would agree it is due to our various defilements *(kleśa)* caused by false views and attachments. It follows naturally that liberation is to be achieved through the extirpation of these defilements. In light of the doctrine of identification outlined above, the Mādhyamika position would be that liberation, which results from the realization of the Truth, should be achieved right in ordinary practices in the empirical world, but with defilements extirpated. This need to extirpate defilements is, in fact, strongly asserted by Nāgārjuna in the *Kārikā:*

> There is *mokṣa* (release or liberation) from the destruction of *karmaic* defilements which are but conceptualization. These arise from mere conceptual play *(prapañca)* which are in turn banished in *śūnyatā.*[28]

Nāgārjuna's position is clear; defilements must first be destroyed or extirpated before liberation can be achieved. This is spoken of in a strong practical sense. Defilements obstruct our liberation; liberation is nothing but the liberation from sufferings and defilements. Liberation and defilements cannot stand together, so, liberation can be achieved only in the extirpation of defilements. And, because conceptual play is what gives rise to defilements, it should be banished or extirpated as well. The urge to extirpate conceptual play and false views in order to attain liberation or *nirvāṇa* is seen throughout the *Kārikā*. Kalupahana, in his comment quoted in the previous section, speaks of freedom or liberation in terms of the absence of certain constraints, such as greed, hatred and confusion. These constraints can indeed be taken as defilements, and an absence of them tends to denote their extirpation.

The need to extirpate defilements in attaining liberation is also detailed in the TCTL:

> The ultimate Truth of the entities is permanent and immovable. However, due to various defilements such as ignorance, etc., sentient beings deviate from the ultimate Truth and commit distortions. The Buddhas and saints teach [the *Dharma*] with various expediencies, destroying defilements such as ignorance, etc., enabling sentient beings to regain the ultimate Nature which is not different from the original. This is called "Suchness." When the ultimate Nature combines with ignorance, deviation occurs. Hence the impurity [of everything]. If ignorance, etc. are extirpated and authentic Nature attained, this is called "Dharma Nature" *(Dharmatā)*, which is the pure and ultimate Realm. This [practice of extirpation] is called "penetration into the Dharma Nature."[29]

In this quotation, ultimate Truth *(shih-hsiang)*, ultimate Nature *(shih-hsing)*, Suchness *(ju)*, authentic Nature *(chen-hsing)*, ultimate Realm *(shih-chi)*, and Dharma Nature *(fa-hsing)* are synonymous, and their common ground is Emptiness. The crucial point here is that deviations and distortions arise from the combination of the ultimate Truth and such defilements as ignorance. The deviations and distortions will cause suffering and keep beings in the life-death cycle. The ultimate Truth (or simply Truth) originally immanent in beings can be restored to its purity by the extirpation of defilements. Consequently, liberation is attained.

Therefore, the extirpation of defilements is an important practice in the Mādhyamika in achieving liberation. This practice of extirpation of defilements is closely connected with the issue of the identification of the unworldly and worldly as explicated in Mādhyamika. However, we must cautiously note that this practice does not imply that the world itself must be extirpated as well, although both the defilements and the world are empirical in nature and are, consequently, often associated with each other. In this respect, the author of the TCTL makes the following distinction:

> In [the practice] of the Prajñāpāramitā [wisdom], what is extirpated is merely false views, not the four causes.[30]

The false views pertain to defilements, while the four causes represent the empirical world of causal relation.[31] In the practice of the Prajñāpāramitā wisdom to realize the Truth, what is extirpated is the defilements, not the empirical world itself, because it is in the empirical world that Emptiness can be realized.

Nāgārjuna himself has also expressed his objection to extirpating the empirical world. He states in the *Kārikā:*

> You will thus destroy all the everyday practices relative to the empirical world because you will have destroyed the *śūnyatā* of relational origination.[32]

In this verse, Nāgārjuna refutes his opponent, who tends to negate the doctrines of Dependent Origination and Emptiness. Nāgārjuna's point is that the empirical world as such is possible in virtue of these doctrines. If these doctrines are negated, the empirical world will be destroyed and nihilism will result. Nāgārjuna is by no means a nihilist, in view of his emphasis on the realization of the supreme Truth in ordinary practices in this empirical world. He would certainly be in favor of preserving the nature or realm of the empirical world. This positive attitude toward the empirical world is in line with the idea of *t'i-fa,* or embodying the *dharmas* in realizing Emptiness, with which Chih-i characterizes the Common Doctrine.

5. Chih-i on the issue of identification: no-extirpation

Let us now take a pause and sum up Mādhyamika's position with regard to the issue of identification of the unworldly and worldly. It identifies *nirvāṇa* and the life-death cycle to the extent that the supreme Truth (or simply the Truth) must be realized in ordinary practices in the empirical world. It holds that defilements must be extirpated before liberation can be achieved. In the Mādhyamika context, identification is the identification of *nirvāṇa* or liberation with the life-death cycle, *not* with defilements. In view of the fact that defilements are part of *saṃsāric* existence or the life-death cycle, we have to make a distinction that the identification in question is one of liberation not with the defilements, but with the rest of the life-death cycle.

Must we extirpate defilements in achieving liberation? It is true that defilements often obstruct liberation in ordinary life, and that liberation is precisely the liberation from defilements. But can we not imagine a situation in which we achieve liberation *via* overcoming or transcending defilements instead of extirpating them? Both Nāgārjuna and the author of the TCTL are not aware of this possibility and take a completely dim view of defilements. Let us bear this point in mind and come to a discussion of Chih-i's conception of identification.

In view of Chih-i's intimacy with the TCTL, which was the center of study in his early period, and his high appreciation of the idea of *t'i-fa* of the Common Doctrine, a close relationship between him and the Mādhyamika with regard to the issue of identification can be ascertained. He states:

> The *Pañcaviṃśatisāhasrikā-prajñāpāramitā-sūtra* says, "It is that form itself is Emptiness, not that Emptiness is attained in the eradication of form." The *Ta-chih-tu lun* explains, "Form is the life-death cycle, while Emptiness is *nirvāṇa*. The realm of the life-death cycle and that of *nirvāṇa* are one and not two." Does this [oneness] not indicate that the delusive and pure are harmonized?[33]

This vividly reveals his awareness of the same realm shared by the life-death cycle and *nirvāṇa*. He sees the life-death cycle as containing delusive *(jan)* elements and *nirvāṇa* as pure *(ching)*. The harmonization of the delusive life-death cycle and pure *nirvāṇa* signifies a relationship of identification.

With regard to the realization of the Truth, Chih-i is in line with the Mādhyamika in asserting that the Truth should be realized in the empirical world, not apart from it. He states this claim in the following manner:

> The Dharma Nature and all *dharmas* are the same without difference. . . . To keep away from the mundane *dharmas* and yet seek the ultimate Truth [elsewhere] is similar to avoiding this Emptiness and seeking Emptiness elsewhere. The mundane *dharmas* are themselves the ultimate *Dharma* [i.e., the Truth]. There is no need to forsake the mundane and adhere to the sacred.[34]

The non-difference between, or the identification of, the sacred Dharma Nature and mundane *dharmas* implies that the Truth and the empirical world share the same realm, or that it is in the empirical world that the Truth is to be realized.

There is no doubt about Chih-i's deep worldly concern for the realization of the Truth, but he goes even further. He claims that, in the attainment of *nirvāṇa* or liberation, even defilements should not be extirpated. That is, liberation and defilements can co-exist, without the former being hindered by the latter. This famous idea of no-extirpation *(pu-tuan)* is seen throughout Chih-i's major works in various expressions; for example, "To attain *nirvāṇa* without extirpating defilements," "Defilements are *Bodhi* (i.e., wisdom of enlightenment)," "Ignorance is wisdom," "The realm of the devils is the realm of the Buddha," "To initiate wisdom and liberation without extirpating ignorance and delusive love *(tṛṣṇā)*."[35] These expressions, though numerous and touching on various subjects, can be summed up in two basic patterns: "to attain the pure without extirpating the impure" and "the impure is the pure." In both patterns, the impure may denote ignorance, defilements and so on; the pure may denote *nirvāṇa,* liberation, etc. Both patterns can be construed as expressive of the identification of *nirvāṇa* or liberation and defilements. Identification as such is, indeed, a radical form in relating the unworldly and worldly.

It is this radical attitude that makes Chih-i different from the Mādhyamika with regard to the issue of identification. As summed up earlier, the Mādhyamika holds that the Truth should be realized in the empirical world, insisting that the extirpation of defilements is a necessary condition to liberation. Their identification is one involving *nirvāṇa* and the life-death cycle. Chih-i recognizes this worldly association but admits the existence of defilements in liberation. Therefore, his identification is not only one of *nirvāṇa* and the life-death cycle, but also one of *nirvāṇa* and defilements, which are commonly regarded as harmful to liberation. It is this latter form of identification that Chih-i emphasizes vigorously. In Chih-i's view, defilements are not necessarily harmful. Rather, they may have two positive significances. These issues will reveal the unique structure of Chih-i's thought and his deep practical interest.

6. The expedient significance of defilements

The first significance of defilements for Chih-i is that they can be taken as expedient measures for educational purposes. This expedient significance of defilements has both active and passive aspects. With regard to the active aspect, Chih-i states:

> If the body extirpates defilements and enters *nirvāṇa,* like [the prisoner who] breaks the wall and escapes, [it will mean that one] fears life and death, failing to use defilements to perform Buddha affairs. The bodhisattva, with the wisdom to Buddhahood, enters [*nirvāṇa*] without extirpating [defilements]. He is like one who, acquiring supernatural power, is not obstructed by a wall. It means to use defilements in performing Buddha affairs. This is called "to enter *nirvāṇa* without extirpating defilements."[36]

Chih-i mentions the role of performing Buddha affairs and associates it with defilements. What are Buddha affairs *(fo-shih)?* Although Chih-i does not enumerate them, it is obvious that they have much to do with promoting the realization of the Truth and the attainment of Buddhahood among sentient beings. With regard to this role, defilements can serve as expedient measures. How this happens is not detailed in Chih-i's major works, but it is not difficult to imagine that defilements include evil deeds, which can be undertaken expediently to convert evil sentient beings. In Chapter IV, section 7 we pointed out that the Buddha or bodhisattva, in the process of converting robbers, may assume the apparition of a robber and perform evils with them in order to enhance the intimacy with the robbers, which is conducive to their conversion and attainment of Buddhahood. Defilements can be expedient in this sense, and the conversion and attainment of Buddhahood of robbers are by all means Buddha affairs. The performance of evil deeds in this way is not evil at all. As an expedient measure, it is justifiable from the viewpoint of the Buddha affair that is the end.

This active aspect of the expedient significance of defilements refers to something to be used or adopted, whether it be a deed or a form, while the passive aspect is quite different. Chih-i refers to this latter aspect and remarks:

> In tackling the rebels, for an example, the rebels are [indeed] the root of exploits. In destroying the rebels, one attains high rank and great wealth. Likewise, the immeasurable greed and sensuous desires are the seed of Buddhahood. [They] enable the bodhisattva to produce countless doors to the *Dharma*. More firewood makes the flames [rise] fiercely, and the dung fertilizes flowers. This is why [we say] that greed and sensuous desire are the Way. If [one] extirpates greed and sensuous desire and abides in the Emptiness of greed and sensuous desire, how can [he] produce all doors to the *Dharma*?[37]

Defilements can help produce the doors to the *Dharma (fa-men)* to promote Buddha affairs, but defilements are not something to be used. In promoting Buddha affairs, they play the expedient role of a trigger, not in an active and mechanical sense, but in a passive and dialectical sense. This "trigger" initiates the acts for Buddhahood. That is, it is because there are defilements that practical measures have to be undertaken to overcome them, and it is due to the overcoming of these defilements that one attains Buddhahood. Buddhahood cannot be established on nullification. Rather, it is mainly based on the endeavors for overcoming defilements. The same is also true with high rank and great wealth, which are available merely through doing something, such as destroying the rebels. It is in this sense that defilements serve expediently as a dialectical trigger in promoting Buddha affairs, just as the rebels do in initiating great honour and wealth. The term "passive" in "passive aspect" indicates the passive signficance of defilements in promoting Buddha affairs. That is, defilements do not actively and directly initiate Buddha affairs. Rather, Buddha affairs are initiated on the basis of "overcoming defilements."

Chih-i, here, is creating an analogy between defilements and the rebels. However, a significant problem remains. That is, high rank and great wealth are achieved through the destruction of the rebels, who will vanish for good as a result; on the other hand, Buddha affairs are achieved by overcoming and yet maintaining defilements. There is, therefore, a discrepancy in the analogy, of which Chih-i apparently was not aware. The issue of overcoming and yet maintaining defilements will be discussed in detail below.

Chih-i sometimes distinguishes between the active and passive aspects of defilements, but sometimes he does not. In his remark that greed and sensuous desire enable the bodhisattva to produce the doors to the *Dharma,* for example, both aspects may be involved. Greed and sensuous desire, being the major defilements, obviously play the role of a dialectical trigger. This is the passive aspect. But the doors to the *Dharma* may denote certain concrete defilements to be used. This is the active aspect. In either aspect, the expedient significance of defilements is beyond doubt.

In view of the expedient significance of defilements, it is natural for Chih-i to suggest the idea of no-extirpation of defilements in entering *nirvāṇa.*[38] Obviously, no-extirpation presupposes a special understanding of the nature of defilements. This understanding precedes the use of defilements and renders their use possible. In the quotation immediately preceding the above one, Chih-i compares the bodhisattva's wisdom to a supernatural power. He elaborates the analogy as follows:

> [Someone] asked, "If you do not extirpate the *karma* resulting from the assemblage of defilements, how can you obtain liberation?" [I] answered, "It is like someone in prison [who wants to escape]. If he has not acquired supernatural power, he must break the wall in order to escape. But if he has acquired supernatural power, he can leave and enter the prison without obstruction, leaving the wall unbroken.[39]

Chih-i's point is that the attainment of liberation in the form of no-extirpation is based on a special wisdom which is not obstructed by, but rather embraces, defilements. This wisdom tends to understand that defilements originate from causal relations and do not have permanent Self Nature. They are empty in nature. Chih-i himself has, in fact, identified the nature of ignorance—the major defilement—as empty.[40] Chun-i T'ang also points out that the liberation explicated by Chih-i indicates the understanding of the empty nature of defilements.[41] Ultimately speaking, because defilements are empty, they cannot affect and harm us; because they are empty, we can use them at our disposal. It is due to such an understanding that we can be free from the obstruction of defilements, can manipulate them, and make them beneficial. When we can do this, defilements become a positive instrument to us and there is no need to extirpate them.

7. Identification of Dharma Nature and ignorance in and of themselves

The expedient significance opens for defilements a new facet in which they can be soteriologically beneficial. Yet this also indicates conditionality; it has to be justified by the end. When the end is completely fulfilled, the expediency can be dispensed with. Theoretically speaking, when every sentient being acquires liberation, and there is nothing to enlighten, defilements will lose their expedient significance automatically and will have to be extirpated. In view of this conditionality, the idea of no-extirpation is not ultimate, and the identification based on this idea cannot be guaranteed.

There is, for Chih-i, yet another significance of defilements that opens a completely different picture for the identification. Chih-i goes so far as to declare that Dharma Nature and ignorance are identical and are simply different aspects of the same thing. In this context, Dharma Nature and ignorance stand for liberation and defilements, respectively. The relationship between Dharma Nature and ignorance is just like that between water and ice. Chih-i remarks:

> The defilement of ignorance is originally Dharma Nature. Due to stupidity and confusion, Dharma Nature turns into ignorance and gives rise to various perversions, [the duality of] good and evil, etc. It is like water turning into solid ice in cold weather, or the mind having various dreams in sleep.[42]

Dharma Nature and ignorance are therefore different states of the same thing under different conditions. This relationship is similar to that of water and ice, which are two different states of the same thing, i.e., H_2O, under different temperatures. Chih-i particularly warns that Dharma Nature and ignorance do not refer to two different things:

> There is merely [the difference of] names and words [between Dharma Nature and ignorance]. How can there be the identification of two things? [The situation is] like a pearl which will produce water when it is put toward the moon, and produce fire when it is put toward the sun. If it is not put [toward them], there will be no water nor fire. The thing has never been divided, but the pearl of both water and fire is there.[43]

Chih-i's point is that Dharma Nature and ignorance are not two entities divided from one source, but result from the single source that acts or is acted upon differently. For Chih-i, this case is like water and fire, which do not result from the division of the pearl, but from different manipulations of a single pearl. This pearl image does not communicate to us clearly, but what we should pay attention is Chih-i's reduction of the difference of Dharma Nature and ignorance to an issue of names and words. That is, the difference is nominal, not substantial. The question "How can there be the identification of two things?" does not conflict with the identification of Dharma Nature and ignorance. Rather, it entails a rejection of the identification of Dharma Nature and ignorance in *the sense* that Dharma Nature and ignorance are taken as two separate things. This sense is, for Chih-i, a misunderstanding of the nature of Dharma Nature and ignorance.

It is in the sense of not being two separate things, but being different states of the same thing, that Chih-i identifies Dharma Nature and ignorance. In his terminology, this is an identification of Dharma Nature and ignorance in and of themselves *(tang-t'i)*. Chih-i himself has stated that the various perversions are in and of themselves Dharma Nature.[44] The perversions spoken of here are the perversions of the Truth, which originate from ignorance. Identification as such is, in fact, the most radical form in which ignorance or defilements acquire their positive significance.[45]

In the identification as such, liberation or enlightenment consists in a transition of states; namely, from the prevalence of ignorance to the overcoming of ignorance and the revelation of Dharma Nature. This transition does not take place smoothly, but rather involves a moral or religious struggle between Dharma Nature and ignorance. Consequently, the character of this identification must be understood in a practical and dynamic context, making Chih-i's identification one of the most difficult issues in Buddhist philosophy and practice. To cope with this crucial point, let us quote Chih-i:

> In evil there is good; apart from evil there is no good. It is the overturning of various evils upon which the tenability of good is based. The situation is like the bamboo in possession of the potency of fire. This potency is not actual fire, therefore the bamboo does not burn. But when the potency meets subsidiary causes and is actualized, the bamboo can burn things. [Likewise,] evil is [the potency of] good,

> though it has not yet become actually [good]. When it meets subsidiary causes and is actualized, it can overturn evil. Similar to the potency of fire in the bamboo, which burns the bamboo when actualized, the potency of good in evil will overturn the evil when actualized. Therefore the aspect of evil potency is identical to the aspect of good potency.[46]

Chih-i makes an analogy between evil and the bamboo, and good and fire. Evil embraces the potency of good, just as the bamboo embraces the potency of fire. Good reveals itself on the basis of overturning evil, just as fire comes into reality on the basis of burning the bamboo. Chih-i's point is that good and evil do not make terms with each other, but are constantly in a struggle. Good must overturn evil in order to prevail, and good can prevail only by the overturning of evil. It follows that the overturning of evil is a necessary and sufficient condition for the prevalence of good. But the overturning of evil does not imply extirpation of evil. The former means to overcome evil, obstructing it from prevailing and affecting our life; the latter contains a sense of annihilation, i.e., to extinguish evil completely so that it can never come again. In Chih-i's view, evil should not be extirpated because good is tenable merely in evil; apart from evil, there is no good. This relationship between evil and good is not spoken of in expedient or instrumental terms. Evil should not be extirpated, not because it is expedient to the realization of good; rather, this relationship is spoken of in terms of the identification of evil and good in and of themselves. Evil and good pertain to the same thing and thus cannot be separated from each other. If there is no evil, neither will there be any good. Therefore, evil should not be extirpated.[47]

There is then a constant struggle, yet there is also a constant association of good with evil. Good and evil stand for Dharma Nature and ignorance, respectively. There is a similar struggle and association of Dharma Nature with ignorance. Speaking both logically and practically, there is hardly a common point on which the struggle and association of Dharma Nature with ignorance can come to terms. Struggle is the struggle of Dharma Nature with ignorance to overturn the latter, or at least to get away from it. However, there is simultaneously a relationship between the pure Dharma Nature and impure ignorance, which are identified in and of themselves. There is a sophisticated antinomy of the constant struggle and the persistent association between the two poles of Dharma Nature and ignorance. This antinomy makes Chih-i's thought extremely difficult to comprehend, and, consequently, it has hardly been dealt with seriously by scholars.

8. The mind and its acts

The solution to this antinomy cannot be found in either side, or even both sides, of Dharma Nature and ignorance. It can be found solely in a third possible condition, which synthesizes Dharma Nature and ignorance. Because the identification in question is one of Dharma Nature and ignorance in and of themselves, referring to different states of the same thing, the third condition must be nothing but the mind, which embraces Dharma Nature and ignorance. Concerning this mind, Chih-i states:

> This mind is [where] ignorance, Dharma Nature, *Dharma-dhatū,* the ten realms of existence, the one hundred categories of *dharmas* and countless [states of] concentration and deconcentration are all embraced in one single moment. Why? Because of the delusion toward Dharma Nature, there are all evil *dharmas* such as deconcentration and confusion, etc.; and because of the awakening to Dharma Nature, there are all *dharmas* of concentration. . . . There is no difference in nature between not awakening and awakening [to Dharma Nature], concentration and deconcentration.[48]

Chih-i tries to enumerate all sorts of states of existence and to sum them up in terms of concentration and deconcentration, which he relates to the pure Dharma Nature and impure ignorance, respectively. His point is that whether a person is in the state of concentration or of deconcentration depends on whether or not he awakens to Dharma Nature; this in turn depends on how his mind acts. When Chih-i claims that there is a non-difference in nature between not awakening and awakening to Dharma Nature (i.e., between deconcentration and concentration), he is pinpointing the mind and its activities. If it acts in accordance with Dharma Nature, it will result in enlightenment; if not, ignorance will occur. Dharma Nature and ignorance seem to be two opposing aspects of a cycle in which the mind rotates. It is in the context of this mind that Dharma Nature and ignorance are identified with each other; likewise, the struggle and association of Dharma Nature with ignorance are spoken of in this context. This struggle and association are not taken in an isolated and ultimate sense. They are related to the mind as two forms of relationship of Dharma Nature and ignorance embraced in the mind.

In relating the struggle and association of Dharma Nature with ignorance to the mind, Chih-i delineates:

> When ignorance determines Dharma Nature, the one mind [differentiates into] all kinds of mind. This is like one who is asleep. When one realizes that ignorance is Dharma Nature, all kinds of mind [will return to] the one mind. This is like one who is awake.[49]

Although Chih-i does not specify the association and struggle of Dharma Nature with ignorance, such implications are undeniable. "Ignorance determines Dharma Nature" implies the association of Dharma Nature with ignorance, in which the former is submissive to the latter. This is expressive of the differentiation of the one mind into all kinds of mind. In Chih-i's terminology, "one mind" *(i-hsin)* usually denotes the pure mind in an absolute sense, while "all kinds of mind" *(i-ch'ieh hsin)* denotes the delusive mind in a relative sense. The pure mind and delusive mind are, however, not two separate minds. Rather, they are different manifestations resulting from different acts of the same mind. Chih-i's point here is that when ignorance determines Dharma Nature, the mind will act ignorantly. In this case, the mind is delusive. On the contrary, when one realizes that ignorance is essentially not different from Dharma Nature and acts in conformity to the latter, one's mind will be pure. This implies a struggle of Dharma Nature with ignorance, in which the former triumphs over the latter.

In view of the fact that Dharma Nature and ignorance are simultaneously embraced in the mind, their association is unavoidable. Because they are opposite to each other in nature—Dharma Nature is pure, while ignorance is impure or delusive—their struggle is likewise unavoidable. Depending on the outcome of the association and struggle, the mind acts ignorantly of or in conformity to Dharma Nature. Dharma Nature and ignorance equally indicate a direction along which the mind may act; as a consequence, they are identical to each other. The annoying antinomy can therefore find a solution in the mind and its acts.

It should be cautiously noted here that the claim regarding Dharma Nature and ignorance as embraced in the mind does not imply that they appear simultaneously in our actual life. If they did, the mind would then act in conformity to both Dharma Nature and ignorance simultaneously. This is impossible and would render the identification of Dharma Nature and ignorance into an antinomy. The implication is, rather, that either Dharma Nature or ignorance will prevail, subject to how the mind acts. Theoretically speaking, the mind has complete freedom to conform or be opposed to Dharma Nature, achieving enlightenment or remaining ignorant correspondingly. Nevertheless, the achievement of enlightenment or revelation of Dharma Nature must stand on the overturning of ignorance. In the revelation of Dharma Nature, ignorance has nowhere to conceal itself. The revelation of Dharma Nature and overturning of ignorance take place at the same time. This has also been pointed out by Chih-i himself:

> When Dharma Nature is revealed, ignorance will be transformed into wisdom.[50]

> When ignorance is transformed, it will become wisdom, like ice thawing and turning into water. It is not something else coming from another place. Both [ignorance and wisdom] are embraced in the mind in one single moment.[51]

When ignorance is overturned, it will be transformed into wisdom or light, which is precisely the light of Dharma Nature. This means the revelation of Dharma Nature. As a matter of fact, the overturning of ignorance and the revelation of Dharma Nature are two facets of the same event: an act of the mind. Both ignorance and Dharma Nature are embraced in the mind. It is the mind which acts ignorantly; it is also the same mind that overturns its ignorance and simultaneously reveals its Dharma Nature. When Chih-i states that it is the overturning of various evils upon which the tenability of good is based (cf. above), he is also referring to the two facets: overturning of various evils, and making the good tenable in terms of the act of the mind. It is in this sense that Chih-i identifies good and evil (or Dharma Nature and ignorance) in and of themselves and declares that they are not two separate things.

Now we are in a better position to account for the difficult idea of no-extirpation of defilements. Defilements, represented by evil and ignorance, are, together with good and Dharma Nature, what the mind embraces in nature. Their extirpation in an annihilative sense would indicate the extirpation of the mind as well. Such a condition would further result in the extirpation of good and Dharma Nature, rendering *nirvāṇa* and liberation impossible. This justifies the assertion "In evil there is good; apart from evil there is no good." Therefore, defilements can only be transcended or overturned. They can never be extirpated.

The idea that the mind embraces both Dharma Nature and ignorance (or the pure and impure) in one single moment is widespread and emphasized in Chih-i's major works as well as the works of his followers.[52] The term "in one single moment" *(i-nien)* actually means "in any single moment." It characterizes the mundane nature of the mind indicated, that is, the mind appearing in any single moment in our daily lives. It is therefore the mind in an ordinary state, not in a special state.

Chih-i's identification of Dharma Nature and ignorance, as shown above, can be situated in the context of the mind. In this kind of context, the identification is clearly expressive of something about the mind; the mind embraces both Dharma Nature and ignorance and consequently may act in conformity to Dharma Nature or ignorantly. It also conveys the message that Dharma Nature or liberation is to be attained right in the moment of the transcendence of ignorance or defilements; what we should work upon is nothing but the ordinary mind in our daily lives. It is not far from us at all. We have no need to leave our ordinary mind and daily experience to seek liberation elsewhere. This message is a very practical one, in the sense that our ordinary mind is the most concrete and intimate subject matter to start with in our soteriological pursuit. Liberation is tenable merely in the overturning of defilements.

In beginning this pursuit, it is evident that there are various defilements and they seem to be everywhere. In practice, one cannot overturn all defilements in the beginning, but must select some of them with which to deal. In the overwhelming "sea of defilements," one is likely to remain in the dark as to the selection of defilements. In such a case, the identification of Dharma Nature and ignorance situated in the context of the mind advises that one may concentrate on the ignorant tendencies arising in one's ordinary mind at any moment. One should watch these ignorant tendencies and try to stop them because, once they are stopped, Dharma Nature is revealed. The outcome will be that the mind treated in this manner will act in full accord with Dharma Nature. With regard to the cultivation of the mind, to make it act along the direction of Dharma Nature and abandon ignorance, Chih-i has suggested his own sophisticated and technical methods. Delineation of these methods, however, exceeds the scope of the present work.

9. Chih-i's criticism of the Common Doctrine

We have discussed in detail the two significant factors of defilements. One refers to their expedient sense; the other is that ignorance and Dharma Nature are embraced in the mind, making the mind the starting point of soteriological pursuits. Because defilements have these two significances, they should not be extirpated. It is in this sense that Chih-i proposes the idea of no-extirpation of defilements, and it is in the context of this idea that Chih-i identifies Dharma Nature with ignorance, or liberation with defilements. No-extirpation is, indeed, an important practice. From it also arises the practical significance of the identification of liberation and defilements.

In light of this identification, Chih-i criticizes the Common Doctrine, which includes the Mādhyamika. This criticism deserves our attention because it can enhance our understanding of the relationship between Chih-i and the Mādhyamika on the issue of identification. However, before going into the criticism, we must explain two technical terms used by Chih-i: the conceivable liberation and the inconceivable liberation.

In light of his unique identification of Dharma Nature and ignorance, Chih-i classifies two forms of liberation, i.e., the conceivable liberation *(ssu-i chieh-t'o)* and the inconceivable liberation *(pu ssu-i chieh-t'o),* favoring the latter form. This classification is mainly based on whether or not liberation is achieved in the pattern of no-extirpation. If the liberation is a no-extirpation one, it is inconceivable; if not, it is conceivable. In fact, Chih-i associates the nature of inconceivability with two features: non-separation from language and no-extirpation of defilements.[53] But it is the latter that he emphasizes to the greatest extent, sometimes explaining inconceivability exclusively in terms of no-extirpation.[54] He goes so far as to claim that only liberation based on the idea of no-extirpation is inconceivable. In response to why this is so, he remarks:

> The Sumeru Mountain enters into the mustard seed, so that the tiny does not obstruct the huge, nor the huge obstruct the tiny. This is why it is called inconceivable. Now, the assemblage of defilements do not obstruct *prajñā* and *nirvāṇa,* nor do *prajñā* and *nirvāṇa* obstruct the assemblage of defilements. This is [also] called "inconceivable."[55]

Nirvāṇa results from the revelation of *prajñā.* Chih-i suggests that *nirvāṇa* and defilements do not obstruct each other, just as the tiny mustard seed and the huge Sumeru Mountain do not obstruct each other. There is a relationship of non-obstruction in both cases. What draws our attention is the suggestion that the pure *nirvāṇa* is not obstructed by the impure defilements, just as a tiny mustard seed is not obstructed by the huge Sumeru Mountain. This relationship is inconceivable to common sense. It entails a special wisdom which tends to see the defilements and Sumeru Mountain as empty in nature and consequently non-obstructive. From the standpoint of such wisdom, defilements do not need to be extirpated. This is quite akin to the analogy explicated earlier, in which Chih-i compares such wisdom with the supernatural power that enables one to escape a prison without being obstructed by a wall. The idea of no-extirpation resulting from non-obstruction as such is what Chih-i denotes with the word "inconceivable."

Chih-i also relates the contrast between conceivable liberation and inconceivable liberation to his classification of Buddhist doctrines. For him, liberation based on the Tripiṭaka Doctrine and the Common Doctrine is conceivable; liberation based on the Gradual Doctrine and the Perfect Doctrine is inconceivable.[56]

Because Chih-i ascribes to the Perfect Doctrine the nature of inconceivability in terms of no-extirpation, it is beyond doubt that he takes the liberation advocated by the Perfect Doctrine as being based on no-extirpation: the identification of Dharma Nature with ignorance, or *nirvāṇa* with defilements. His criticism of the Common Doctrine is also made in the light of this no-extirpation and identification. In this respect, he states:

> [Someone] asked, "If the entering of *nirvāṇa* without extirpating [defilement] is inconceivable, then the Common Doctrine also teaches the no-extirpation of entering *nirvāṇa;* why is that liberation not inconceivable?" [I] answered, "The Common Doctrine does not see the characteristic of defilements. Although it uses the term 'no-extirpation,' it in fact extirpates [defilements], like the case in which light prevails and there is no darkness. This is different from the case in which the tiny size of the mustard seed does not undermine the huge size of Sumeru Mountain."[57]

In this conversation, both the questioner and Chih-i have a particular sūtra in mind when they speak of the Common Doctrine, though it is not specified. It is, however, evidenced by the statement "It uses the term 'no-extirpation,' " which refers to a *sūtra* commonly categorized as belonging to the no-extirpation thinking. What is this *sūtra*? We infer it to be the well-known *Vimalakīrtinirdeśa-sūtra.* This *sūtra* is classified by Chih-i as preaching the Common Doctrine; its text is widely occupied with expressions featuring no-extirpation.[58] Chih-i's point is that the *Vimalakīrtinirdeśa-sūtra* preaches the doctrine of extirpation rather than no-extirpation, because it does not understand the true characteristic of defilements.

Chih-i's criticism of the Common Doctrine is that it fails to understand the true characteristic of defilements and merely extirpates them in liberation; its liberation is therefore in the nature of conceivable liberation, not inconceivable liberation. Chih-i does not elaborate in what specific points this failure of understanding the true characteristic of defilements occurs. Instead, he relates the failure to the situation in which light does not admit darkness and draws a contrast in terms of the tiny mustard seed not undermining the huge Sumeru Mountain. In these two cases, he obviously appreciates the latter and downgrades the former. The relationship of darkness to light is obstruction, while the relationship of the Sumeru Mountain to the mustard seed is one demonstrating non-obstruction. Chih-i's ideal is the relationship of non-obstruction, which he enthusiastically descibes as "inconceivable." Because defilements and liberation are placed in the context of such an inconceivable relationship, the outcome will be that defilements do not obstruct liberation. Therefore, defilements need not be extirpated in liberation.

What does the "characteristic of defilements" denote? In response, we must first remind ourselves that Chih-i is criticizing the Common Doctrine from the standpoint of no-extirpation of defilements, which he ascribes to the Perfect Doctrine. In such a context, we believe the characteristic denotes the two significances of defilements detailed previously. In view of these two significances, Chih-i suggests that the no-extirpation of defilements is higher, and expounds on the identification of liberation with defilements. In Chih-i's view, the Common Doctrine is not aware of these two significances. Rather, it takes defilements to be obstructive and therefore advocates their extirpation.

It is not our concern here to examine whether or not Chih-i's criticism does justice to the *Vimalakīrtinirdeśa-sūtra.* However, because this criticism is directed at the Common Doctrine, it should naturally be directed at the Mādhyamika. Does it do justice to the Mādhyamika?

This question is concerned mainly with the Mādhyamika conception of defilements. Let us examine what the Mādhyamikas, Nāgārjuna in particular, see defilements to be. In the *Kārikā,* Nāgārjuna says that defilements are in the nature of Emptiness *(śūnya).*[59] He also says that defilements are similar to the nature of an imaginary city in the sky, and that they are a mirage and a dream.[60] On some occasions, Nāgārjuna says that defilements are devoid of real nature (Skt., *tattva;* Ch., *shih*).[61] Piṅgala speaks of this *shih* in terms of Self Nature and explains that defilements are devoid of Self Nature.[62] Both Nāgārjuna and Piṅgala tend to see defilements as empty in nature, which is quite understandable in light of the standpoint of Dependent Origination. That is, all things or entities, including defilements, originate from the relationship of dependence upon others and are therefore devoid of Self Nature and are empty.

In the *Kārikā,* there is no indication that defilements have the two specific significances. Nāgārjuna's attitude toward the extirpation of defilements in liberation is clear and firm. We can conclude, therefore, that Chih-i's criticism of the Common Doctrine definitely applies to Nāgārjuna.

10. No-extirpation and the Middle Way-Buddha Nature

As seen above, Chih-i's identification of liberation and defilements is spoken of in the context of no-extirpation of defilements, which is an extremely important practice in his system. Accordingly, the identification in question is a practical issue. Its major concern is the attainment of the soteriological goal: liberation. We may also say that, for Chih-i, liberation is basically attained in the practice of no-extirpation. But Chih-i also declares that liberation is attained in the realization of the Middle Way-Buddha Nature (cf. Chapter IV. 1). There must be a close relationship between no-extirpation and the Middle Way-Buddha Nature; it must be possible that the practice of no-extirpation is directly related to the realization of the Middle Way-Buddha Nature. Because the two significances of defilements are the basis of no-extirpation, such a relationship cannot be made clear without taking them into account.

We will discuss this relationship by referring to two points, focusing on the two significances of defilements. First, one of the three characteristics of the Middle Way-Buddha Nature is that it embraces all *dharmas*. These *dharmas* may not necessarily be confined to the good and the pure. They may include the evil and the delusive, i.e., defilements. Accordingly, the realization of the Middle Way-Buddha Nature entails the realization, or at least the preservation, of defilements. This, however, does not indicate that one may act delusively in an ultimate and isolated sense. Rather, defilements should be preserved because they may serve as expedient measures in teaching certain sentient beings. This has been detailed in our chapter on the Middle Way-Buddha Nature. Chih-i's message is, indeed, that with the expedient significance, defilements can be very helpful in promoting Buddha affairs, among which the teaching of sentient beings is an important item. It is obvious that the expedient significance of defilements can be situated in the context of the realization of the Middle Way-Buddha Nature and also provides a better understanding of the all-embracing nature of the Middle Way-Buddha Nature.

Another characteristic of the Middle Way-Buddha Nature is that it is functional. The realization of the Middle Way-Buddha Nature is impossible apart from the exertion or manifestation of its function. As pointed out previously, this function focuses on the transformation of the empirical world, sentient beings in particular. "The bodhisattva. . . . puts the sentient beings into correct places with the perfect function."[63] In doing so, the bodhisattva may use various methods and skills. The expedient significance of defilements could, no doubt, facilitate the bodhisattva in dealing with difficult cases. That is, the bodhisattva may first assume defilements or act delusively to obtain an intimacy with evil sentient beings and try to convert them gradually. In this sense, defilements *as expediencies* may contribute to the conversion of sentient beings, and their significance can be affirmed in the realization of the Middle Way-Buddha Nature.

Second, in the realization of the Middle Way-Buddha Nature, which embraces both the pure and the delusive *dharmas* or elements, the major task is to reveal the pure elements and overcome the delusive. But how are we to do this in the midst of various pure and delusive *dharmas?* The other significance of defilements suggests that we can start our task with our ordinary mind, which embraces Dharma Nature and ignorance in any single moment. It is the act of this mind that determines whether we are in enlightenment or in delusion. We must watch this mind with full attention, to see that it does not act ignorantly, but acts in the light of Dharma Nature. If it acts ignorantly, it will be a delusive mind; if it acts in the light of Dharma Nature, it will be a pure mind. This pure mind is in fact the True Mind *(chen-hsin),* which Chih-i identifies with Buddha Nature.[64] Because Buddha Nature is not different from the Middle Way-Buddha Nature, this pure mind is not different from the Middle Way-Buddha Nature. Accordingly, the realization of the Middle Way-Buddha Nature can be achieved through the attainment of the pure mind, which is based on practice in terms of our ordinary mind. The concern of such practice is the restoration of Dharma Nature and the overcoming or overturning of ignorance or defilements.

We have related the two significances of defilements to the Middle Way-Buddha Nature in practical terms. This is not surprising at all, because the no-extirpation of defilements is of a deeply rooted practical character.

11. Extirpation and no-extirpation of defilements

Finally, let us wind up our discussion of the difficult issue of identification by reflecting on two questions: Why does Nāgārjuna insist on the extirpation of defilements in liberation? Is the no-extirpation of defilements a positive development of the extirpation of defilements?

With regard to the realization of the Truth or attainment of *nirvāṇa,* Nāgārjuna does not differentiate *nirvāṇa* from the life-death cycle, tending to identify them with each other. His advice is that the Truth should be expressed and attained in ordinary practices in the empirical world, and that liberation can be achieved on the condition that defilements are extirpated. To express and attain the Truth right in ordinary practices reveals the immanent character of the Truth. That is, the Truth is not at all far from us and the empirical world. It also indicates that the Truth is an intimate soteriological goal to us. But this intimacy seems to be restricted by the extirpation of defilements. Nāgārjuna tends to put defilements outside of ordinary practices. In his view, the Truth is immanent in ordinary practices, not in defilements. As pointed out earlier, he was not aware of the two significances of defilements, but aware of their empty nature. Like most Buddhists, he is likely to take defilements to be a great hindrance to enlightenment. It is therefore understandable that he insists on the extirpation of defilements.

Defilements, like other things or events, are involved in the nature of Dependent Origination and are therefore empty. It is also true that, in most cases, they are harmful to our pursuit for enlightenment because they often obstruct us from revealing the luminosity of Dharma Nature or Buddha Nature. Accordingly, defilements can and should be extirpated. But can we not see the issue from another angle? Can we not think that, due to their empty nature, defilements ultimately cannot harm us and need not be extirpated? Furthermore, if defilements are empty in nature, being devoid of the unchangeable and immovable Self Nature, can they not then be subject to our manipulation and made beneficial in certain circumstances?

Chih-i must have considered these questions carefully, and his response is affirmative. The crucial point seems to be that he does not take an exclusively negative view of defilements. He tends to think that the harm resulting from defilements can be avoided by the wisdom of non-obstruction, which can be cultivated through practice. This is similar to the case in which the wall of a prison does not prevent a prisoner with supernatural power from obtaining freedom. Chih-i also discovers the two significances of defilements, which are helpful in our pursuit for liberation. It is from this background that Chih-i proposes the practice of no-extirpation of defilements and identifies *nirvāṇa* or liberation with defilements. As remarked previously, this identification does not reject in any sense Nāgārjuna's non-difference or identification of *nirvāṇa* and the life-death cycle, advising us to attain the Truth in ordinary practices. In view of Chih-i's high appreciation of the *t'i-fa* thinking of the Mādhyamika, it seems certain that he would applaud this manner of attaining the Truth wholeheartedly. Furthermore, he is eager to incorporate the employment of defilements into these ordinary practices. Nāgārjuna was not aware of the possibility and implication of this incorporation.

Based on this understanding, we may conclude that Chih-i does not reject Nāgārjuna on the issue of non-difference or identification. On the basis of Nāgārjuna's conception of non-difference or identification of *nirvāṇa* and the life-death cycle, Chih-i establishes his own conception of identification which greatly enhances its comprehensiveness and flexibility in adopting appropriate methods to cope with particular cases. In Chih-i's new conception of identification, defilements are something not to be extirpated, but to be overcome, transcended and manipulated. This identification, indeed, opens a new picture for the practitioner in his pursuit of the soteriological goal. It is in this sense that we may affirm that Chih-i's identification based on the no-extirpation of defilements is a positive development of Nāgārjuna's non-difference or identification, which entails the extirpation of defilements. In other words, the practice of no-extirpation of defilements is a positive development beyond that of extirpation of defilements.

CHAPTER VIII

Conclusion

In the preceding pages we have discussed the three basic questions proposed in the Introduction. The first two questions concerning the concept of Truth were dealt with in Chapters II to IV, while the third one concerning the realization of the Truth in terms of philosophical methods was dealt with in Chapters V to VII. In comparison, we spent more space on the discussion of the third question, but this does not mean that the third question is more important than the first two, nor that the issue of philosophical method is more crucial than that of the concept itself. Rather, this is because the discussion of the philosophical methods involves more related problems which are complicated and necessarily call for more clarifications and elaboration. Speaking both logically and practically, the conception or understanding of the Truth precedes and determines the method of its realization. As shown in our discussions, Chih-i's understanding of the Truth (*shih-hsiang* or the Middle Way-Buddha Nature) is different from that of Nāgārjuna, who takes Emptiness or the Middle Way to be the Truth. Accordingly, in the realization of the Truth, Chih-i's methods are different from Nāgārjuna's, demonstrating that the issue of concept is more fundamental than that of philosophical method.

Although it is undeniable that Chih-i inherits much from the Mādhyamika's understanding and realization of the Truth, his affiliation with the Mādhyamika in thought is far outweighed by his difference from this School, as is evidenced mostly in his unique conception of the Middle Way-Buddha Nature, the Truth or ultimate Truth for him. As delineated in Chapter IV, he ascribes three characteristics—namely, permanence, function and all-embracement of *dharmas*—as belonging to the Middle Way-Buddha Nature. These characteristics are unanimously spoken of in the context of Buddha Nature. Because the Middle Way (itself the Way or Truth) is identified with Buddha Nature, it follows that the Truth possesses these characteristics; the Truth is permanent, functional and all-embracing in nature. Nāgārjuna does not mention the concept of Buddha Nature in his *Kārikā;* the Truth for him, whether it be Emptiness or the Middle Way, has nothing to do with these characteristics.

Among these characteristics of the Middle Way-Buddha Nature, it is the functional nature that is depicted and elaborated most often in Chih-i's works, the FHHI and MHCK in particular. This is evidence of Chih-i's special emphasis on the functional or dynamic aspect of the Truth. In view of the fact that this nature is basically delineated in terms of the transformation of sentient beings undertaken by bodhisattvas, Chih-i's deep concern about the welfare of sentient beings and their residence, the empirical world, is beyond doubt.

But how can Truth be functional or dynamic? Or, how can Truth initiate actions? Chih-i's understanding is that Truth can be construed not only as a Principle, which tends to be static, but also as a pure Mind that can act. He identifies the Buddha Nature with the pure Mind and consequently speaks of the various functions of the Middle Way-Buddha Nature. Buddha Nature is not different from the Middle Way, which is revealed as a Principle in the transcendence of extremes, the pure Mind, therefore, is not different from, but is identified with the Middle Way. This identification of the pure Mind with the Middle Way or Principle is comparable to the fundamental idea of Neo-Confucianism that the Mind is the Principle *(hsin chi li).* This idea, advocated by Lu Hsiang-shan and Wang Yang-ming, characterizes the Chinese way of philosophizing with regard to the issue of Truth. That is, Truth is not only the Principle, but also the Mind.[1] Roughly speaking, Chih-i's identification of the pure Mind and Middle Way can be taken as a Buddhist expression of this idea.

Does Nāgārjuna touch the issue of pure Mind? In the *Kārikā,* Nāgārjuna does mention the mind, but in a negative tone:

> Where mind's functional realm ceases, the realm of words also ceases. For, indeed, the essence of existence *(dharmatā)* is like *nirvāṇa,* without origination and destruction.[2]

Nāgārjuna speaks here not only of the mind *(citta),* but also of the mind's functional realm *(citta-gocara).* Kumārajīva renders the latter as *hsin-hsing,* which means actions of the mind. The functions or actions of the mind, however, have to be stopped in order to attain the Dharma Nature *(dharmatā)* or the Truth. This mind is by all means delusive. Piṅgala also comments on *citta-gocara* or *hsin-hsing* in the following way:

> All actions of the mind are delusive. Because of the delusiveness, they should be eliminated.[3]

Nāgārjuna is definitely aware of the issue of mind, but only as a delusive mind. There is no sign in the *Kārikā* that he has the idea of pure Mind, much less the identification of the pure Mind with the Middle Way. He does not understand the Truth, whether it be Emptiness or the Middle Way, in terms of the pure Mind. Accordingly, his Truth is not functional or dynamic.

Chih-i also differs significantly from the Mādhyamika in the issue of the realization of the Truth. The most striking feature of this issue is seen in his conception of expediency. That is, even defilements can play important roles in transforming sentient beings, as long as they are employed properly and kept under control. Defilements can be of highly expedient value on many occasions, a value that is all-embracing in the sense that there is nothing that cannot be utilized. This conception of expediency, focusing on the radical but constructive attitude toward defilements or evils, is unique in Indian and Chinese Buddhism.

Hurvitz understands Chih-i as both a Mādhyamika and a confirmed dhyāna-practitioner.[4] A dhyāna-practitioner is one who practises meditation, with a major concern for the concentration of the mind. This practice is akin to Chih-i's cessation *(chih)* and contemplation *(kuan)*. This understanding of Chih-i is correct, in view of his inheritance from the Mādhyamika doctrine as well as the extremely deep concern and involvement he had in the practice of cessation and contemplation. But he is more than a Mādhyamika. His unique conception of the nature of Truth and its realization enabled him to go far beyond the Mādhyamika and found a new school of Buddhism, the T'ien-t'ai School, thus opening up a new era in the development of Buddhism.

Finally, we wish to wind up this conclusion by discussing the central element or concept in Chih-i's thought. Throughout the present work, we hold firmly that the central concept in Chih-i's system of thought is the Middle Way-Buddha Nature, which has ever-abidingness, meritorious function and embracing various *dharmas* as its characteristics. This position is quite different from what is held by other scholars, who emphasize the threefold pattern found in the Threefold Truth and Threefold Contemplation and tend to see it as most central in Chih-i's thought.[5] They fail to recognize the extremely important role played by the Middle Way-Buddha Nature in the formation of Chih-i's system. Our understanding with regard to this issue is, as stated previously, that Chih-i's Threefold Contemplation is worked out in the perspective of the Middle Way-Buddha Nature,[6] and that Emptiness, the Provisional and the Middle Way, the three elements comprising in the Threefold Truth, are nothing but three aspects of the Middle Way-Buddha Nature, and their meanings are contained in the latter's three characteristics.[7] Moreover, the threefold pattern tends to have a methodological role in relation to the realization of the Middle Way-Buddha Nature. In view of this, we take the Middle Way-Buddha Nature to be more primary and fundamental than the threefold pattern. Only the Middle Way-Buddha Nature, with its characteristics, can account for the Threefold Contemplation and Threefold Truth.[8] This Middle Way-Buddha Nature cannot be reduced to anything else.

NOTES

Notes to Chapter One

1. The Sanskrit term *Mādhyamika* is usually used by modern scholars to denote the School of Nāgārjuna. It also signifies the doctrine of Emptiness (*śūnyatā*) as expounded by Nāgārjuna. It can also refer to a person who subscribes to the doctrine of this school. In the present work, the term *Mādhyamika* covers all three meanings, with particular emphasis on the doctrinal aspect. Another variation is *Madhyamaka*, which refers specifically to the thought or philosophy espoused by Nāgārjuna. For details about the term *Madhyamaka*, see Ruegg, pp. 1–3.

2. MHCK, chap. 1, T.46.1b.

3. Leon Hurvitz maintains that, of all the philosophical tendencies in Buddhism, it was the Mādhyamika more than any other that molded Chih-i's thought (Hurvitz, p. 24).

4. In the development of Buddhism in China, it was necessary to reconcile and integrate the different and even contradictory doctrines transmitted from India, so that they could all be regarded as true teachings of the Buddha. This was usually done by classifying the doctrines and viewing them as instructions of the Buddha given to different listeners by means of various methods used for different occasions. This sort of work is called "classification of the Buddhist doctrines". Cf. Chih-i's WMCHS, chap. 6, T.38.561b–c, where the author explains why different doctrines were taught by the Buddha. With regard to the translation of *pieh-chiao* as "Gradual Doctrine", see chapter VI, section 3 in the present work.

5. David J. Kalupahana has rendered *dharma* with different terms, such as "phenomena" (Kalupahana, pp. 29, 34, 46), "entity" (Ibid., p. 39), "elements" (Ibid., pp. 51, 84, 85), "elements of experience" (Ibid., p. 51), and "thing" (Ibid., p. 71). No specific reasons are given for such different renderings.

6. For a detailed description of Nāgārjuna's works, cf. Ramanan, pp. 34–37, in which K. Venkata Ramanan suggests that the works that can be attributed to Nāgārjuna may be classified into six categories. Cf. also Yūichi Kajiyama, "Chūgan shisō no rekishi to bunken" 中觀思想の歴史と文献, in A. Hirakawa, et al., ed., *Chūgan shisō*, Tokyo: Shunjusha, 1982, pp. 4–5. One of the most extensive studies of Nāgārjuna's works was done by D.S. Ruegg. Cf. Ruegg, pp. 9–33.

7. Ramanan, p. 42.

8. The Sanskrit text of the *Kārikā* has never appeared by itself. The one available now is incorporated in Candrakīrti's commentary of the *Kārikā* titled *Prasannapadā*. According to some Japanese scholars, even the *Kārikā* found in the *Prasannapadā* is not necessarily the same as the original text. The *Kārikā* text, on which Bhāvaviveka's *Prajñāpradīpa* is based, is slightly different from the one found in the *Prasannapadā*. Cf. Susumu Yamaguchi, "Chūronge no shohon taishō kenkyū yōron" 中論偈の諸本対照研究要論, in his *Chūgan bukkyō ronkō*, Tokyo: Kōbundo Shobō, 1944, pp. 1–28. Cf. also Yūichi Kajiyama, "Chūgan shisō no rekishi to bunken," op. cit., p. 7. For an exhaustive enumeration of modern studies on the *Prasannapadā*, cf. Yūichi Kajiyama, ibid., pp. 76–77.

9. Cf. his *Le Traité de la grande Vertu de Sagesse de Nāgārjuna*, vol. 3. Louvain: Université de Louvain, 1970, Preface.

10. Ramanan, p. 13.

11. Ibid., pp. 45–46.

12. Ibid., p. 13.

13. 25.57b.

14. T.25.756c.

15. For a good introduction to Kumārajīva's life and thought, cf. Yung-t'ung T'ang, *Han wei liang-chin nan-pei-ch'ao fo-chiao-shih* 漢魏兩晋南北朝佛教史, Peking: Chung-hua, 1955, chap. 10, pp. 278–340; Robinson 1967, chap. 3, pp. 71–95.

16. For instance, T.25.61b, 64b, 97b, 107a, 198a, 245c, 338c, as well as others. In some cases, the quotations are made with slight literary changes.

17. E.g., the *catuṣkoṭi*, i.e., the Four Alternatives (T.25.61b), the Eight Negations (T.25.97b), the concepts of Emptiness, Provisional Name and Middle Way (T.25.107a), and the relation between *saṃsāra* and *nirvāṇa* (T.25.198a, 338c).

18. For a brief description of TCTL's doctrinal contents, cf. Ramanan, pp. 44–45. Ramanan has suggested that the principal themes of Nāgārjuna's works are Emptiness and the Middle Way (Ibid., p. 35). For a detailed description of Emptiness and the Middle Way expounded in the TCTL, cf. below (Chapter II, "Emptiness and the Middle Way in Mādhyamika").

19. According to Tetsuei Satō's statistics, Chih-i quotes the TCTL 114 times in his FHHI, 103 times in MHCK, 59 times in FHWC, and 83 times in his early work, *Tz'u-ti-ch'an men* 次第禪門. Satō regards the TCTL as the predominant Buddhist text that Chih-i worked on during his early period (Satō, pp. 96–97).

20. As far as we are aware, each of these works is mentioned no more than two times throughout all of Chih-i's major writings. *Shi-er-men lun* is mentioned and quoted in the FHHI, chap. 8 (T.33.779a–c); *Shi-chu-pi-p'o-sha lun* is mentioned in the FHWC, chap. 5 (T.34.65a) and chap. 7 (T.34.96c); the *Pai-lun* is mentioned in the WMCLS, chap. 1 (T.38.568a).

21. For a brief description of the commentaries to the *Kārikā*, cf. Kajiyama, pp. 143–146. Cf. also Yūichi Kajiyama, "Chūgan shisō no rekishi to bunken", op. cit., pp. 9–14.

22. For example, WMCHS, chap. 3, T.38.535c, and chap. 6, T.38.557c; WMCLS, chap. 5, T.38.626a.

23. I.e., WMCHS, chap. 3, T.38.535c.

24. Satō, pp. 25–27; also Preface, pp. 1–3. For a comprehensive biography of Chih-i, cf. Hurvitz and Jikō kyōdo, *Tendai daishi no shōgai* 天台大師の生涯. Tokyo: Regulus Library, 1975.

25. Satō elsewhere regards the *Hsiao chih-kuan* 小止觀 as written by Chih-i himself. Cf. Satō, p. 263.

26. Satō elsewhere regards the *Liu miao-men* 六妙門 as representing Chih-i's thought. Ibid., pp. 151–172.

27. A commentary on the Prajñāpāramitā, i.e., the *Chin-kang-po-je-ching shu* 金剛般若經疏, was alleged to be the work of Chih-i. Satō rejects this idea and places this work in the third category. (Ibid., p. 412)

28. Ibid., p. 77.

29. Ibid., p. 554.

30. Ibid., p. 290.

31. Ibid., p. 27, pp. 44–45.

32. [天台智者]....稱: "我位居五品弟子,事在法華." (*Kuo-ch'ing pai-lu*, chap. 3, T.46.811b) This *Kuo-ch'ing pai-lu* 國清百錄, compiled by Kuan-ting, is a record of the subjects of Chih-i's lectures during his sojourn in the T'ien-t'ai Mountain.

33. T.46.686a.

34. T.46.688a.

35. T.46.681a–b.

36. Satō, pp. 236–237.

Notes to Chapter Two

1. See, for example, Ramanan, p. 35; Inada, p. 144. The fact that Kajiyama titled his book on Mādhyamika *Kū no ronri*, i.e., *Logic of Emptiness*, also shows his primary emphasis of this concept.

2. *Kārikā-P*, p. 503. This declaration is from a very famous verse in the *Kārikā*, which we will deal with in detail when we come to the discussion of Mādhyamika's conception of the Middle Way.

3. It is interesting to note that *śūnya*, the Sanskrit term for "empty," means "zero" in a mathematical sense. Cf. also Matilal, pp. 151–152; Ruegg, p. 3.

4. Ruegg, p. 45.

5. Ibid., p. 14.

6. Inada, p. 98. *svabhāvaḥ kṛtako nāma bhaviṣyati punaḥ katham, akṛtrimaḥ svabhāvo hi nirapekṣah paratra ca.* (*Kārikā-P*, pp. 260–262), cf. Kumārajīva's

rendition 性若是作者,云何有此義?性名為無作,不待異法成. (CL, 15:2, T.30.19c). All references to the translations of the *Kārikā* will come from Inada unless specified otherwise. The corresponding Sanskrit original and Kumārajīva's Chinese translation of the *Kārikā* will also appear with each translation.

7. Inada, p. 99. *yadyastitvaṃ prakṛtyā syānna bhavedasya nāstitā, prakṛteranyathābhāvo na hi jātūpapadyate.* (*Kārikā-P*, p. 271), cf. Kumārajīva's rendition 若法實有性,後則不應無;性若有異相,是事終不然. (CL, 15:8, T.30.20b).

8. Ruegg, p. 2, note 5.

9. Inada, p. 92. *bhāvānāṃ niḥsvabhāvatvamanyathābhāvadarśanāt, asvabhāvo bhāvo nāsti bhāvānāṃ śūnyatā yataḥ.* (*Kārikā-P*, p. 240), cf. Kumārajīva's rendition 諸法有異故,知皆是無性;無性法亦無,一切法空故. (CL, 13:3, T.30.18a). Strictly speaking, according to Sanskrit grammar, the first half of the verse should read, "The entities' nature of having no Self Nature is from the perception of varying characters."

10. Nāgārjuna elsewhere has made these two propositions separately. The major theme of chapter 15 of the *Kārikā* is to propose and argue that entities do not have Self Nature. Cf. verses 1, 2, 8, 9 (*Kārikā-P*, pp. 259–262, 271–272; CL, 15:1,2,8,9, T.30.19c,20b). Cf. also Kajiyama, pp. 77–81. As regards the proposition that entities are empty, cf. *Kārikā-P*, p. 505; CL, 24:19, T.30.33b.

11. Inada, p. 67. *pratītya yadyadbhavati tattacchāntaṃ svabhāvataḥ.* (*Kārikā-P*, p. 159), cf. Kumārajīva's rendition 若法衆緣生,即是寂滅性. (CL, 7:17, T.30.10c).

12. 衆緣所生法,無自性,故寂滅.寂滅名為無. ... 從衆緣生法,無自性.無自性故空. (T.30.10c).

13. Cp. *Kārikā-P*, p. 503 and CL, 24:18, T.30.33b.

14. Kajiyama, p. 65. Here, he refers to the verse in the *Kārikā* that discusses the characteristics of the Truth (Skt., *tattvasya lakṣaṇa*; Ch., *shih-hsiang* 實相). Cf. *Kārikā-P*, p. 372; CL, 18:9, T.30.24a.

15. Inada, p. 147. *svabhāvadyadi bhāvānāṃ sadbhāvamanupaśyasi, ahetupratyayān bhāvāṃstvamevam sati paśyasi.* (*Kārikā-P*, p. 503), cf Kumārajīva's rendition 若汝見諸法,決定有性者,即為見諸法,無因亦無緣. (CL, 24:16, T.30.33b). It should be noted that, in the first half of the verse, Kumārajīva's translation does not fully correspond to the original grammatically. The Sanskrit text reads, "If you see entities' true being from the standpoint of Self Nature (*svabhāvat*)"; whereas Kumārajīva translates, "If you see various entities as determinately having Self Nature." Nevertheless, both texts are concerned with the same perversion that one may commit in ascribing to entities a Self Nature, which actually does not exist.

16. 若法決定有性,則應不生不滅.如是,法何用因緣?若諸法從因緣生,則無有性.是故諸法決定有性,則無因緣.(T.30.33b).

17. We have no intention to give a detailed exposition of Dependent

Origination here. For further examination of this concept, see Kajiyama, pp. 67–75, in which the views of Nāgārjuna and other Mādhyamikas are introduced. For an excellent philosophical explication of this concept, see Ruegg, pp. 43–46, p. 43 in particular.

18. Ramanan, p. 294.

19. 諸法因緣和合生.是和合法無有一定法,故空.何以故?因緣生法無自性.無自性故,即是畢竟空.是畢竟空從本以來空,非佛所作,亦非餘人所作. (T.25.581b–c). There are still other places in the TCTL, where the same conception of Emptiness is expressed. Cf. T.15.207c, T.25.211a.

20. 性名自有, 不待因緣. 若待因緣, 則是作法, 不名為性. 諸法中皆無性. ...一切諸法性不可得故, 名為性空. (T.25.292b). The TCTL also discusses Nature Emptiness elsewhere, T.25.716b–c.

21. This Nature Emptiness indeed corresponds to *svabhāva-śūnya*, which appears in the Sanskrit text of the *Hṛdaya-sūtra*. For the Sanskrit *Hṛdaya-sūtra*, cf. E. Conze, *Thirty Years of Buddhist Studies*, Oxford: Bruno Cassirer, 1967, pp. 148–167.

22. Inada, p. 93. *śūnyatā sarvadṛṣṭīnāṃ proktā niḥsaraṇaṃ jinaiḥ*. (*Kārikā-P*, p. 247), cf. Kumārajīva's rendition 大聖說空法, 為離諸見故. (CL, 13:9, T.30.18c). *Dṛṣṭi* in Buddhist texts usually denotes false views, as seen in Inada's rendition of the verse. Kumārajīva does not specify its false nature in his Chinese translation; he simply renders the term as "view" (*chien* 見). However, in the final chapter of the *Kārikā*—which discusses false views exclusively—he renders its title, *Dṛṣṭi parīkṣa*, as *Kuan hsieh-chien p'in* 觀邪見品, meaning the chapter of observing the false views. He obviously takes *dṛṣṭi* to be *hsieh-chien* 邪見, viz., false view. Cf. *Kārikā-P*, p. 571; CL, 27, T.30.36c. If not specified otherwise, we will take *dṛṣṭi* to be false view.

23. 大聖為破六十二諸見,及無明、愛等諸煩惱,故說空. (T.30.18c).

24. These sixty-two various views are found in the *Brahmajāla-sutta* (in *Dīgha-nikāya*, i, 1) in Primitive Buddhism. We cannot discuss them further because of limited space. For an explication of them, cf. H. Nakamura, et al. ed., *Shin butten kaidai jiten* 新・佛典解題事典. Tokyo: Shunjūsha, 1965, pp. 63–64.

25. Inada, p. 115. *aparapratyayaṃ śāntaṃ prapañcairaprapañcitaṃ, nirvikalpamanānārthametattattvasya lakṣaṇam*. (*Kārikā-P*, p. 372), cf. Kumārajīva's rendition 自知不隨他,寂滅無戲論,無異無分別,是則名實相. (CL, 18:9, T.30.24a). In the Sanskrit verse, the term "*śānta*" (quiescence) is used instead of "*śūnyatā*" (Emptiness). These terms are, however, identical in the *Kārikā*, as pointed out earlier.

26. Inada, p. 39. *anirodhamanutpādamanucchedamaśāśvataṃ, anekārthamanānārthamanāgamamanirgamaṃ. Yaḥ pratītyasamutpādaṃ prapañcopaśamaṃ śivaṃ, deśayāmāsa saṃbuddhastaṃ vande vadatāṃ varaṃ*. (*Kārikā-P*, p. 11), cf. Kumārajīva's rendition 不生亦不滅,不常亦不斷,不一亦不異,不來亦不出(去).能說是因緣,善滅諸戲論;我稽首禮佛,諸說中第一. (CL, 1, T.30.1b).

27. The problems of false views in the understanding of the Truth have also been discussed by many scholars. Cf. Ramanan, p. 41; Matilal, pp. 147–148.

28. For the Chinese and Sanskrit texts, see note 22 above.

29. Cf. T.30.18c. For the Chinese text, see note 23 above.

30. Inada, p. 93. *śūnyatā sarvadṛṣṭīnāṃ proktā niḥsaraṇaṃ jinaiḥ, yeṣāṃ tu śūnyatādṛṣṭistānasādhyān babhāṣire.* (*Kārikā-P*, p. 247), cf. Kumārajīva's rendition 大聖說空法, 為離諸見故; 若復見有空, 諸佛所不化. (CL, 13:9, T.30.18c).

31. 大聖為破六十二諸見, 及無明、愛等諸煩惱, 故說空. 若人於空復生見者, 是人不可化. (T.30.18c). Cf. also the previous section.

32. T.30.33b.

33. In this regard, Ruegg also points out that the term *śūnyatādṛṣṭi* denotes a speculative view that hypostatizes Emptiness. (Ruegg, p. 2)

34. Mou 1977, p. 1208. (My translation).

35. Robinson 1967, p. 43.

36. Nakamura, p. 172.

37. Ibid., loc. cit.

38. 有人罪重, 貪著心深, 智慧鈍故, 於空生見, 或謂有空, 或謂無空. 因有無還起煩惱. (T.30.18c).

39. Cf. Nakamura, pp. 171–173.

40. 空破一切法, 唯有空在. 空破一切法已, 空亦應捨. 以是故, 須是空空. 復次, 空緣一切法, 空空但緣空. 如一健兒, 破一切賊; 復更有人, 能破此健人. 空空亦如是. 又如服藥, 藥能破病. 病已得破, 藥亦應出. 若藥不出, 則復是病. 以空滅諸煩惱病; 恐空復為患, 是故以空捨空, 是名空空. (T.25.288a). Cf. also Ramanan, p. 329.

41. 行者以有為患, 用空破有, 心復貴空. 著於空者, 則墮斷滅. 以是故, 行是空以破有, 亦不著空. (T.25.396a).

42. Inada, p. 13.

43. Sprung 1979, p. 13.

44. Ruegg, p. 44.

45. Kalupahana, p. 49.

46. For a very brief description of this concept in early Buddhism, cf. Inada, pp. 21–22; Nakamura, pp. 151–152.

47. 衆因緣生法, 我說即是空(無), 亦為是假名, 亦是中道義. (CL, 24:18, T.30.33b).

48. *Kārikā-P*, p. 503.

49. Toshio Andō says that the meaning of this verse in its original form is that various things are Emptiness, Emptiness is a Provisional Name, and Provisional Name is the Middle Way. (*Tendai shōgu shisō ron* 天台性具思想論, Kyoto: Hōzōkan, 1953, p. 68). I am arguing that this interpretation is by no means correct.

50. In Buddhism, Provisional Name is used to distinguish entities from

each other. It signifies the nature of provisionality and lack of ultimacy. For an extensive discussion of this concept, cf. the present work, Chapter VI on the Threefold Contemplation.

51. 衆緣具足和合而物生. 是物屬衆因緣, 故無自性; 無自性故空. 空亦復空. 但為引導衆生故, 以假名說. 離有、無二邊故, 名為中道. (T.30.33b).

52. Inada, p. 98. *bhāvasya cedaprasiddhirabhāvo naiva sidhyati, bhāvasya hyanyathābhāvamabhāvaṃ bruvate janaḥ.* (*Kārikā-P*, p. 267), cf. Kumārajīva's rendition 有若不成者, 無云何可成?因有有法故, 有壞名為無. (CL, 15:5, T.30.20a).

53. Inada, p. 99. *svabhāvaṃ parabhāvaṃ ca bhāvaṃ cābhāvameva ca, ye paśyanti na paśyanti te tattvaṃ buddhaśāsane.* (*Kārikā-P*, p. 267), cf. Kumārajīva's rendition 若人見有無, 見自性他性, 如是則不見, 佛法真實義. (CL, 15:6, T.30.20a).

54. Inada, p. 99. *kātyāyanāvavāde cāstīti nāstīti cobhayaṃ, pratisiddhaṃ bhagavatā bhāvābhāvavibhāvinā.* (*Kārikā-P*, p. 269), cf. Kumārajīva's rendition 佛能滅有無, 如化迦旃延, 經中之所說, 離有亦離無. (CL, 15:7, T.30.20b).

55. Ruegg, pp. 16–17.

56. Cf. T.25.538b, 551a, 581b, 610a, 622a, 714b, and others.

57. Cf. T.25.171c, 331b, 348a, 370b, 466a, 492c (cp. Ramanan, p.88), 587a, 607a–b, 648c, 732c, 747a, and others.

58. Cf. T.25.59a–b, 110a, 170a, 291a (cp. Mou 1977, p. 47 on commencement and non-commencement), 370a (cp. Ramanan, p. 108 on eternalism and annihilationism), 711b, 732c, and others.

59. 如是等衆生著有見、無見. 是二種見虛妄非實, 破中道. 譬如人行狹道, 一邊深水, 一邊大火. 二邊俱死. 著有、著無, 二事俱失. 所以者何?若諸法定實有, 則無因緣. ...若無法是實, 則無罪福, 無縛無解, 亦無諸法種種之異. (T.25.331b).

60. 佛弟子捨二邊, 處中道行. (T.25.538b).

61. 是有無二見捨, 以不戲論慧, 行於中道, 是名慧眼. (T.25.348a).

62. For instance, T.25.370a–b, 387a, 607b, 732c, and others.

63. T.25.466a.

64. See note 36 above.

Notes to Chapter Three

1. For example, in MHCK, T.46.30b, 31c, 34a–b, 47c, 69c, 74c–75b, 79c, 128a–b; in FHHI, T.33.682c–683a, 702c–703c, 737b, 742a–c, 784a–790c; in FHWC, T.34.3b; and many places in SCI and WMCHS.

2. In this work, for example, seven points are proposed with regard to the explication of the theory. These points are: explanation of the names of the four Doctrines, examination of the interpreted, [i.e., the Principle,] clarification of the penetration into the Principle through the four doors, clarification of the classification of different positions [of the four Doctrines], explication of expediency and ultimacy, summary of the contem-

plation of the mind, and finally, harmonization of various *sūtras* and *śāstras*. Cf. T.46.721a. Indeed, the full name of this work, *Ssu-chiao i*, suggests that this is the work devoted to the explication of the meaning of the four Doctrines classified by Chih-i.

3. Cf. WMCHS, chap. 3, T.38.533a–b; SCI, chap. 1, T.46.723c. In the SCI, Chih-i even goes as far as to quote the *sūtras* and *śāstras* generally (T.46.723c) and specifically (T.46.723b), in order to justify the four types of Buddhist doctrines.

4. For an extensive study of the various ways of classifying the Buddhist doctrines before Chih-i, see Hurvitz, pp. 214–229.

5. For a brief overall estimation of the characteristic of Chih-i's classification theory, see T'ang, pp. 1111–1116.

6. Andō, pp. 92–111; Tamura, pp. 81–97; Hurvitz, pp. 248–271.

7. Hurvitz, p. 264.

8. In Chih-i's works, although reference is frequently made to these four types of Buddhist doctrine, a clear enumeration and explanation of them are often lacking. The first chapter of SCI (T.46.721a–722b) and the third chapter of WMCHS (T.38.532b–533a) are the exceptions; they enumerate the four Doctrines and deal with their implications in detail. Yet there are some crucial points missing. Indeed, there is not a single paragraph in Chih-i's works that gives a satisfactory description, including all the important points. Many crucial points, such as those concerning Chih-i's conception of Buddha-Nature and No-emptiness, are scattered here and there. Our observation and reflection of Chih-i's classification theory will consequently be based on the SCI, the WMCHS, and those scattered expressions found throughout Chih-i's works.

9. Cf. FHHI, chap. 1, T.33.688a–b. Incidentally, a special point should be mentioned with regard to Chih-i when he speaks of the way of realizing the Truth advocated by the Tripiṭaka Doctrine in terms of *hsi-fa ju-k'ung*. The term *hsi* 析 usually means "to analyze;" Hurvitz describes this way as "analytic." (Hurvitz, p. 260) In Chih-i's use, however, *hsi* means more than to analyze because it must cover the implications of disintegration and elimination. This point will be made clearer later.

10. FHHI, chap. 8, T.33.785b; SCI, chap. 3, T.46.730a–b.

11. FHHI, chap. 2, T.33.703c.

12. Cf. the chapter below, in which the concept of Middle Way-Buddha Nature is treated in full. It should be noted that such predicates as "negative, static and transcendent" on the one hand and "positive, dynamic and immanent" on the other are our own terminology to describe Chih-i's understanding of the concepts of Emptiness and the Middle Way. Why this terminology is used will be accounted for in due course.

13. *Fa-chieh tz'u-ti ch'u-men*, op. cit., chap. 2, T.46.681a–b. For an excellent elaboration of the difference between *hsi-fa* and *t'i-fa*, cf. T'ang, pp. 1134–1135.

14. The contrast of the terms "dullness" and "skillfulness," are seen throughout Chih-i's works, e.g., FHHI, chap. 1, T.33.688a–b, 690a; chap. 8, T.33.785b; MHCK, chap. 1, T.46.5c, 7b; SCI, chap. 3, T.46.730a–b; chap. 12, T.46.766b; WMCHS, chap. 2, T.38.526a–b. They are also mentioned in Chegwan's TTSCI, T.46.778a. Chegwan was traditionally regarded as a faithful interpreter of Chih-i, but see the criticism by Shindai Sekiguchi that is summarized in David Chappell, ed., *Outline of T'ien-t'ai Fourfold Teachings* (Tokyo: Dai-ichi shobo, 1983), Introduction.

15. FHHI, chap. 6, T.33.754c; chap. 8, T.33.784c; FHWC, chap. 1, T.34.5a; WMCHS, chap. 2, T.38.526a–b.

16. FHHI, chap. 9, T.33.790c.

17. 實有時無真,滅有時無俗. (FHHI, chap. 2, T.33.702c).

18. 二諦義不成. (Ibid.).

19. 即俗而真. (Ibid.).

20. 體法即真. (FHHI, chap. 1, T.33.690a).

21. MHCK, chap. 3, T.46.33a. Cf. also TTSCI, T.46.778a.

22. Cf. FHWC, chap. 2, T.34.17a.

23. WMCLS, chap. 1, T.38.579b.

24. SCI, chap. 9, T.46.752a.

25. SCI, chap. 3, T.46.729c.

26. Chih-i raises Buddha Nature as the determining factor on many occasions. See, for example, his general observation of the four types of doctrine (SCI, chap. 1, T.46.726a–b), of both the Gradual Doctrine and the Perfect Doctrine (FHHI, chap. 8, T.33.785b), and of the Gradual Doctrine alone (MHCK, chap. 6, T.46.75a). He also states that practitioners of both the Gradual Doctrine and the Perfect Doctrine see No-emptiness, which is Buddha Nature (FHHI, chap. 8, T.33.781c). In the WMCHS, in which the concept of Middle Way-Buddha Nature is often mentioned, Chih-i points out that the Common Doctrine does not understand the nature of Middle Way-Buddha Nature (chap. 4, T.38.546b), that the Gradual Doctrine understands it (chap. 4, T.38.540b), and that the Perfect Doctrine penetrates the realm of the supreme Truth of Middle Way-Buddha Nature (chap. 4, T.38.541b).

27. The permanency, dynamism and immanence of Buddha Nature will be discussed in detail in the next chapter.

28. Andō, pp. 102–106.

29. Ibid., pp. 106–111.

30. For *li-pieh*, see FHHI, chap. 1, T.33.688a–b; chap. 1, T.33.690a; chap. 3, T.33.710b. For *tz'u-ti*, see FHWC, chap. 1, T.34.5a; WMCLS, chap. 1, T.38.576a; FHHI, chap. 1, T.33.688a–b. For *li-chieh hsiu-hsing*, see WMCHS, chap. 3, T.38.538b–c; SCI, chap. 9, T.46.752a; TTSCI, T.46.778a.

31. FHHI, chap. 8, T.33.785a.

32. Hurvitz, p. 262.

33. For *yüan-tun* cf. FHHI, chap. 1, T.33.688a–b. For *pu tz'u-ti* cf. FHWC, chap. 1, T.34.5a.

34. FHWC, chap. 1, T.34.5a.

35. FHHI, chap. 8, T.33.781c.

36. WMCHS, chap. 4, T.38.542b.

37. FHHI, chap. 7, T.33.764a–b.

38. WMCHS, chap. 4, T.38.544b.

39. Cf. SCI, chap. 1, T.46.721a–722b; WMCHS, chap. 4, T.38.544b–c; chap. 6, T.38.560c–561c; and other locations.

40. Hurvitz, p. 260.

41. For the sake of brevity, we cannot explicate these four types of realization of the Four Noble Truths and their respective relationships to the four Doctrines. For details of these issues, cf. FHHI, chap. 2, T.33.701a–b; SCI, chap. 2, T.46.725b–726b. Chih-i even goes so far as to regard these four types of realizing the Four Noble Truths as wisdom. Cf. FHHI, chap. 4, T.33.720c–721b. For a brief but excellent description of these various types of approaches to the Four Noble Truths, cf. Tamura, pp. 90–91.

42. 法若有生，亦可有滅．法本不生，今則不滅． (FHHI, chap. 4, T.33.721a).

43. *Kārikā-P*, p. 11; CL, chap. 1, T.30.1c.

44. *Kārikā-P*, p. 12; CL, 1:1, T.30.2b. For the employment of the negative of the Four Alternatives, cf. Chapter V in the present work.

45. 即事而真, 非滅後真. (FHHI, chap. 2, T.33.701a).

46. 中論品品別意, 而俱會無生. (MHCK, chap. 8, T.46.117a).

47. SCI, chap. 1, T.46.722a.

48. We have no intention of discussing the close doctrinal relationship, as it has already been pointed out by many scholars. For instance, Robinson admits that to a certain extent Nāgārjuna expounds the teachings of some important *Prajñāpāramitā-sūtras*. (Robinson 1967, pp. 61–65) Kajiyama suggests that Nāgārjuna inherits and accepts the world of mystical intuition expressed in the *Prajñāpāramitā-sūtras*. (Kajiyama, p. 34) Inada regards Nāgārjuna as the heir to the teachings of the *Prajñāpāramitā-sūtras*. (Inada, p. 21) And, according to Sprung, such scholars as E. Conze, N. Dutt, M. Winternitz, E. Frauwallner, *et al.*, all agree that there is a most intimate and creative relationship between Nāgārjuna's thought and the philosophy of the *Prajñāpāramitā-sūtras*. (Sprung 1979, p. 26)

49. [龍樹]以不可得空，洗蕩封著，習應一切法空．是名與般若相應. (FHHI, chap. 5, T.33.742b). For the meaning of the expression "unattainable Emptiness," see below.

50. FHHI, chap. 3, T.33.713c; chap. 9, T.33.792b–c.

51. FHHI, chap. 10, T.33.813b.

52. SCI, chap. 2, T.46.727b; WMCHS, chap. 3, T.38.534b–c.

53. See Chapter 2, section 7 above, where the Sanskrit original and Kumārajīva's translation of the verse are quoted.

54. [龍樹]以不可得空，洗蕩封著，...淨諸法已，點空說法，結四句相. (FHHI, chap. 5, T.33.742b).

55. Inada, p. 147. *sarvaṃ ca yujyate tasya śūnyatā yasya yujyate, sarvaṃ na yujyate tasya śūnyaṃ yasya na yujyate.* (*Kārikā-P*, p. 500) Cf. Kumārajīva's rendition 以有空義故，一切法得成；若無空義者，一切則不成. (CL, 24:14, T.30.33a).

56. Inada, p. 147.

57. 智者見空，復應見不空. 那得恒住于空? (FHHI, chap. 5, T.33.738a).

58. 無相教明空蕩相，未明佛性常住，猶是無常. (FHHI, chap. 10, T.33.801c). This criticism is directed at the teaching of no-characteristic, which Chih-i identifies with the Prajñāpāramitā. This identification is evidenced in the compound terms *po-je wu-hsiang chiao* 般若無相教 (FHHI, chap. 10, T.33.803b) and *wu-hsiang po-je chiao* 無相般若教 (FHHI, chap. 10, T.33.803c), which Chih-i views as one of the three Buddhist teachings. For a fluent explanation of these teachings, see Taya, p. 154b.

59. FHHI, chap. 2, T.33.700c; WMCHS, chap. 3, T.38.538b–c; WMCHS, chap. 6, T.38.555c.

60. It is interesting to note that the concept of No-emptiness (Skt., *aśūnya*; Ch., *pu-k'ung* 不空) also appears in the Kārikā (*Kārikā-P*, p. 511; T.30.34a; *Kārikā-P*, p. 512; T.30.34b; *Kārikā-P*, p. 521; T.30.34c). This No-emptiness, however, is spoken of in terms of substantiality, and thus is different from Chih-i's. That is, Nāgārjuna's No-emptiness is the opposite of Emptiness, which is the negation of the metaphysical substantiality, or, in other words is non-substantiality. It follows that No-emptiness is another form of substantiality. Chih-i's No-emptiness, however, is identified with Buddha Nature, which is not a substantiality in any metaphysical sense.

61. FHHI, chap. 2, T.33.702c–703b. For a comprehensive explication of this division, see Mou 1977, pp. 648–665; Swanson, pp.146–150.

62. 破著空故，故言不空. 空著若破，但是見空，不見不空. 利人謂不空是妙有，故言不空. 利利人聞不空，謂是如來藏，一切法趣如來藏. (FHHI, chap. 2, T.33.703a).

63. Chih-i is in fact well aware of this thought of the Emptiness of Emptiness. In MHCK (chap. 4, T.46.38c), he quotes the famous verse of the CL, in which the Emptiness of Emptiness is clearly expressed (CL, 13:9, T.30.18c). (Chih-i's quotation of this verse is slightly different in wording from the original, but this slight difference is not significant.) In the same work he also stresses that the sickness of Emptiness is also to be emptied. (空病亦空. MHCK, chap. 5, T.46.51a)

64. Mou 1977, pp. 661–662.

65. For an explication of *miao-yu*, cf. H. Nakamura, ed., *Shin Bukkyō jiten* 新・佛教辭典. Tokyo: Seishin Shōbō, 1976, p. 297a.

66. 圓人聞不空， 即知具一切佛法， 無有缺減， 故言一切趣不空也. (FHHI, chap. 2, T.33.703b). Here, "all Buddhist *dharmas*" (*i-ch'ieh fo-fa* 一切佛法) include worldly entities. Indeed, when Chih-i speaks of "em-

bracing *dharmas*", he usually refers to the worldly entities. The concept of "embrace" (*chü* 具) will be treated fully in the next chapter.

67. Though the term "Buddha Nature" appears occasionally in the Prajñāpāramitā text (e.g., T.25.420b, 491c, 715b, and others), it is not mentioned in the TCTL itself. This shows that although the author of the TCTL is aware of the concept of Buddha Nature, he does not pay any attention to it.

68. 離斷常名中道，非佛性中道. (MHCK, chap. 1, T.46.7a). Swanson has also discussed Chih-i's understanding of the Middle Way but we are not satisfied with his discussions. He remarks:

> Reality is one in that all is lacking in substantial Being; its nature is that of emptiness. However, this emptiness is not a complete nothingness but consists of the conventional existence of things which arise and perish interdependently according to causes and conditions. These aspects of emptiness and conventional existence are not contradictory opposites, but are synonymous and integrated. In T'ien-t'ai terminology this is called the "Middle Path." Thus all of reality is empty—it is one. All of reality has conventional existence—it is many. Reality is simultaneously empty and conventionally existent—it is the Middle Path. (Swanson, p. 125)

Swanson is discussing Chih-i's Threefold Truth; accordingly, "T'ien-t'ai terminology" in the quotation should denote Chih-i's terminology. Swanson sees the Middle Path or Middle Way as the synthesis of Emptiness and conventional existence of things, which is all right. Chih-i's Middle Way does carry a synthetic implication, as will be seen in the present work, Chapter VI below. However, Swanson fails to recognize that he mainly understands Chih-i's use of the Middle Way only in terms of transcendence of such extremes as annihilation and eternalism. Swanson is also unaware of Chih-i's understanding of the Middle Way in terms of Buddha Nature.

69. For instance, FHWC, chap. 1, T.34.8a; chap. 8, T.34.120a; chap. 10, T.34.145c; MHCK, chap. 1, T.46.6c; WMCLS, chap. 8, T.38.672c; chap. 9, T.38.690a; T.38.695a; chap. 10, T.38.695c–696a; T.38.701c.

70. 若不定有，則非有；若不定無，則非無. 非有者，非生也，非無者，非滅也. 出于有無之表，是名中道. 與中論同. (MHCK, chap. 5, T.46.66b).

71. 通教真諦，空中合論. (MHCK, chap. 3, T.46.35a).

72. 如通教所明二諦，含中道在真諦中. (WMCLS, chap. 10, T.38.702b).

73. 若計有中道，則於中道有病. 此病亦空，故言中道亦空. (WMCLS, chap. 8, T.38.672c).

74. Cf. notes 62 and 63 above.

75. This accusation is mainly made in FHHI, for instance, chap. 2, T.33.704a (Swanson, pp.247–248), T.33.704c–705a (Swanson, pp.252–253); chap. 5, T.33.740a, T.33.746b; chap. 7, T.33.762c; chap. 9,

T.33.787c–788a. This accusation is also applicable to the Tripiṭaka Doctrine.

76. For details about the five types of the Threefold Truth teaching, cf. FHHI, chap. 2, T.33.704c–705a. For a delineation of these five types of the Threefold Truth, cf. Swanson, pp. 150–152.

77. 當教論中, 但異空而已. 中無功用, 不備諸法. (FHHI, chap. 2, T.33.704c–705a).

78. For the use of *chieh*, cf. section 7.

79. Mou also points out that *tang-chiao* here should denote the Common Doctrine. Cf. Mou 1977, p. 749.

80. For details concerning these two attributes and the identification of the Middle Way with the Buddha Nature, cf. the next chapter.

81. 二諦無中道體. 故明真時, 則永寂如空, 明有時, 如石裏有金, 石金有異. (WMCLS, chap. 10, T.38.702c).

82. 諸佛依二諦, 為衆生說法: 一以世俗諦, 二第一義諦. (CL. 24:8, T.30.32c). Cf. also *Kārikā-P*, p. 492. This Twofold Truth teaching will be dealt with in great detail in Chapter IIV.

83. Mou 1977, p. 562.

Notes to Chapter Four

1. 藏、通觀生、無生, 入偏真理, 名為真實. 別、圓觀無量、無作, 入中道佛性, 名為真實. WMCLS, chap. 3, T.38.607b.

2. With regard to the terms *sheng*, *wu-sheng*, *wu-liang* and *wu-tso*, we basically adopt the translation of Leon Hurvitz. Cf. Hurvitz, p. 252.

3. 解脫者, 即見中道佛性. (WMCLS, chap. 8, T.38.674b). Elsewhere, Chih-i points out that liberation is the realization of the Middle Way, the realization of Buddha Nature, and abiding in *Parinirvāṇa*. (WMCWS, chap. 23, Z.28.273b) He also claims that the liberation of the Buddhas is that the Middle Way-Self Nature-Pure Mind is not polluted by defilements. (WMCWS, chap.20, Z.28.223a) With regard to the concept of Middle Way-Self Nature-Pure Mind, see below (section 4).

4. 別圓入中, 即是佛道. (Ibid., chap. 9, T.38.683b).

5. Earlier in the same chapter a clear definition of the Buddha Way (*fo-tao* 佛道) is given. (Ibid., chap. 9, T.38.683a)

6. 佛性即中道. (FHHI, chap. 6, T.33.761b). As a matter of fact, the identification of the Middle Way and Buddha Nature was first proposed by the *Mahāparinirvāṇa-sūtra* 大般涅槃經, not by Chih-i. Cf. T. 12.767c–768a; 768c. However, this *Sūtra* does not elaborate on the identification; it merely mentions the permanent nature of Buddha Nature.

7. I.e., in WMCLS, T.38.569b, 593a–b, 614a, 630c, 674b, 688b and 691b; in *Fa-chieh tz'u-ti ch'u-men*, T.46.688a.

8. Cf. FHHI, chap. 5, T.33.735b, SCI, chap. 12, T.46.764b and WMCLS, chap. 9, T.38.688b.

9. Dharma Body is one of the important concepts characterizing Indian Mahāyāna Buddhism. For an excellent explication of this concept, see Nagao's "On the Theory of Buddha-body," *The Eastern Buddhist*, 6:1, (May 1971), pp. 25–53.

10. 盧舍那佛處蓮華海，共大菩薩．皆非生死人．(FHHI, chap. 7, T.33.772c).

11. 滅者即解脫，解脫必有其人．人即法身，法身不直身．(FHHI, chap. 7, T.33.776b).

12. 生身九惱，飢、渴、寒、熱、疾病等事．所以身小有疾，須用牛乳．阿難不知是法性身，謂有疾是實，故持鉢乞乳．...不聞法身金剛之體，常住湛然．(WMCLS, chap. 5, T.38.632a). The quotation states that Ānanda 阿難, a faithful disciple of the Buddha, did not understand the permanent Dharma Body. Ānanda was traditionally regarded as an advocate of the Tripiṭaka Doctrine and scriptures.

13. 真法身無此疾也．(Ibid., loc. cit.)

14. 如來身者，金剛之體，即法身常身．所以喻金剛者，體堅用利，徹至本際．堅譬法身不為妄、惑、生、死所侵，常住不變．利喻法身智德，般若照用之功，無所不備．徹至本際譬法身斷德，解脫終窮，惑障斯斷．(WMCLS, chap. 5, T.38.632a–b). Similar descriptions can be seen in WMCWS, chap. 15, Z. 28. 137b.

15. E.g., in FHHI, chap. 5, T.33.736a; chap. 10, T.33.804b, 805c, 806a.

16. 中道即法身．(WMCLS, chap. 8, T.38.674b). 如來行是名行實．所見中道，即一究竟，同於如來所得法身，無異無別．(MHCK, chap. 3, T.46.33a).

17. SCI, chap. 12, T.46.766c.

18. FHHI, chap. 10, T.33.801c.

19. FHHI, chap. 3, T.33.709c; chap. 4, T.33.731a; chap. 6, T.33.749b; WMCLS, chap. 6, T.38.654a. Cf. section 7 in the preceding chapter.

20. Mou 1977, p. 1207.

21. Cf. also FHHI, chap. 2, T.33.704c–705a.

22. WMCHS, chap. 5, T.38.551b.

23. Ibid., T.38.550c.

24. MHCK, chap. 6, T.46.81b.

25. FHHI, chap. 7, T.33.774a.

26. For *kung-yung*, cf. FHHI, chap. 5, T.33.732b. For *li-yung*, cf. FHHI, chap. 1, T.33.683a; MHCK, chap. 1, T.46.2a–b. For *yung*, cf. FHHI, chap. 1, T.33.685a, 685b, 686c, 689c–690a; WMCHS, chap. 4, T.38.541c; MHCK, chap. 6, T.46.81b.

27. 功論自進，用論益物．合字解者，正語化他．(FHHI, chap. 5, T.33.736c). Chih-i is discussing the position of the Perfect Doctrine, the fourth point of which is *kung-yung*. (Ibid., T.33.732b)

28. 自行二智照理理周，名為力；二種化他二智鑒機機遍，名為用．(FHHI, chap. 1, T.33.683a).

29. Cf. FHHI, chap. 1, T.33.681c–682a. Hurvitz translates *yung* discussed in the fourth part of FHHI as "practical manifestation." (Hurvitz, p. 206) "Function" seems to be more straightforward than "practical manifestation" in transmitting the original meaning of *yung*.

30. 若豎功未深, 横用不廣, 豎功若深, 横用必廣. 譬如諸樹, 根深則枝潤, 華葉亦多. (FHHI, chap. 5, T.33.736c).

31. 用是化他. (FHHI, chap. 1, T.33.685a).

32. 用是益他. (Ibid., T.33.685b).

33. 若住于空, 則於衆生永無利益. 志存利他. 即入假之意也. (MHCK, chap. 6, T.46.75c).

34. E.g., T.46.75c, 78a, b, 80a, etc.

35. T.46.75c.

36. T.46.76a–79a.

37. MHCK, chap. 6, T.46.75c, 77c, 80a.

38. 菩薩本不貴空而修空, 本為衆生故修空. 不貴空, 故不住, 為益衆生, 故須出. (Chap. 6, T.46.79c). For the following discussion in this paragraph, I am indebted to Inada's comments on a draft of the present work.

39. 不度衆生, 故不能用. (FHHI, chap. 1, T.33.689c). This is actually Chih-i's criticism of those who favor the Tripiṭaka Doctrine. It can be inferred that, for Chih-i, to function is nothing but saving sentient beings.

40. 菩薩聞圓法, 起圓信, 立圓行, 住圓位, 以圓功德, 而自莊嚴. 以圓力用建立衆生. ... 云何圓建立衆生? 或放一光, 能令衆生得即空即假即中益, 得入、出、雙入出、不入出益. 歷行、住、坐、卧、語、默、作, 亦如是. ... [龍王] 興種種雲, 震種種雷, 耀種種電, 降種種雨. 龍於本宮, 不動不搖, 而於一切, 施設不同. 菩薩亦如是. 內自通達即空即假即中, 不動法性, 而令獲種種益, 得種種用, 是名圓力用建立衆生 (MHCK, chap. 1, T.46.2a–b). To enhance readability, I did not translate the expressions *ju*, *ch'u*, *shuang ju-ch'u*, *pu ju-ch'u* 入、出、雙入出、不入出 word for word, but used "the method of the Four Alternatives" to stand for them. See Chapter V below.

41. It should be noted that the term *chien-li* 建立 here, which we translate as "put into correct places," is used in an entirely soteriological sense. It is difficult to find a good corresponding phrase in English. "Establish" and "build up" may be options. However, neither term is adequate.

42. That is, 知病, 識藥, 授藥. These steps are delineated in great detail in Chih-i's elaboration of the bodhisattva's endeavor to enter the provisional world (*ju-chia*) and provide remedies for the sickness of sentient beings. Cf. MHCK, chap. 6, T.46.76a–79a.

43. 我見為諸見本, 一念惑心為我見本; 從此惑心, 起無量見, 縱横稠密, 不可稱計. 為此見故, 造衆結業, 墮墜三途, 沈迴無已. (MHCK, chap. 6, T.46.76a).

44. 病相無量, 藥亦無量. (Ibid., T.46.77a).

45. 一一法有種種名、種種相、種種治, 出假菩薩皆須識知. 為衆生故, 集衆法藥, 如海導師. 若不知者, 不能利物. 為欲知故, 一心通修止、觀、大悲、誓願及精進力. (Ibid., T.46.77c). Here, Chih-i qualifies the bodhisattvas as *ch'u-chia*, which actually means *ju-chia*, as pointed out above.

46. 隨其病故, 授藥亦異. 謂下、中、上、上上. 下根. ...智慧鈍故, 斷婬怒癡, 名為解脫, 是為授因緣生法之藥. ...次中根人授藥者. ...為說因緣即空, ...授即空藥. 上根人授藥者, ...次第斷五住, 得入中道, 是為授即假藥. ...上上根授藥者, ...為如理直說, 善如空生, 障如空滅,入究竟道,是名授即中藥. (Ibid., T.46.78c–79a).

47. Chih-i often mentions the bodhisattvas' symbolic remedies for the diseases of sentient beings. Cf. FHHI, chap. 4, T.33.721b; MHCK, chap. 5, T.46.56c, 75c, 79c–80a. The example delineated above, which includes the three steps, is the most detailed and systematic one in this point.

48. MHCK, chap. 6, T.46.81c.

49. For an Indian interpretation of the theory, See Murti, *The Central Philosophy of Buddhism*, pp. 284–287; Nagao, "On the Theory of Buddha-body," *The Eastern Buddhist*, 6:1 (May 1971), pp. 25–53. For Chih-i's explication of this theory, see FHWC, chap. 9, T.34.128a, 129c. We are not in a position to discuss this theory in detail here, but a few words should be stated about the translation of the three forms of body. *Dharma-kāya* or *fa-shen* can naturally be translated as Dharma Body. With regard to *saṃbhoga-kāya* or *pao-shen*, and *nirmāṇa-kāya* or *ying-shen*, both W.T. de Bary and W.E. Soothill associate them with "bliss" and "transformation," respectively. (W.T. de Bary, ed., *The Buddhist Tradition in India, China and Japan*, New York: Vintage Books, 1972, p. 196; W.E. Soothill et al., comp., *A Dictionary of Chinese Buddhist Terms*, Taiwan: Buddhist Culture Service, 1971, p. 77) "Bliss" refers to the bliss or reward of the Buddha, while "transformation" points to the transformation of sentient beings by the Buddha. These are acceptable renderings which our translations follow.

50. 初得法身本故, 即體起應身之用. (FHHI, chap. 7, T.33.764c).

51. Hurvitz has translated *pen* 本 as origin in contrast with *chi* 迹, "traces." (Hurvitz, p. 206) We think that such a rendition of *pen* is also applicable in the present context.

52. 法身為體, 應身為用. (WMCHS, chap. 4, T.38.545b).

53. 由于應身, 得顯法身. (FHHI, chap. 7, T.33.764c). 由此法身, 故能垂不思議應用之迹, 由此應用, 能顯法身. (WMCHS, chap. 4, T.38.545b).

54. 應以佛身得度, 即作佛身說法, 授藥; 應以菩薩、二乘、天龍八部等形得度, 而為現之. (MHCK, chap. 6, T.46.79c).

55. MHCK, chap.4, T.46.41c, chap. 7, T.46.89a; FHWC, chap. 8, T.34.114a; WMCLS, chap. 1, T.38.577b, chap. 2, T.38.590a, chap. 4, T.38. 620b, chap. 6, T.38.643c, 646c, chap. 8, T.38.672b, 676c, chap. 9, T.38.690a, 691a, chap. 9, T.38.691c.

56. FHHI, chap. 2, T.33.703a; FHWC, chap. 2, T.34.19b; MHCK, chap. 9, T.46.127b; WMCLS, chap. 4, T.38.622a, chap. 7, T.38.661a, chap. 9, T.38.688b.

57. WMCLS, chap. 10, T.38.702a, chap. 10, T.38.703a; *Fa-chieh tz'u-ti ch'u-men*, chap. 3, T.46.697b.

58. FHHI, chap. 6, T.33.757b.

59. MHCK, chap. 4, T.46.37b.

60. FHWC, chap. 3, T.34.43c.

61. Hurvitz translates *ju-shih* 如是 as "such-like." (Hurvitz, p. 205) The *ju-shih* is, in fact, a philosophical category.

62. 如是性者, 性以據內, 總有三義. 一、不改名性. 無行經稱不動性, 性即不改義也. 又性名性分, 種類之義, 分分不同, 各各不可改. 又性是實性, 實性即理性 (MHCK, chap. 5, T.46.53a). For a description of the ten categories, see Kumārajīva's translation of *Fa-hua ching*, T.9.5c. For an extensive explication of the ten categories, see Hurvitz, pp. 280–308.

63. 若觀心即是佛性, 圓修八正道, 即寫中道之經. 明一切法悉出心中, 心即大乘, 心即佛性. (MHCK, chap. 3, T.46.31c). The Eightfold Noble Path (Skt., *āryāṣṭāṅgo-mārgaḥ*; Ch., *pa cheng-tao* 八正道) was originally taught by the Buddha. On one occasion, Chih-i also claims that the Buddha Nature is the Self Nature-Pure Mind. (WMCWS. chap.7, Z.27.951a)

64. WMCHS, chap. 4, T.38.541a.

65. 如是力者, 堪任力用也. 如王力士, 千萬技能, 病故謂無, 病差有用. 心亦如是, 具有諸力, 煩惱病故, 不能運動. 如實觀之, 具一切力. 如是作者, 運為、建立名作. 若離心者, 更無所作. 故知心具一切作也. (MHCK, chap. 5, T.46.53b). We translate *li* 力 and *tso* 作 as "force" and "action", respectively; Hurvitz translates them as "power" and "function" (Hurvitz, p. 280). Our renditions are, we think, more faithful to the original meanings of *li* and *tso*. The term *li*, or "force," is closely related to function. When force operates, it will initiate function. Since the description of the ten categories in the *Fa-hua ching* is not seen in the Sanskrit text of the *Saddharma-puṇḍarika-sūtra*, there is no way of tracing back to the original word in order to refine the meaning of *li*.

66. It should be noted that Chih-i has in mind two levels of mind: the pure and the delusive. The one in question here is the pure Mind. As a matter of fact, with regard to the understanding of the Truth in terms of the Mind, Chih-i identifies the Buddha Nature with the Mind as delineated above. In addition, he straightforwardly identifies the Middle Way as the Principle with the Mind. (WMCWS, chap. 7, Z.27.951a). He also articulates two compound terms, "Middle Way-True Mind" (*chung-tao chen-hsin* 中道真心) (WMCWS, chap. 16, Z.28.148b) and "Middle Way-Self Nature-Pure Mind" (*chung-tao tzu-hsing ch'ing-ching-hsin* 中道自性清淨心) (WMCWS, chap.20, Z.28.223a), to highlight this identification. However, he does not elaborate on these cases.

67. 却前兩種二諦, 以不明中道故. 就五種二諦, 得論中道, 即有五種三諦. 約別入通, 點非有漏非無漏, 三諦義成. 有漏是俗, 無漏是真, 非有漏非無漏是中. 當教論中, 但異空而已. 中無功用, 不備諸法. 圓入通三諦者, 二諦不異前,點非[有]漏非無漏,具一切法,與前中異也.別三諦者,開彼俗為兩諦,對真為中,中理而已.圓入別三諦者,二諦不異前,點真中道,具足佛法也.圓三諦者,非但中道具足佛法,真俗亦然. (FHHI, chap. 2, T.33.704c–705a). For further understanding of this delineation, see the previous chapter. Cf. also Mou 1977, 748–750.

68. 此中但理,不具諸法. (FHHI, chap. 3, T.33.709c).

69. FHHI, chap. 3, T.33.714a.

70. FHHI, chap. 5, T.33.743c.

71. FHHI, chap. 5, T.33.743a, chap. 8, T.33.783b; WMCHS, chap. 6, T.38.558c.

72. We are not in a position to discuss this doctrine in detail. Cf. I. Ogawa, *Busshō shisō* 佛性思想, (Kyoto: Buneidō, 1982) for an explication of this doctrine.

73. Cf. FHHI, chap. 6, T.33.757b; FHWC, chap. 5, T.34.72a; WMCLS, chap. 3, T.38.598c.

74. 佛性即是法性. (WMCLS, chap. 8, T.38.681a).

75. 一色一香, 無非中道. 中道之法, 具一切法. (MHCK, chap. 4, T.46.42b).

76. 若知諸法不生,即具一切佛法. (WMCLS, chap. 9, T.38.684b). The same remark is also found in WMCWS, chap. 25, Z.28.306a.

77. The assertion that the Buddha Nature embraces all *dharmas* is reminiscent of the expression of *hsing-chü* 性具, or *hsing pen-chü* 性本具, which the T'ien-t'ai scholars regarded as representing the major thought of their School. As a matter of fact, this expression carrying the message that the Buddha Nature embraces all *dharmas* or entities is not found in Chih-i's major works. (Although *hsing-chü* does appear in WMCWS, chap. 11, Z.28.69a, its message is quite different. There, Chih-i is discussing the possibility that greed, hatred and ignorance essentially embrace all Buddhist *dharmas*. *Hsing* 性 is used as an adverb, meaning "essentially," rather than a noun to denote the Buddha Nature.) *Hsing-chü* as such was obviously proposed by the T'ien-t'ai advocates after Chih-i, with the intention of strengthening the all-embracing nature of the Buddha Nature. It should be noted, however, that their understanding of this all-embracing nature may not be the same as Chih-i's. Cf. *Kuan-yin-ching-hsüan-i-chi hui-pen* 觀音經玄義記會本, chap. 2, Z.55.81a–b.

78. Cf. his *Chin-kang pei* 金剛錍, T.46.784c.

79. Incidentally, the passive meaning of the term "embrace" (viz., "possessed by") was originally suggested by Yün-hua Jan in his comments on the draft form of this thesis. Our further studies evidenced that it is a significant suggestion.

80. *Maitreya* or *tz'u* means to "bestow happiness," whereas *karuṇa* or *pei* means to "withdraw suffering." In Chih-i's works, however, they are al-

ways used interchangeably. Therefore, we will use compassion to stand for *tz'u*, or *pei*, or both, if not specified otherwise.

81. 若住於空, 則無淨佛國土. (MHCK, chap. 6, T.46.75c).

82. Cf. MHCK, chap. 6, T.46.81a.

83. 上兩觀慈, 慈有邊表, 如來慈者, 即無齊限. ... 是如來藏諸法都海. (Ibid., loc. cit.)

84. [實相]多所含受, 故名如來藏. ...[實相]含備諸法, 故名如來藏. (FHHI, chap. 8, T.33.783b).

85. 一切衆生心中具足一切法門. 如來明審照其心法, 按彼心說無量教法從心而出. (MHCK, chap. 3, T.46.32a).

86. 若觀心即是佛性, 圓修八正道, 即寫中道之經, 明一切法悉出心中, 心即大乘, 心即佛性. (Ibid., T. 46.31c). This description was also quoted in note 63. On this occasion Chih-i is introducing the four types of contemplating the Mind from the four Doctrines he classifies.

87. Cf. MHCK, chap. 6, T.46.81a–c. For a discussion of the "great function without limits" cf. section 2 above.

88. 所言方便者, 為成實慧, 故須方便也. 方是智所詣之偏法, 便是善巧權用之能. 善巧權用諸法, 隨機利物, 故云方便. (WMCWS, chap. 9, Z. 28. 16a.)

89. This evil implication is reminiscent of the T'ien-t'ai idea that the Buddha Nature embraces evil (*hsing-o* 性惡). Among the works traditionally attributed to Chih-i, this idea is found only in the *Kuan-yin hsüan-i* (T.34.882c–883a). As this *Kuan-yin hsüan-i* is not a reliable source for the study of Chih-i's thought (cf. the Introduction of the present work), we are not in a position to discuss the idea of *hsing-o*. Y. Tamura, however, claims that this idea can be regarded as representing the thought of Chih-i himself. Cf. Tamura, p. 121.

90. Cf. above the previous chapter, section 9.

91. 不離於生死, 而別有涅槃. (CL, 16:10, T.30.21b). It should be noted here that Kumārajīva's translation does not completely conform to the Sanskrit original. Cf. *Kārikā-P*, p. 299; Inada, p. 103.

92. Inada, p. 158. *na saṃsārasya nirvāṇātkiṃ cidasti viśeṣaṇam, na nirvāṇasya saṃsārātkiṃ cidasti viśeṣaṇam.* (*Kārikā-P*, p. 535) Cf. Kumārajīva's rendition 涅槃與世間, 無有少分別, 世間與涅槃, 亦無少分別. (CL, 25:19, T.30.36a).

93. Inada, p. 158. *nirvāṇasya ca yā koṭiḥ saṃsārasya ca, na tayorantaraṃ kiṃ citsusūkṣmamapi vidyate.* (*Kārikā-P*, p. 535) Cf. Kumārajīva's rendition 涅槃之實際, 及與世間際, 如是二際者, 無毫釐差別. (CL, 25:20, T.30.36a).

94. For our detailed discussion of the Middle Way and Emptiness of the Mādhyamika, see Chapter II above.

95. FHHI, chap. 8, T. 33. 783b.

96. 若有大乘圓機, 即雨中道實相甘露, 即開佛知見, 見佛性, 住大涅槃也. (WMCWS, chap. 4, Z.27.905b). 正觀中道,得佛性,成師子吼三昧也. (WMCWS, chap. 4, Z.27.913a). 菩薩觀中道,見佛性故,非凡夫人也. (WMCWS, chap. 13, Z.28.97a). 解脫者見中道,即是見佛性,即住大涅槃. (WMCWS, chap. 23, Z.28.273b). 菩薩從初心修此[空、假]二觀,是權義,得入中道,見於佛性,是實義. (WMCWS, chap. 25, Z.28.316b–317a).

97. Cf. note 66 in this chapter.

98. Cf. note 66 in this chapter.

Notes to Chapter Five

1. Robinson 1967, pp. 50–58; Robinson 1957, pp. 301–303; Kajiyama, pp. 82–84, pp. 115–120; Ramanan, pp. 160–170; R. Pandeya, "The Logic of *Catuṣkoṭi* and Indescribability", in his *Indian Studies in Philosophy*, Delhi: Motilal Banarsidass, 1977, pp. 89–103; S.S. Chakravarti, "The Mādhyamika *Catuṣkoṭi* or Tetralemma", *Journal of Indian Philosophy*, 8 (1980), pp. 303–306; Yu-kwan NG, "The Arguments of Nāgārjuna in the light of Modern Logic," *Journal of Indian Philosophy*, 15 (1987), pp. 363–384.

2. Inada, p. 115. *sarvaṃ tathyaṃ na vā tathyaṃ tathyaṃ cātathyameva ca, naivātathyaṃ naiva tathyametadbuddhānuśāsanaṃ*. (*Kārikā-P*, P. 369) Cf. Kumārajīva's rendition 一切實非實,亦實亦非實,非實非非實,是名諸佛法. (CL, 18:8, T.30.24a).

3. According to the Sanskrit original and Kumārajīva's translation, the subject of all four alternatives is the same: "everything" (Skt., *sarvam*; Ch., *i-ch'ieh* 一切). This verse is also quoted in the TCTL a number of times, with slight changes. For instance, 一切實一切非實,及一切實亦非實,一切非實非不實,是名諸法之實相 (T.25.61b), and 一切諸法實,一切法虛妄,諸法實亦虛,非實亦非虛 (T.25.338c). In these two quotations, it is clearly shown that "everything" is the subject throughout the four alternatives. Robinson, however, takes the subject of the third alternative to be "something." (Robinson 1957, p. 303; Robinson 1967, p. 57) His understanding of this rendering is questionable.

4. Inada, p. 115. *ātmetyapi prajñapitamanātmetyapi deśitaṃ, buddhairnātmā na cānātmā kaścidityapi deśitaṃ*. (*Kārikā-P*, p. 355) For the Chinese text please see the following footnote.

5. 諸佛或說我, 或說於無我, 諸法實相中, 無我無非我. (CL, 18:6, T.30.24a).

6. 諸法不生不滅, 非不生非不滅, 亦不生滅非不生滅, 亦非不生滅非非不生滅. (T.25.97b). The Arabic numerals have been added by us for the sake of clarity.

7. Ibid., loc. cit.

8. Robinson 1967, p. 56

9. 諸佛無量方便力,諸法無決定相,為度衆生,或說一切實,或說一切不實,.... (T.30.25a).

10. Robinson 1967, p. 56.

11. Cf. the above section for the verse.
12. *Po-je-teng lun-shih*, chap. 11, T.30.106c.
13. Robinson 1967, p. 56.
14. Kajiyama, p. 117.
15. Ibid.
16. 內外諸入色等境界, 依世諦法, 說不顚倒, 一切皆實. 第一義中, 內外入等, 從緣而起, 如幻所作, 體不可得, 不如其所見故, 一切不實. 二諦相待故, 亦實亦不實. 修行者證果時, 於一切法得真實無分別故, 不見實與不實, 是故說非實非不實. (Chap. 11, T.30.108a).
17. Inada, p. 39. *na svato nāpi parato na dvābhyāṃ nāpyahetutaḥ, utpannā jātu vidyante bhāvāḥ kvacana ke cana.* (*Kārikā-P*, p. 12) Cf. Kumārajīva's rendition 諸法不自生, 亦不從他生, 不共不無因, 是故知無生. (CL, 1:1, T.30.2b). The same verse also appears elsewhere in the *Kārikā*. (*Kārikā-P*, p. 421; CL, 21:12, T.30.28c) Incidentally, the verse has been quoted in the TCTL, with slight modifications 諸法. ...非自作, 非彼作, 非共作, 非無因緣. (Chap. 6, T.25.104b).
18. T.30.2b.
19. 不自生者, 萬物無有從自體生, 必待衆因. ...自無故他亦無. 何以故? 有自故有他. 若不從自生, 亦不從他生. 共生則有二過: 自生、他生故. 若無因而有萬物者, 是則為常, 是事不然. 無因則無果. (Ibid).
20. 衆緣中無自性. 自性無故, 不自生. 自性無故, 他性亦無. 何以故? 因自性有他性. 他性於他, 亦是自性. (Ibid).
21. Ibid.
22. Kulapahana, p. 28.
23. Inada, p. 157. *paraṃ nirodhādbhagavān bhavatītyeva nohyate, na bhavatyubhayaṃ ceti nobhayaṃ ceti nohyate.* (*Kārikā-P*, p. 534) Cf. Kumārajīva's rendition 如來滅度後, 不言有與無, 亦不言有無, 非有及非無. (CL, 25:17, T.30.35c).
24. Inada, p. 157. *tiṣṭhamāno 'pi bhagavān bhavatītyeva nohyate, na bhavatyubhayaṃ ceti nobhayaṃ ceti nohyate.* (*Kārikā-P*, p. 534) Cf. Kumārajīva's rendition 如來現在時, 不言有與無, 亦不言有無, 非有及非無. (CL, 25:18, T.30.35c).
25. Sprung 1979, p. 7.
26. For an enumeration of the negative of the Four Alternatives, cf. my article "The Arguments of Nāgārjuna in the Light of Modern Logic," op. cit.
27. 畢竟空義, 無有定相, 不可取. 不可傳釋得悟. 不得言有, 不得言無, 不得言有無, 不得言非有非無 (TCTL, chap. 55, T.25.448b). Based on Kumārajīva, perhaps it is more appropriate to render 畢竟空義, 無有定相, 不可取 the first sentence as: "The meaning of ultimate Emptiness consists in *the nature of* being devoid of definite forms and should not be clung to."
28. For example, chap. 2, T.25.74c–75a; chap. 7, T.25.110a. In the

former case, the Four Alternatives is employed to present fourteen difficult questions to which the author gives no response, remarking that these have nothing to do with the Truth. In the latter case, four kinds of views are raised through the Four Alternatives. They are all false views, and it follows that the Four Alternatives is irrelevant to the Truth.

29. They are mentioned, for instance, in the Chinese version of the *Saṃyutta-nikāya*, the *Cha a-han ching* 雜阿含經, chap. 13, T.2.86a.

30. Cf. notes 2 and 17 above.

31. It is said that, before Chih-i, a person revered as Fu Ta-shi 傅大士 in the Chinese Buddhist circle had composed a short poem in which the issues of the Four Alternatives and No-origination were touched on. Cf. Chan-jan, *Chih-kuan i-li* 止觀義例, T.46.452c. Cf. also T. Andō, *Tendai shōgu shisō ron*, p. 26. Fu Ta-shi was a vague personality, and the poem ascribed to him is too brief to reveal what the issues of the Four Alternatives and No-origination are exactly about.

32. E.g., SCI (T.46.729a–730a, 731c–732a, 747a, 751c, 760a); FHHI (T.33.682b–c, 687a, 782b, 784a–790b). It is also mentioned in MHCK (T.46.20c–21a, with the third alternative lacking, 53c); WMCHS (T.38.520c, 528b, 557b–558b); WMCLS (T.38.695a). On these occasions, the Four Alternatives is taken as conducive to the realization of the Truth.

33. E.g., MHCK (T.46.4c, 8a, 21c–22a, 29a, 46c, 54a–b, 54c, 63c–64b, 70b, 82a, 82b–c, 111b, 127b). It is also mentioned in WMCHS (T.38.525a–b, 526c, 528b, 550a); WMCLS (T.38.564a, 638c–639a); FHHI (T.33.696a–b, 699c); *Fa-chieh tz'u-ti ch'u-men* (T.46.691b). On these occasions, the negative of the Four Alternatives is regarded as the method through which the Truth can be approached.

34. For details, cf. FHHI, chap. 8, T.33.784a–785b; SCI, chap. 8, T.46.747a; chap. 9, T.46.751c.

35. 故知諸佛說法, 無不約此四門. 若實者, 即是法性實理, 用有為門. 若非實, 即是約畢竟空為門. 若亦實亦不實, 即是上文無明即明, 明即畢竟空, 即是亦實亦不實為門. 若非實非不實, 即空有雙非之義, 如用中道非空非有為門. 如是四門, 為向道之人, 聞說即悟. (WMCLS, chap. 9, T.38.695a).

36. SCI, chap. 4, T.46.731c.

37. SCI, chap. 3, T.46.729a.

38. 尋佛三藏, 赴緣多種, 尋其正要, 不出四門入道. 其四門者, 一者有門, 二者空門, 三亦有亦空門, 四非有非空門 (SCI, chap. 4, T.46.731c).

39. 四教各明四門, 雖俱得入道, 隨教立義, 必須逐便. 若是三藏教四門, 雖俱得入道, 而諸經論多用有門. 通教四門雖俱得入道, 而諸經論多用空門. 別教四門雖俱得入道, 而諸經論多用亦有亦空門. 圓教四門雖俱得入道, 而諸經論多用非有非空門也. (SCI, chap. 4, T.46.731c–732a).

40. 今明佛法四門, 皆得入一理, 但有二種不同. 一者, 三藏、通教兩種四門, 同入偏真之理. 二者, 別、圓兩教四門, 同入圓真之理 (SCI, cahp. 3, T.46.730a).

41. SCI, chap. 3, T.46.730a–b.

42. 三界人見三界為異, 二乘人見三界為如, 菩薩人見三界亦如亦異, 佛見三界非如非異, 雙照如異. 今取佛所見為實相正體也. (FHHI, chap. 1, T.33.682b–c).

43. [四門]皆是赴機異說. (FHHI, chap. 9, T.33.791a). This is a conclusion Chih-i arrived at after discussing in great detail the issue of penetration into the Truth through the four doors. Cf. FHHI, chap. 9, T.33.784a–790b.

44. 實相尚非是一, 那得言四?當知四是入實相門耳. (FHHI, chap. 8, T.33.784a).

45. 四句立名, 是因待生, 可思可說. ...[絕待止觀]待對既絕, 即非有為. 不可以四句思, 故非言說道, 非心識境. (MHCK, chap. 3, T.46.22a). Chih-i is discussing here the relationship between the relative and absolute cessation and contemplation.

46. This cautious evaluation of the Four Alternatives is seen in Chih-i's discussion of the supreme Meaning (Skt., *siddhānta*; Ch., *hsi-t'an* 悉檀), which refers to the Truth or *shih-hsiang*. Chih-i divides this supreme Meaning into the unspeakable and speakable. With regard to the speakable one, he enumerates the four alternatives and concludes that all of them are conducive to the understanding of the Truth. 第一義悉檀者, 有二種: 一、不可說; 二、可說. ... 約可說者, 一切實, 一切不實, 一切亦實亦不實, 一切非實非不實, 皆名諸法之實相. (FHHI, chap. 1, T.33.687a).

47. 若定謂是有, 即是著法. 乃至定謂是非有非無, 亦名著法者. ... 若定言諸法非有非無者, 是名愚癡論. (FHWC, chap. 10, T.34.141b).

48. 諸法不自生, 那得自境智?無他生, 那得相由境智?無共生, 那得因緣境智?無無因生, 那得自然境智?若執四見著, 愚惑紛論, 何謂為智? 今以不自生等破四性. 性破, 故無依倚, 乃至無業苦等. 清淨心常一, 則能見般若 (MHCK, chap. 3, T.46.29a–b).

49. The expression "mutual dependence," or *hsiang-yu* 相由, sounds somewhat unnatural in the context in question. Chih-i assoicates self-origination with "knowledge of the self as its object," or *tzu-ching chih* 自境智. He should associate other-origination with "knowledge of the other as its object," or *t'a-ching chih* 他境智, rather than "knowledge of mutual dependence as its object," or *hsiang-yu-ching chih* 相由境智. Accordingly, it seems possible and indeed better to take *hsiang-yu* as *t'a* 他, or "other."

50. 觀此欲心, 為從根生?為從塵生?為共為離?若從根生, 未對塵時, 心應自起, 若從塵生, 塵既是他, 於我何預?若共生者, 應起兩心, 若無因生, 無因不可. 四句推欲, 欲無來處. ... 畢竟空寂. (MHCK, chap. 6, T.46.70b).

51. 夫心不孤生, 必託緣起. 意根是因, 法塵是緣, 所起之心, 是所生法 (MHCK, chap. 1, T.46.8a).

52. 妄謂心起. 起無自性, 無他性, 無共性, 無無因性. 起時不從自、他、共、離來. (Ibid., loc. cit.)

53. MHCK, chap. 6, T.46.81c–82c. This threefold process is one of the most complicated examples in which Chih-i employs the negative of the Four Alternatives to reveal the Truth. It is far beyond the scope of this thesis to elaborate this process. For a delineation and elaboration of this process, cf. T'ang, pp.1168–1170.

54. *Kuan-hsin lun*, T.46.586a.

55. For this verse, cf. *Kārikā-P*, p. 11; CL, chap. 1, T.30.lb; Inada, p. 39. It has been discussed in Chapters II and III above.

56. Cf. Chapter III, section 5 and note 46.

57. This argument is mostly found in the MHCK, e.g., chap. 1, T.46.8a; chap. 5, T.46.54b; chap. 5, T.46.63c–64b; chap. 6, T.46.70b. In MHCK, chap. 5, T.46.63c–64b, this argument is articulated in a very subtle and detailed manner.

58. MHCK, chap. 5, T.46.49a–b. For a detailed denotation of the five aggregates, eighteen realms and twelve entrances, cf. H. Nakamura, *Bukkyōgo daijiten* 仏教語大辞典, vol. I, Tokyo: Shoseki, 1975, 355a, 660c, 657c.

59. 心是惑本, 其義如是. 若欲觀察, 須伐其根, 如炙病得穴. 今當去丈就尺, 去尺就寸, 置色等四陰, 但觀識陰. 識陰者心是也. (MHCK, chap. 5, T.46.52a–b). Here, *chang* 丈, *ch'ih* 尺 and *ts'un* 寸 are units of length. A *chang* is ten *ch'ihs*, and a *ch'ih* is ten *ts'uns*. A *ts'un* is about the size of one inch or three centimeters.

60. The practical significance of the emphasis of the mind in the employment of the negative of the Four Alternatives has also been pointed out by Chun-i T'ang. However, he does not elaborate the significance. Cf. T'ang, p. 1159.

61. [解脫]不從自脫起, 故不從自性以立名. 不從他脫起, 故不約他性以立名. 解脫不從自、他起, 故不從共性以立名. 解脫不從離自、他無因緣起, 故不約無因緣性以立名. ...解脫不依四邊起. (WMCHS, chap. 5, T.38.550a).

62. Cf. the above section as well as notes 50 and 52.

Notes to Chapter Six

1. Chih-i explicitly relates his Threefold Contemplation to the *Kārikā* in two places: MHCK, chap. 3, T.46.25b; chap. 5, T.46.55b. When he mentions the *Kārikā*, he particularly refers to the verse titled by the T'ien-t'ai tradition as the "verse of the Threefold Truth" (*San-ti chieh* 三諦偈). In this verse, the concepts of Emptiness, Provisional Name and Middle Way are given. Cf. CL, 24:18, T.30.33b; *Kārikā-P*, p.503. Cf. also Chapter II.7 above. Chih-i's point is that this verse is expressive of the Threefold Contemplation. However, he claims elsewhere that the name of the Threefold Contemplation comes from the *sūtra*, *Pu-sa-ying-lo-pen-yeh ching* 菩薩瓔珞本業經. (WMCHS, chap. 2, T.38.525c) This *sūtra* is, according to Satō, a

forgery composed in China rather than in India. (Satō, pp. 699–703) Satō also points out that the establishment of this *sūtra* was under the influence of CL, i.e., the *Kārikā*. (Ibid., pp. 702–703) It should also be noted that the Threefold Contemplation has been related to Fu Tai-shi 傅大士, who composed a poem in which the Threefold Contemplation is mentioned. (Cf. Chan-jan, *Chih-kuan i-li* 止觀義例, T.46.452c. Cf. also Satō, pp. 717–718 and T. Andō, *Tendai shōgu shisō ron*, pp. 26–27). However, despite the fact that the name "Threefold Contemplation" appears in Fu Ta-shih's poem, there is no sign as to what this Threefold Contemplation denotes. Moreover, Fu Ta-shih was a vague personality in Chinese Buddhist circles. In view of these two points, we do not think that a rigid relationship between Chih-i and Fu Ta-shih, with regard to the issue of Threefold Contemplation, can be acknowledged.

2. Inada, p. 134. *śūnyamiti na vaktavyamaśūnyamiti vā bhavet, ubhayaṃ nobhayaṃ ceti prajñaptyarthaṃ tu kathyate*. (*Kārikā-P*, p. 444) Cf. Kumārajīva's rendition 空則不可說，非空不可說，共不共叵說，但以假名說. (CL, 22:11, T.30.30b).

3. Cf. Monier Monier-Williams, *A Sanskrit-English Dictionary*, Delhi, Patna, Varanasi: Motilal Banarsidass, 1974, p. 659.

4. Sprung 1979, p. 17. Sprung also expresses his understanding of Provisional Name elsewhere, Sprung 1977, pp. 245–246, for example.

5. Matilal, p. 150.

6. 五衆和合，假名衆生. (TCTL, chap. 81, T.25.630b) It should be noted that Provisional Name in Chinese, *chia ming* 假名, remains unchanged in its verb form.

7. 離二邊故，假名為中道. (TCTL, chap. 80, T.25.622a).

8. 諸法和合，假名為老. (TCTL, chap. 80, T.25.622b). Cp. Ramanan's freer and more detailed rendition: "All the necessary causal factors gather together and hence, depending on this togetherness, there comes into being the state called old-age." (Ramanan, p. 244)

9. 凡夫顛倒見故有. 智者於有為法不得其相，知但假名. (TCTL, chap. 31, T.25.289a).

10. 如頭、足、腹、脊和合故，假名為身. (TCTL, chap. 89, T.25.691a).

11. 假名有者，如酪有色、香、味、觸四事. 因緣合故，假名為酪. 雖有不同因緣法有，雖無亦不如兔角龜毛無. (TCTL, chap. 12, T.25.147c). Our translation is made in reference to Ramanan's. Cf. Ramanan, p. 83.

12. TCTL, chap. 61, T.25.495b. Cp. Ramanan, p. 87.

13. [須菩提]不壞假名，而說諸法實相. ... 菩薩知一切法假名，則應般若波羅蜜學. 所以者何?一切法但有假名，皆隨順般若波羅蜜畢竟空相故. (TCTL, chap. 55, T.25.453a).

14. 不壞假名，而說諸法實相. This idea appears in the Chinese translation of the *Pancaviṃśatisāhasrikā-prajñāpāramitā-sūtra*, of which the TCTL is the commentary. Cf. TCTL, chap. 55, T.25.452a.

15. 以觀觀於境，則一境而三境；以境發於觀，則一觀而三觀. ... 觀三即一，發一即三，不可思議. (MHCK, chap. 3, T.46.25b).

16. 一心三觀所成三智，知不思議三境. (MHCK, chap. 3, T.46.26b).

17. 所觀之假者，有二種假，攝一切法. 一者愛假，二者見假. (WMCHS, chap. 2, T. 38. 525c).

18. WHCHS, chap. 2, T.38.525c.

19. 無而虛設. (Ibid., T.38.525b).

20. MHCK, chap. 5, T.46.63b.

21. 法界洞朗，咸皆大明，名之為觀. (MHCK, chap. 5, T.46.56c).

22. 法性寂然名止，寂而常照為觀. (MHCK, chap. 1, T.46.1c–2a). "Cessation" (*chih* 止) and "contemplation" are often enumerated together in Chih-i's works as the two practical methods through which to attain the Truth. Indeed, the MHCK is named after these two methods. We do not particularly delineate cessation in the present work, because, with regard to this method, there is no close connection witnessed between Chih-i and Mādhyamika.

23. 觀以觀達為義，亦是觀穿. 言觀達者，達衆生本源淸淨，如從假入空觀之所照達. 雖復凡聖有殊，同歸空寂，一如無二. ... 觀穿義者，菩薩從假入空時，貫穿俗諦見思之磐石，滯眞無知之沙，無明覆蔽一實之礫，洞徹無礙. 即是窮至心性本際金剛. (WMCLS, chap. 8, T.38.672b). 觀以觀穿為義，亦是觀達為能. 觀穿者，穿見思、恒沙、無明之惑，故名觀穿也. 觀達者，達三諦之理也. (WMCHS, chap. 2, T.38.525c).

24. [二乘]止觀，雖出生死，而是拙度，滅色入空. 此空亦得名止，亦得名非止非不非，而不得名觀. 何以故？灰身滅智，故不名觀. (MHCK, chap. 3, T.46.23c–24a).

25. Hurvitz, p. 315.

26. K. Tamaki, *Shin hasoku no tenkai*, Tokyo: Sankibo-busshorin, 1961. "Introduction" (English version), p. 11.

27. W.T. de Bary, ed., *The Buddhist Tradition in India, China and Japan*, New Yrok: Vintage Books, 1972, p. 165.

28. Chung-yuan Chang, *Original Teachings of Ch'an Buddhism*, New York: Vintage Books, 1971, pp. 12, 39.

29. Ibid., loc. cit.

30. 所照為三諦，所發為三觀，觀成為三智. (MHCK, chap. 5, T.46.55c).

31. E.g., FHHI, chap. 9, T.33.789c; MHCK, chap. 3, T.46.26b, 28c; FHWC, chap. 2, T.34.22c. It is extremely difficult to translate these three sorts of wisdom (*chih* 智) into another language literally. In order to avoid misunderstandings, we do not venture a translation. Chih-i acknowledges that the Threefold Wisdom in the present context comes from the TCTL (SCI, chap. 1, T.46.723c), and we do find that its three components are discussed there (TCTL, chap. 27, T.25.258c–259b). However, because of the ambiguity in its discussion, it is not easy to decide what the exact denotations of these three components might be. For further discussion of

the Threefold Wisdom, Cf. Swanson, p.116; pp. 276–277, note 5. Swanson, however, does not render the *i-ch'ieh-chung chih* as the wisdom of both universality and particularity. He renders it as universal wisdom, to which we refer the *i-ch'ieh chih*.

32. 觀有三. 從假入空, 名二諦觀. 從空入假, 名平等觀. 二觀為方便道, 得入中道, 雙照二諦, 心心寂滅, 自然流入薩婆若海, 名中道第一義諦觀. (MHCK, chap. 3, T.46.24b). Cp. Swanson's rendition and explanations with ours. (Swanson, pp. 118–120) For a discussion of the Threefold Contemplation in connection with the HCK, cf. Nitta, pp. 317–320.

33. 所言二諦者, 觀假為入空之詮, 空由詮會, 能所合論, 故言二諦觀. (Ibid., loc. cit.)

34. 從空入假名平等觀者, 若是入空, 尚無空可有, 何假可入? 當知此觀為化衆生, 知真非真, 方便出假, 故言從空. 分別藥病, 而無差謬, 故言入假. 平等者望前稱平等也. 前觀破假病, 不用假法, 但用真法. 破一不破一, 未為平等. 後觀破空病, 還用假法, 破用既均, 異時相望, 故言平等也. (MHCK, chap. 3, T.46.24c).

35. 前觀假空, 是空生死, 後觀空空, 是空涅槃. 雙遮二邊, 是名二空觀. 為方便道, 得會中道. 故言心心寂滅, 流入薩婆若海. 又初觀用空, 後觀用假, 是雙存方便. 入中道時, 能雙照二諦. (Ibid., loc. cit.) It should be noted that Chih-i here refers the Provisional to *saṃsārā* or the life-death cycle. He obviously sees the Provisional to be the empirical world, and his tendency to substantiate the Provisional is very clear. It is important to note that the description of the Threefold Contemplation appears quite often in Chih-i's works. What we quoted from the MHCK is most concise, but cf. WHCHS, chap. 2, T.38.524c–532a; FHWC, chap. 8, T.34.110c–111a for more details.

36. Cf. note 34.

37. 若一法一切法, 即是因緣所生法, 是為假名, 假觀也. 若一切法即一法, 我說即是空, 空觀也. 若非一非一切者, 即是中道觀. 一空一切空, 無假、中而不空, 總空觀也. 一假一切假, 無空、中而不假, 總假觀也. 一中一切中, 無空、假而不中, 總中觀也. 即中論所說不可思議一心三觀. (MHCK, chap. 5, T.46.55b). This *i-hsin san-kuan* is elsewhere reversed as *san-kuan i-hsin* 三觀一心 (e.g., MHCK, chap. 9, T.46.131b), without any change in meaning.

38. WMCLS, chap. 7, T.38.661c–662a. 但以一觀當名, 解心皆通. (Ibid., T.38.662a).

39. 三諦具足, 只在一心. 分別相貌, 如次第說, 若論道理, 只在一心. 即空即假即中, 如一刹那, 而有三相. (MHCK, chap. 6, T.46.84c–85a). A few words should be given to explain the translation of the term *tao-li* 道理 in the quotation above. It is difficult to find a straightforward rendition for this term. In the *A New Practical Chinese-English Dictionary* edited by Shih-ch'iu Liang, the renditions given for this term are "reason," "rationality," the "right way," and the "proper way." (p. 1112) None of them is good

enough. In the context in question, Chih-i contrasts *tao-li* with *hsiang-mao* 相貌 or features of the three Truths, viz., Emptiness, the Provisional and the Middle Way. *Hsiang-mao* tends to denote what appears to be and is therefore external, while *tao-li* signifies the internal and true nature or principle of something. Therefore, we translate *tao-li* as "true principle." It should also be pointed out that in the expression *i-hsin san-kuan*, or Threefold Contemplation in one single Mind, the term *hsin* 心 may denote either the pure Mind or the delusive mind. If it denotes the pure Mind, this pure Mind will be the acting subject in the epistemic aspect of the Contemplation, and consequently the origin of the Threefold Wisdom (cf. the previous section). In this context, the expression in question means that the pure Mind by itself can realize Emptiness, the Provisional and the Middle Way simultaneously. However, if *hsin* stands for the delusive mind, this delusive mind will be the object acted on in the epistemic aspect of the Contemplation. It is not different from the so-called *nien* 念, or "intention," which usually appears delusive in our daily life. In this context, *i-hsin san-kuan* means that the mind or intention, though tending to be delusive, is contemplated as being in the nature of Emptiness, Provisionality and the Middle Way simultaneously. This interpretation by all means presupposes an acting or contemplating subject, whether it be titled the pure or impure Mind. As for the phrase *chi-k'ung chi-chia chi-chung*, it makes equal sense in either context of the *i-hsin san-kuan*. In the former context, the phrase reveals the simultaneous illumination of Emptiness, the Provisional and the Middle Way by the pure Mind; in the latter context, the phrase signifies that the delusive mind is penetrated and its nature as Emptiness, Provisionality and Middle Way is realized simultaneously. In Chih-i's works, the former context seems more dominant. In our study we will focus on this context, in which hsin is construed as the pure Mind.

40. This is evidenced by the observation that the phrase *chi-k'ung chi-chia chi-chung* appears extremely often in Chih-i's most important works. For instance, it appears 13 times in the FHHI (T.33.692c, 695b, 714a, 721b, 726a, 733a, 739a, 736b, 777b, 781a, 781b, 789c, 811b); 18 times in the MHCK (T.46.7b, 8c, 25b, 31c, 41b, 67b, 84b, 85a, 87b, 88b, 88c, 95b, 99c, 100a, 100c, 128b, 130c, 131b); and 4 times in the FHWC (T.34.4c, 5a, 17a, 25a). It is important to note here that this phrase appears only in Chih-i's works established in his later period, such as the FHHI, MHCK, FHWC, WMCHS and WMCLS. This fact shows that the idea of the simultaneous Threefold Contemplation was not developed until Chih-i's thought became mature. In the works established in Chih-i's early period, the simultaneity of the realization of the Threefold Contemplation is not mentioned. With regard to the object of the Threefold Contemplation, i.e., the Threefold Truth, cf. Nitta, pp. 497–512 for a detailed delineation. Nitta's delineation is made with reference to the FHHI, MHCK and FHWC.

41. 一實諦即空即假即中.…一實諦者, 即是實相. 實相者即經之正體也. 如是實相即空假中. (FHHI, chap. 8, T.33.781b).

42. WMCLS, chap. 7, T.38.661c–662a.

43. 不權不實, 不優不劣, 不前不後, 不並不別, 不大不小. (MHCK, chap. 3, T.46.25b).

44. 智即是境, 境即是智, 融通無礙. (FHHI, chap. 3, T.33.714a).

45. Tamura, p. 79. The English translation from the Japanese original is mine.

46. 空觀通於小、大、偏、圓. (MHCK, chap. 6, T.46.85b).

47. For more delineation about *shuang-che* and *shuang-chao*, cf. section 5 above.

48. 初, 從假入空, 是破法折伏義也. 次, 從空入假, 是立法攝受. 中道正觀, 即是教化衆生, 入實慧也. 入實者, 名法久住, 法久住者, 則法身常存. (WMCLS, chap. 3, T.38.597b).

49. 法久住者, 令見佛性, 住大涅槃. (Ibid., T.38.597a–b). Similar remarks in note 48 and here are also found in the WMCWS, chap. 9, Z.28.19a.

50. WMCLS, chap. 3, T.38.597a.

51. Ibid., loc. cit.

52. For instance, FHHI, chap. 1, T.33.682c; MHCK, chap. 5, T.46.67b. In the former case, Chih-i says, "It is stated in the *Chung-lun* [i.e., the *Kārikā*] that the *dharmas* originating from major and subsidiary causes are Emptiness, the Provisional and the Middle Way simultaneously." 中論云: 因緣所生法, 即空即假即中.

53. 中論偈云: 因緣所生法, 我說即是空, 此即詮真諦, 亦名為假名, 即詮俗諦也, 亦是中道義, 即詮中道第一義也. 此偈即是申摩訶衍, 詮三諦之理. (SCI, chap. 2, T.46.728a). The same description is also seen in WMCHS, chap. 3, T.38.535a. Transcendent Truth (*chen-ti* 真諦) can be otherwise termed "absolute Truth," and conventional Truth (*su-ti* 俗諦) "relative Truth." The last sentence in this description also accounts for the title "the verse of the Threefold Truth."

54. 因緣所生法, 我說即是空, 破法折伏也. 亦名為假名, 立法攝受也. 亦是中道義, 教化衆生, 令法得久住. (WMCLS, chap. 3, T.38.597a). A similar remark is also found in the WMCWS, chap. 9, Z.28.18a.

55. For instance, FHHI, T.33.682c, 695c, 758a; MHCK, T.46.1b–c, 5c–6a, 7a, 28b, 31b; FHWC, T.34.3a, 4a; SCI, T.46.724a, 727b, 728a, 728b; WMCHS, T.38.525a; WMCLS, T.38.597a–b.

56. Cf. note 53.

57. We have made a detailed analysis of the Sanskrit original of the verse of the Threefold Truth earlier. Cf. Chapter II.7 above.

58. It should be noted cautiously that Chih-i is less to blame than Kumārajīva for the misinterpretation of the verse. In the latter's Chinese translation of the verse, Emptiness, the Provisional Name and the Middle

Way are treated as equal predicates of Dependent Origination. It is natural for Chih-i to take a parallel view of these three concepts and see them as expressive of three Truths, in view of the Truth nature ascribed to Emptiness. From this misinterpretation, it is also shown that Chih-i did not consult the Sanskrit original of the verse, but got to know the Mādhyamika *via* Kumārajīva's translations. Chih-i probably did not know Sanskrit.

59. With regard to the relationship between Nāgārjuna's thought—the thought revealed in the Threefold Truth verse in particular—and Chih-i's threefold structure shown in his Threefold Contemplation and Threefold Truth, Swanson holds a view quite different from ours. He favors a positive and close relationship between Chih-i and Nāgārjuna in this matter, divulging that the threefold structure is already implicit in the *Kārikā* (Swanson, pp. 14–15) and claiming that Chih-i's interpretation is a Chinese attempt to search out the meaning of the verse to make Mādhyamika philosophy intelligible (Ibid., p. 8). In view of our studies and arguments shown above, we would tend to emphasize Chih-i's difference from Nāgārjuna, rather than his similarity. This difference does not necessarily mean a deviation.

Notes to Chapter Seven

1. Cf. below for the details of these assertions.

2. The practical importance of this identification in Buddhism is obvious. There was, in fact, hardly a Mahāyāna Buddhist school that could deny such an identification. Inada has remarked that the understanding of this relationship is the constant challenge and the most profound feature of the Mahāyāna Buddhist philosophy. (Inada, p. 12)

3. Yin-shun has also spoken of the Twofold Truth in methodological terms. He says that the doctrine of the Twofold Truth is the basic method in leading sentient beings from ignorance to enlightenment. (*Chung-kuan chin-lun*. Taipei: Hui-jih Chiang-t'ang, 1971, p. 205) The doctrine of the Twofold Truth in this context mainly denotes that of the Mādhyamika, which preaches the non-difference of the Truth of Emptiness and the world of conventionality.

4. Inada, p. 158. The Sanskrit original of these verses has been given in Chapter IV. 7.

5. Cf. Chapter IV. 8 and note 91 above.

6. Inada, p. 156. *ya ājavaṃjavībhāva upādāya pratītya vā, so 'pratītyānupādāya nirvāṇamupadiśyate*. (*Kārikā-P*, p. 529) Cf. Kumārajīva's rendition 受諸因緣故, 輪轉生死中; 不受諸因緣, 是名為涅槃. (CL, 25:9, T.30.35b). Cp. Matilal, p. 156.

7. Murti, *The Central Philosophy of Buddhism*. London: George Allen and Unwin Ltd., 1955, p. 274.

8. Sprung 1979, pp. 19, 260.

9. E. Conze, *Buddhist Wisdom Books*. London: George Allen and Unwin Ltd. 1958, p. 81.

10. For an extensive elaboration of this identification, see ibid., pp. 81–85.

11. It should be noted that Tibetan sources also mention the relationship between Emptiness and form. In a delineation that Emptiness and form do not differ from each other, Vimalamitra remarks that there is no respective external entity (*bāhyārtha*) of form and Emptiness. That is to say, Emptiness is not external to form, and *vice versa*. Cf. A. Wayman, "Secret of the Heart Sutra," in L. Lancaster, ed., *Prajñāpāramitā and Related Systems*. Berkeley Buddhist Studies Series. Printed in Korea, 1977, p. 143. (Wayman renders *śūnyatā* as "voidness," rather than "Emptiness.") That Emptiness and form are not external to each other means that there is no Emptiness apart from form, and there is no form apart from Emptiness. That there is no Emptiness apart from form may bear the practical implication that Emptiness can be realized only in form, whose realm is precisely that of Emptiness. The consequence is the identification of Emptiness and form in terms of sharing the same realm.

12. 佛告須菩提: 色即是空, 空即是色. ...空即是涅槃, 涅槃即是空. 中論中亦說: 涅槃不異世間, 世間不異涅槃, 涅槃際世間際, 一際無有異故. (T.25.198a).

13. Inada, p. 146. *dve satye samupāśritya buddhānāṃ dharmadeśanā, loka-saṃvṛtisatyaṃ ca satyaṃ ca paramārthataḥ*. (*Kārikā-P*, p. 492) Cf. Kumārajīva's rendition 諸佛依二諦, 為衆生說法, 一以世俗諦, 二第一義諦. (CL, 24:8, T.30.32c).

14. Inada, p. 146. *ye 'nayorna vijānanti vibhāgaṃ satyayordvayoḥ, te tattvaṃ na vijānanti gambhīraṃ buddhaśāsane*. (*Kārikā-P*, p. 494) Cf. Kumārajīva's rendition 若人不能知, 分別于二諦, 則于深佛法, 不知真實義. (CL, 24:9, T.30.32c).

15. Cf., for instance, M. Sprung, ed., *The Problems of Two Truths in Buddhism and Vedānta*. Dordrecht: D. Reidel, 1973; T.R.V. Murti, *The Central Philosophy of Buddhism*, pp. 228–255; Kajiyama, pp. 130–136; Ruegg, pp. 42–47; Kalupahana, pp. 67–70, 331–335.

16. Matilal, p. 153.

17. Inada, p. 146. *vyavahāramanāśritya paramārtho na deśyate, paramārtha-manāgamya nirvāṇaṃ nādhigamyate*. (*Kārikā-P*, p. 494) Cf. Kumārajīva's rendition 若不依俗諦, 不得第一義; 不得第一義, 則不得涅槃. (CL, 24:10, T.30.33a).

18. T.32.14a.

19. T.30.33a.

20. Kajiyama, p. 131.

21. H. Ui, *Ui Hakuju chōsaku senshū*, Vol. 4, "Japanese Translation of the Sanskrit Text of Madhyamakakārikā." Tokyo: Taito Press, 1974, p. 51.

22. Kalupahana, p. 333.
23. Murti, p. 19.
24. Ibid., p. 17.
25. Monier Monier-Williams, *A Sanskrit-English Dictionary*, p. 158b.
26. Cf. note 17.
27. Kalupahana, pp. 89–90.
28. Inada, p. 114. *karmakleśakṣayānmokṣa karmakleśā vikalpataḥ, te prapañcātprapañcastu śūnyatāyāṃ nirudhyate.* (*Kārikā-P*, pp. 349–350) Cf. Kumārajīva's rendition 業煩惱滅故,名之為解脫.業煩惱非實,入空戲論滅. (CL, 18:5, T.30.23c).
29. 諸法實相常住不動.衆生以無明等諸煩惱故,於實相中,轉異邪曲.諸佛賢聖種種方便說法,破無明等諸煩惱,令衆生還得實性,如本不異,是名為如.實性與無明合,故變異,則不清淨.若除却無明等,得其真性,是名法性,清淨實際,名入法性中. (T.25.298c–299a).
30. 般若波羅蜜中,但除邪見,而不破四緣. (T.25.297b).
31. It is commonly maintained by all Buddhist schools that the empirical world is formed *via* the assemblage of causes (*pratyaya*). The Yogācāra School goes further by articulating a sophisticated theory of four causes to account for this issue. In this theory, the causes are divided into major cause, i.e., *hetu-pratyaya* and subsidiary causes, the latter of which are again specified as *ālambana-pratyaya, samanantara-pratyaya* and *adhipati-pratyaya*. For details, cf. Dharmapāla's *Vijñaptimātratāsiddhi-śāstra* (*Ch'eng-wei-shih lun* 成唯識論), chap. 7, T.31.40a–41a.
32. Inada, p. 152. *sarvasaṃvyavahārāṃśca laukikān pratibādhase, yatpratītyasamutpādaśūnyatāṃ pratibādhase.* (*Kārikā-P*, p. 513) Cf. Kumārajīva's rendition 汝破一切法,諸因緣空義,則破于世俗,諸餘所有法. (CL, 24:36, T.30.34b).
33. 大品云: 即色是空,非色滅空.釋論解云: 色是生死,空是涅槃.生死際、涅槃際一而無二.此豈非染淨俱融? (FHHI, chap. 10, T.33.805a).
34. 法性與一切法無二無別. ...離凡法更求實相,如避此空,彼處求空.即凡法是實法,不須捨凡向聖. (MHCK, chap. 1, T.46.6a–b).
35. The idea that the condition of liberation is identical to defilements—whether the latter be termed ignorance, delusive love, etc.—or that liberation is achieved without extirpating defilements appears so often in Chih-i's works that one would tend to think that it is the major feature of Chih-i's thought. This is particularly true with the MHCK, in which this idea is seen at least eighteen times: T.46.9a, 11c, 14b, 21b, 47c, 49c, 56b, 82c, 100b, 103b–c, 104c, 116b, 126c, 127a, 128c, 129a, 131a, 140b.
36. 若身子(等)斷惑入般,如破壁得出,怖畏生死,不能用煩惱而作佛事.菩薩以趣佛慧,不斷而入,如得道者壁不能礙.是則還用煩惱以為佛事.是名不斷煩惱而入涅槃. (WMCLS, chap. 4, T.38.612b). The term *te-tao che* 得道者 is very taoistic in tone. It seems to mean a person who has acquired or realized the Way. However, in view of the fact that the text

describes such a person in terms of being not obstructed by a wall, we understand him to be a person who has acquired the supernatural power of penetrating the wall without obstruction.

37. 譬如對寇,寇是勳本.能破寇故,有大功名,得大富貴.無量貪欲是如來種,亦復如是.能令菩薩出生無量百千法門.多薪火猛,糞壤生華.貪欲是道,此之謂也.若斷貪欲,住貪欲空,何由生出一切法門? (MHCK, chap. 4, T.46.47a).

38. In this respect, Chih-li 知禮 (A.D. 960–1028), an outstanding follower of Chih-i, goes even further by associating "the door to the *Dharma*" with the idea that Buddha Nature embraces evil (cf. Chapter IV, note 89) in order to form a sophisticated idea of "Evil Nature as the door to the *Dharma*" (*hsing-o fa-men* 性惡法門). In this idea, defilements are emphasized as an important element to be practiced. Chih-li states: "Defilements and the life-death cycle are the evils to be practiced. All of them are Evil Nature as the door to the *Dharma*. Therefore there is no need to extirpate and reverse them. However, the other masters do not know this Evil Nature; they consequently need to reverse the evil to the good, extirpate the evil and realize the good." (*Shih-pu-erh-men chih-yao ch'ao* 十不二門指要鈔, T.46.707b)

39. 問曰: 若不斷煩惱結業,云何而得解脫?答曰: 譬如未得神通之人,若在牢獄,必須穿牆破壁,方得走脫.若是得神通之人,處在牢獄,雖不穿牆破壁,而出入無礙也. (WMCHS, chap. 5, T.38.550c–551a).

40. 畢竟空即是無明之性. (WMCLS, chap. 10, T.38.701a).

41. T'ang, p. 1174.

42. 無明癡惑, 本是法性. 以癡迷故, 法性變作無明, 起諸顛倒, 善不善等; 如寒來結水, 變作堅冰, 又如眠來變心, 有種種夢. (MHCK, chap. 5, T.46.56b).

43. 但有名字, 寧復有二物相即耶? 如一珠, 向月生水, 向日生火; 不向, 則無水火. 一物未曾二, 而有水火之珠耳 (MHCK, chap. 6, T.46.83a).

44. 當體諸顛倒即是法性. (MHCK, chap. 5, T.46.56b).

45. With respect to the form of identification, Chih-li enumerates three types: combination of two things (*erh-wu hsiang-he* 二物相合); mutual reverse of the back and front (*pei-mian hsiang-fan* 背面相翻); and complete identification in and of the related matters (*tang-t'i ch'üan-shih* 當體全是). Chih-li regards the final type as the authentic identification. (*Shih pu-erh-men chih-yao ch'ao*, T.46.707b. For an explication of these three types of identification, cf. Tamura, pp. 121–122) Obviously, the first two types treat the matters as two separate things, while the third one treats the matters as two different states of the same thing. Chih-li certainly refers Chih-i's identification in question to this third type.

46. 由惡有善,離惡無善.翻于諸惡,即善資成.如竹中有火性,未即是火事,故有而不燒.遇緣事成,即能燒物.惡即善性,未即是事.遇緣成事,即能翻惡.如竹有火,火出還燒竹.惡中有善,善成還破惡.故即惡性相是善性相

也 (FHHI, chap. 5, T.33.743c–744a). In the text, *hsing* 性 and *shih* 事 are enumerated to represent the opposite states of potency and actuality of entities, respectively. In view of this, we render *hsing* as "potency" rather than "nature," the latter being the more common rendition of *hsing*.

47. Again, there is a problem in the analogy, as remarked by Yün-hua Jan in his comments on the draft of the present work: "The bamboo contains the potency of fire, yet when fire comes from the bamboo, the latter will be destroyed by fire. If this is the case, how could the impurity or defilement (i.e., bamboo) remain without extirpation?" His point is that when fire burns the bamboo, the latter will be destroyed and vanish completely, while evil or defilement, when overturned by good, does not vanish completely. This is a discrepancy of which Chih-i was not aware. It should also be noted that the issue of good and evil carries a practical and soteriological sense, while the issue of fire and bamboo carries an ontological sense. As will be shown below, both evil and good have a common ground or origin, i.e., the mind. Because the mind never vanishes completely, both evil and good always have the opportunity to prevail. As for the bamboo and fire, a common ontological origin does not exist. Although Chih-i asserts that the mind embraces *dharmas* (see below) that may include fire and bamboo, the assertion is not in an ontological sense. That is, the mind does not produce fire and bamboo and so is not the ontological origin of them. There is no sign in Chih-i's works that he is interested in any ontological issue.

48. 此心是無明、法性、法界、十界、百法、無量定亂，一念具足．何以故？由迷法性，故有一切散亂惡法，由解法性，故有一切定法．...迷解定散，其性不二. (MHCK, chap. 9, T.46.131a).

49. 無明法法性，一心一切心，如彼惛眠．達無明即法性，一切心一心，如彼醒寤. (MHCK, chap. 5, T.46.55c).

50. 法性顯，則無明轉變為明. (MHCK, chap. 6, T.46.82c–83a).

51. 無明轉，即變為明，如融冰成水．更非遠物，不餘處來．但一念心普皆具足. (MHCK, chap. 1, T.46.9b).

52. In the *Ssu-nien chu*, for example, this idea is crystallized into a highly sophisticated compound concept titled "the mind of ignorance and Dharma Nature in one single moment" (*i-nien wu-ming fa-hsing hsin* 一念無明法性心). Cf. *Ssu-nien chu*, chap. 4, T.46.578a–c. This work, publicized under Chih-i's name, was written by his followers. Cf. our Introduction.

53. 思議解脫即是離文字之解脫．...若不思議解脫即是不離文字之解脫．...若離文字之解脫，即是斷煩惱入涅槃．不離文字之解脫，即不斷煩惱而入涅槃. (WMCHS, chap. 5, T.38.550a–b). At this point, we may remind ourselves that Chih-i has spoken of the Four Alternatives and its negative in terms of conceivability and inconceivability, respectively. Cf. Chpater V. 7 above.

54. 雖言斷盡，無所可斷，不思議斷．不斷無明愛取，而入圓淨涅槃；不斷名色七支，而入性淨涅槃；不斷行有善惡，而入方便淨涅槃.…是名不可思議境也. (MHCK, chap. 9, T.46.127a). 不斷凡夫陰身，而能成就法身，即是不思議. (WMCLS, chap. 3, T.38.607a). It is interesting to note that in the former quotation, Chih-i paradoxically titles the liberation based on the idea of no-extirpation "inconceivable extirpation" (*pu ssu-i tuan* 不思議斷). "Extirpation" (*tuan* 斷) here simply means liberation. It should not be taken to mean the same as the "extirpation" in the idea of no-extirpation.

55. 須彌入芥，小不障大，大不礙小，故云不思議耳. 今有煩惱結惑，不障智慧涅槃，智慧涅槃不礙煩惱結惑，乃名不思議. (WMCHS, chap. 5, T.38.550b).

56. 若思議解脫，即是三藏教、通教三乘人所得二種涅槃灰身滅智解脫也. 若是不思議解脫，即是別、圓兩教菩薩諸佛所得大般涅槃常寂，即是不思議之解脫也. (WMCHS, chap. 5, T.38.550b–c).

57. 問曰：若不斷而入是不思議者，通教亦說不斷而入涅槃，何故非不思議解脫？答曰：通教不見惑相，名為不斷，而實是斷. 如明時實自無暗. 不同有芥子之小不妨須彌之大也. (WMCHS, chap. 5, T.38.550b). A few words about the word *fang* 妨 in the statement that the tiny size of a mustard seed does not "undermine" the huge size of Sumeru Mountain. This word has two meanings: obstruct and undermine, as in *fang-ai* 妨礙 and *fang-hai* 妨害, respectively. Accordingly, the statement may mean that the tiny mustard seed does not undermine the huge Sumeru Mountain, or that the tiny mustard seed does not obstruct the huge Sumeru Mountain. As will be seen below, this statement carries an inconceivable sense. It is manifest or conceivable that the tiny mustard seed does not obstruct the hugh Sumeru Mountain. Consequently, this statement should carry the first meaning: the tiny mustard seed does not undermine the huge Sumeru Mountain. In fact, the assertion that the Sumeru Mountain "enters into" the mustard seed, which Chih-i associates with the inconceivable nature (cf. note 55 above), entails the meaning that the tiny mustard seed "absorbs" the huge Sumeru Mountain and thus that the former "does not undermine" the latter. These arguments support our translation of fang as "undermine."

58. Chih-i has not explicitly specified that the *Vimalakīrtinirdeśa-sūtra* pertains to the Common Doctrine. In his commentary to this *sūtra*, the WMCLS, he speaks of it in terms of *Fang-teng* 方等 (Skt., *Vaipulya*), which in Chinese Buddhist circles represents a group of Mahāyāna sūtras. (Chap. 9, T.38.684a) Both Hurvitz and Tamura have also noted that Chih-i regards the *Vimalakīrtinirdeśa-sūtra* as a *Fang-teng* sūtra. (Hurvitz, pp.224, 234; Tamura, p. 94) In addition, in the SCI, Chih-i enumerates the Mahāyāna sources expressive of the Common Doctrine, including the *Fang-teng* sūtras. (Chap. 1, T.46.722a) The same enumeration is repeated in Chegwan's TTSCI. Cf. T.46.778a. It is therefore certain that Chih-i relates the *Vimalakīrtinirdeśa-sūtra* to the Common Doctrine in his classification, and that he takes it to be a Common Doctrine sūtra.

59. Inada, p. 110; *Kārikā-P*, p. 327; CL, 17:27, T.30.23a–b.
60. Inada, p. 112; *Kārikā-P*, p. 334; CL, 17:31, T.30.23c.
61. *Kārikā-P*, pp. 326, 453; CL, 17:26, T.30.23a; 23:2, T.30.31a.
62. T.30.23a; T.30.31a.
63. Cf. Chapter IV. 3 above.
64. Cf. Chapter IV above.

Notes to Chapter Eight

1. We are not in a position to deal with this proposition here. For a profound and extensive delineation of it, cf. Tsung-san Mou, *Ts'ung Lu Hsiang-shan tao Liu Chi-shan* 從陸象山到劉蕺山. Taiwan: Student Book Co. Ltd., 1979. Cf. the first chapter, pp. 3–78 in particular.

2. Inada, p. 115. *nivṛttamabhidhātavyaṃ nivṛtte cittagocare, anutpannāniruddhā hi nirvāṇamiva dharmatā.* (*Kārikā-P*, p. 364) Cf. Kumārajīva's rendition 諸法實相中,心行言語斷,無生亦無滅,寂滅如涅槃. (CL, 18:7, T.30.24a).

3. 一切心行皆是虛妄.虛妄故應滅. (T.30.25a).

4. Hurvitz, p. 271.

5. For instance, Satō, pp. 150, 186, 666. Swanson, pp. 8, 17, 155, etc.

6. Cf. Chap. VI. 4 above.

7. Cf. Chap. VI. 7 above.

8. Incidentally, Chih-li has asserted that the word "embrace" (*chü* 具) by itself is capable of fully demonstrating the character of the T'ien-t'ai School. He also elaborates the implication of this word in connection with the concept of permanence. Cf. his *Kuan-yin-ching hsüan-i-chi hui-pen* 觀音經玄義記會本, chap. 2, Z.55.81a–b. "Embrace" and "permanence" here refer to the all-embracement of *dharmas* and ever-abidingness, respectively, which are two characteristics of the Buddha Nature or Middle Way-Buddha Nature. This reflects how a prominent T'ien-t'ai thinker in the later period understood the essential of the School founded by Chih-i.

GLOSSARY

Andō Toshio 安藤俊雄

Ch'an-men chang 禪門章
Ch'an-men k'ou-chüeh 禪門口訣
Ch'an-men yiao-lüeh 禪門要略
ch'ang-chu 常住
ch'ang-chu fo-hsing 常住佛性
ch'e 尺
ch'iao 巧
Ch'ing-kuan-yin-ching shu 請觀音經疏
ch'u 出
ch'u-chia 出假
ch'üan 權
Chan-jan 湛然
chang 丈
chen 真
chen-hsin 真心
chen-hsing 真性
chen-shan-miao se 真善妙色
chen-shih 真實
chen-ti 真諦
Cheng-hsin lun 證心論
cheng-men 正門
chi—immediate, equal 即
chi—quiescence 寂
chi erh ch'ang-chao 寂而常照
chi-k'ung chi-chia chi-chung 即空即假即中
chi-mieh 寂滅
Chi-tsang 吉藏
chia 假
chia-kuan 假觀
chia-ming 假名
chia-ming hsiang 假名相
chia-ming yu 假名有
chia-ti 假諦
chieh—instruct 接
chieh—realm 界
chieh-t'o 解脫
chieh-yin 接引

chien 堅
chien-li 建立
chih 止
Chih-i 智顗
Chin-kuang-ming-ching hsüan-i 金光明經玄義
Chin-kuang-ming-ching wen-chü 金光明經文句
ching—objects 境
ching—pure 淨
Ching-chou 荊州
Ching-ling 金陵
Ching-ming hsüan-i 淨名玄義
Ching-ming-ching shu 淨名經疏
cho 拙
chü 具
chü chu-fa 具諸法
chü i-ch'ieh fo-fa 具一切佛法
chü i-ch'ieh fa 具一切法
chu-fa 諸法
chu-fa chih shih-hsiang 諸法之實相
chu-fo fa 諸佛法
Chüeh-i san-mei 覺意三昧
chung 中
chung shih-li 中實理
chung-kuan 中觀
chung-li 中理
Chung-lun 中論
chung-shih li-hsin 中實理心
chung-tao 中道
chung-tao cheng kuan 中道正觀
chung-tao chih fa 中道之法
chung-tao chih li 中道之理
chung-tao fa-hsing chih li 中道法性之理
chung-tao fa-shen 中道法身
chung-tao fo-hsing 中道佛性
chung-tao i-shih chih li 中道一實之理
chung-tao k'ung 中道空
chung-tao li 中道理
chung-tao t'i 中道體
chung-tao ti-i-i-ti kuan 中道第一義諦觀
chung-ti 中諦

erh-ti 二諦
erh-ti kuan 二諦觀

fa 法
fa chiu-chu 法久住
Fa-chieh tz'u-ti ch'u-men 法界次第初門

fa-hsing 法性
fa-hsing shen 法性身
Fa-hua ching 法華經
Fa-hua hsüan-i 法華玄義
Fa-hua wen-chü 法華文句
Fa-hua-san-mei ch'an-i 法華三昧懺儀
fa-men 法門
fa-shen 法身
fang 方
fang-nao 煩惱
fang-pien 方便
Fang-teng ch'an-fa 方等懺法
fo-fa 佛法
fo-hsing 佛性
fo-hsing ch'ang-chu 佛性常住
fo-hsing cheng-hsin 佛性真心
fo-hsing chung-tao 佛性中道
fo-hsing fa-shen ch'ang-chu 佛性法身常住
Fo-hsing yü po-je 佛性與般若
fo-shih 佛事

hsi 析
hsi-fa 析法
hsi-fa ju-k'ung 析法入空
hsi-lun 戲論
hsi-men 析門
hsiang 相
hsin 心
hsin chi li 心即理
hsin-hsing 心行
hsing 性
hsing-k'ung 性空
hsü-k'ung fo-hsing 虛空佛性
hsüeh ta-fang-pien 學大方便
Hua-fa ssu-chiao 化法四教
Hua-i ssu-chiao 化儀四教
hui 會
Hui-ssu 慧思
Hui-wen 慧文
huo-hsin 惑心

i-ch'ieh chih 一切智
i-ch'ieh chung chih 一切種智
i-ch'ieh fa 一切法
i-ch'ieh fa-men 一切法門
i-ch'ieh hsin 一切心
i-ch'ieh-fa ch'ü ju-lai-tsang 一切法趣如來藏

i-fa—one single *dharma* 一法
i-fa—varying character 異法
i-hsin 一心
i-hsin san kuan 一心三觀
i-nien 一念

jan 染
Jen-wang-ching shu 仁王經疏
ju—entrances, enter 入
ju—Suchness 如
ju-chia 入假
ju-ju 如如
ju-lai tsang 如來藏
ju-lai tz'u-pei 如來慈悲

k'ung 空
k'ung i-fu k'ung 空亦復空
k'ung kuan 空觀
k'ung-k'ung 空空
k'ung-ti 空諦
Kajiyama Yūichi 梶山雄一
Kū no ronri: chūgan 空の理論: 中觀
kuan 觀
kuan-ch'uan 觀穿
Kuan-ching shu 觀經疏
Kuan-hsin lun 觀心論
Kuan-hsin shih-er-pu-ching i 觀心十二部經義
Kuan-hsin-shih fa 觀心食法
Kuan-hsin-sung-ching fa 觀心誦經法
kuan-ta 觀達
Kuan-ting 灌頂
Kuan-yin hsüan-i 觀音玄義
Kuan-yin i-shu 觀音義疏
Kuang-chai Monastery 光宅寺
Kuang-chou 光州
kung 功
kung-yung 功用
kūken 空見

li—beneficence 利
li—force 力
li—principle 理
li-chieh hsiu-hsing 歷劫修行
li-fa 立法
li-hsing 理性
li-pieh 歷別
li-yung 力用
Lu Hsiang-shan 陸象山

men 門
miao-yu 妙有
ming 名
Mo-ho chih-kuan 摩訶止觀
Mou Tsung-san 牟宗三

nieh-p'an 涅槃

p'an-chiao 判教
p'ien 偏
p'ien-chen 偏真
p'ien-men 偏門
p'ing-teng kuan 平等觀
pa-pu 八不
Pai-lun 百論
pao-shen 報身
pi 備
pen 本
pen-chi 本際
pen-t'i 本體
pi-ching k'ung 畢竟空
pieh 別
pieh chieh t'ung 別接通
pieh ju t'ung 別入通
pieh-chiao 別教
pien 便
Po-je-teng lun-shih 般若燈論釋
pu ssu-i 不思議
pu ssu-i chieh-t'o 不思議解脫
pu tz'u-ti 不次第
pu-cho pu-she 不著不捨
pu-k'o-te k'ung 不可得空
pu-k'ung 不空
pu-kai 不改
pu-sheng 不生
pu-ssu 不思
pu-tuan 不斷
pu-tung hsing 不動性
pu-tz'u-ti men 不次第門

San ta-pu 三大部
san-chih 三智
san-fan 三番
san-kuan 三觀
San-lun 三論
san-shen 三身
san-ti 三諦
san-yin fo-hsing 三因佛性

Satō Tetsuei 佐藤哲英
Seng-jui 僧叡
sheng 生
sheng-shen 生身
shih 實
shih ju-shih 十如是
shih-chi 實際
Shih-chu-pi-p'o-sha lun 十住毗婆沙論
Shih-er-men lun 十二門論
shih-hsiang 實相
shih-hsiang cheng-t'i 實相正體
shih-hsing 實性
shih-su ti 世俗諦
shih-ti 世諦
shih-yin 識陰
shuang che 雙遮
shuang-chao 雙照
so-tso 所作
ssu 思
Ssu-chiao i 四教義
ssu-chü 四句
ssu-i 思議
ssu-i chieh-t'o 思議解脱
ssu-men ju-li 四門入理
ssu-men ju-tao 四門入道
Ssu-nien ch'u 四念處
ssu-ti 四諦
su 俗
su-ti 俗諦

t'i 體
t'i-fa 體法
t'i-fa ju-k'ung 體法入空
t'i-men 體門
T'ien-t'ai 天台
T'ien-t'ai Mountain 天台山
T'ien-t'ai School 天台宗
t'ung-chiao 通教
Ta-chih-tu lun 大智度論
Ta-su Mountain 大蘇山
ta-yung-kung-li 大用功力
tan-k'ung 但空
tan-li 但理
tang-chiao 當教
tang-t'i 當體
tao-chung chih 道種智
te 得

Tendai daishi no kenkyū 天台大師の研究
ti 諦
ti-i-i ti 第一義諦
tien-k'ung shuo-fa 點空說法
ts'un 寸
ts'ung-chia ju-k'ung 從假入空
ts'ung-k'ung ju-chia 從空入假
tsang-chiao 藏教
tso 作
Tso-ch'an fang-pien-men 坐禪方便門
tz'u-pei 慈悲
tz'u-ti 次第
tz'u-ti ju-chung 次第入中
tz'u-ti men 次第門
Tz'u-ti-ch'an men 次第禪門
tzu-ching chih 自境智
tzu-hsing 自性

Wa-kuan Monastery 瓦官寺
Wang Yang-ming 王陽明
Wei-mo ching 維摩經
Wei-mo-ching hsüan-shu 維摩經玄疏
Wei-mo-ching lüeh-shu 維摩經略疏
Wei-mo-ching wen-shu 維摩經文疏
wo-chien 我見
wu 無
Wu hsiao-pu 五小部
wu-ch'ing yu-hsing 無情有性
wu-fang ta-yung 無方大用
wu-hsiang chiao 無相教
wu-hsing 無性
wu-liang 無量
wu-sheng 無生
wu-tso 無作

Yang Kuang 楊廣
yin 陰
yin-yüan 因緣
ying 應
ying-shen 應身
yu 有
yu-wei 有為
yüan chieh pieh 圓接別
yüan chieh t'ung 圓接通
yüan ju pieh 圓入別
yüan ju t'ung 圓入通
yüan 圓

yüan-chen 圓真
yüan-chiao 圓教
yüan-tun 圓頓
yüan-tun ju-chung 圓頓入中
yün-wei 運為
yung 用
yung-t'i 用體

BIBLIOGRAPHY

Related to Mādhyamika

Articles:

Baird, Robert D. "The Symbol of Emptiness and the Emptiness of Symbols." *Humanitas*, 8 (1972), pp. 221–42.

Bhattacharya, A.R. "Brahman of Śankara and Śūnyatā of Mādhyamikas." *Indian Historical Quarterly*, 32 (1956), pp. 270–85.

Bugault, Guy. "Logic and Dialectics in the Madhyamakakārikās." *Journal of Indian Philosophy*, 11 (1983), pp. 7–76.

Chakravarti, S.S. "The Mādhyamika *Catuṣkoṭi* or Tetralemma." *Journal of Indian Philosophy*, 8 (1980), pp. 303–06.

Cheng, Hsueh-li. "Nāgārjuna's Approach to the Problem of the Existence of God." *Religious Studies*, 12 (1976), pp. 207–16.

———. "Nāgārjuna, Kant and Wittgenstein: The San-lun Mādhyamika Exposition of Emptiness." *Religious Studies*, 17 (1981), pp. 67–85.

Conze, Edward. "The Ontology of the Prajñāpāramitā." *Philosophy East and West*, 3:2 (1953), pp. 117–30.

———. "Meditation on Emptiness." *The Maha Bodhi* (1955), pp. 203–11.

———. "The Development of Prajñāpāramitā Thought." *Bukkyō to Bunka*, Kyoto, 1960, pp. 24–45.

De Jong, J.W. "The Problem of the Absolute in the Mādhyamika School." *Journal of Indian Philosophy*, 2 (1972), pp. 1–6.

———. "Emptiness." *Journal of Indian Philosophy*, 2 (1972), pp. 7–15.

Dilworth, David A. "Nāgārjuna's catuṣkoṭikā and Plato's Parmenides: Grammatological Mappings of a Common Textual Form." *Journal of Buddhist Philosophy*, 2 (1984), pp. 77–103.

Fuse, K. "Daichidoron ni mieru hokekyō no rikai" 大智度論に見える法華経の理解. *Tōyō Shisō Ronshū*, Tokyo, 1960, pp. 574–82.

Hamilton, C.H. "Encounter with Reality in Buddhist Mādhyamika Philosophy." *Journal of Bible and Religion*, 26 (1958), pp. 13–22.

Harata, S. "Kū(śūnya) ni tsuite" 空 (śūnya) について. *Indogaku Bukkyōgaku Kenkyū*, 23:2 (1975), pp. 251–54.

Hatani, Ryōtai, "Dialectics of the Mādhyamika Philosophy." *Studies on Buddhism in Japan*, Vol. 1, Tokyo, 1939, pp. 53–71.

Heimann, B. "The Significance of Negation in Hindu Philosophical Thought." *B.C. Law Volume*, Part II, Poona, 1946, pp. 408–13.

Hikuma, I. "Ideorogī to shite no 'chū'" イデオロギーとしての「中」. *Indo Shisō to Bukkyō*, Tokyo, 1973, pp. 753–61.

Inazu, Kizō. "Ryūju no chū no tetsugaku" 龍樹の中の哲学. *Indogaku Bukkyōgaku Ronshū*, Tokyo: Saneidō, 1954, pp. 269–76.

Jayatilleke, K.N. "The Logic of Four Alternatives." *Philosophy East and West*, 17 (1967), pp. 69–83.

Jones, Elvin W. "Buddhist Theories of Existents: The Systems of Two Truths." *Mahāyāna Buddhist Meditation: Theory and Practice*, ed. by Minoru Kiyota, Honolulu: The University Press of Hawaii, 1978, pp. 3–45.

Kajiyama, Yūichi. "Chūron ni okeru muga no ronri" 中論における無我の論理. *Jiga to Muga*, ed. by Nakamura Hajime, Kyoto: Heirakuji, 1974, pp. 479–514.

Kamata, Shigeo. "Kūgan no chūgokuteki heni" 空観の中国的變異. *Indogaku Bukkyōgaku Kenkyū*, 16:2 (1968), pp. 522–27.

Kunst, A. "The Concept of the Principle of the Excluded Middle in Buddhism." *Rocznik Orientalistyczny*, 21 (1957), pp. 141–47.

La Vallée Poussin, L.De "Madhyamaka." *Encyclopaedia of Religion and Ethics*, ed. by J. Hastings, 8 (1916), pp. 235–37.

———. "Notes on Śūnyatā and the Middle Path." *Indian Historical Quarterly*, 4 (1928), pp. 161–68.

———. "The Mādhyamika and the Tathatā." *Indian Historical Quarterly*, 9 (1933), pp. 30–1.

Lin, Li Kouan. "Á propos de la Sunyata (La Vide)." *La Pensée Bouddhique*, 5 (1940), pp. 8–12.

Masata, K. "Kū shisō ni okeru hitei no ruikei" 空思想における否定の類型. *Indogaku Bukkyōgaku Kenkyū*, 22:2 (1974), pp. 337–40.

May, Jacques. "La Philosophie Bouddhique de la vacuité." *Studia Philosophia*, 18 (1959), pp. 123–37.

———. "Kant et le Mādhyamika." *Indo-Iranian Journal*, 3 (1959) pp. 102–11.

Mehta, Mahesh. "Śūnyatā and Dharmatā: The Mādhyamika View of Inner Reality." *Development in Buddhist Thought*, ed. by Roy C. Amore, Wilfrid Laurier University Press, 1979, pp. 26–37.

Mitsukawa, Toyoki. "Chūganha ni okeru shaki no ito surumono" 中観派に於ける遮遣の意圖するもの. *Indogaku Bukkyōgaku Kenkyū*, 10:1 (1962), pp. 255–60.

Miyamoto, Shōson. "Study of Nāgārjuna," unpublished Ph.D. dissertation. Oxford University, 1928, pp. 1–96.

———. "Voidness and Middle Way." *Studies on Buddhism in Japan*, Vol. 1, Tokyo, 1939, pp. 73–92.

———. "A Re-appraisal of Pratītya-samutpāda." *Indogaku Bukkyōgaku Ronsō*, Kyoto: Hōzōkan, 1955, pp. 152–64.

———. "The Logic of Relativity as the Common Ground for the Development of the Middle Way." *Bukkyō to Bunka*, Kyoto, 1960, pp. 67–88.

———. "The Buddha's First Sermon and the Original Patterns of the Middle Way." *Indogaku Bukkyōgaku Kenkyū*, 13:2 (1965), pp. 855–45 (Western Section).

———. "The Historico-social Bearings of the Middle Way." *Indogaku Bukkyōgaku Kenkyū*, 14:2 (1966), pp. 996–69 (Western Section).

Mookerjee, Satkari. "The Absolutist's Standpoint in Logic." *The Nava-Nalanda-Mahavihara Research Publication*, Vol. 1, 1957, pp. 1–175.

Mukhopadhya, S. "Doctrine of Shunyata in Mahayana Buddhism." *Prabuddhi Bharata*, 48 (1943), pp. 327–29.

Nagao, Gadjin M. "Chūgan tetsugaku no kompon teki tachiba" 中観哲学の根本的立場. *Tetsugaku Kenkyū*, 31:9 (1947), pp. 1–27; 31:11, pp. 16–49; 32:1 (1948), pp. 1–41; 32:2, pp. 19–38.

———. "An Interpretation of the Term 'saṃvṛti' (Convention) in Buddhism." *Jinbun Kagaku Kenkyūsho (Kyoto University) Silver Jubilee Vol.* (1954), pp. 550–61.

———. "The Silence of the Buddha and its Mādhyamic Interpretation." *Indogaku Bukkyōgaku Ronsō*, Kyoto: Hōzōkan, 1955, pp. 137–51.

———. "On the Theory of Buddha-body." *The Eastern Buddhist*, 6:1 (May 1971), pp. 25–53.

Nakamura, Hajime. "Buddhist Logic Expounded by Means of Symbolic Logic." *Indogaku Bukkyōgaku Kenkyū*, 7:1 (1958), pp. 395–75 (Western Section). More discussion on the same issue by Nakamura can be found in his *Indo Shisō no Shōmondai* (Tokyo: Shūnjusha, 1967, pp. 548–56).

———. "Kū no kōsatsu" 空の考察. *Higata Hakushi Koki Kinen Ronbunshū*, Tokyo, 1964, pp. 171–96.

———. "Chūdo to kūken" 中道と空見. *Bukkyō Shisōshi Ronshū*, Tokyo: Daizō Shuppan Co., 1964, pp. 139–80.

Narain, Harsh. "Śūnyavāda: A Reinterpretation." *Philosophy East and West*, 13:4, pp. 331–38.

Ng, Yu-kwan. "The Arguments of Nāgārjuna in the Light of Modern Logic." *Journal of Indian Philosophy*, 15 (1987), pp. 363–84.

Obermiller, Evgenii E. "The Term Śūnyatā and its Different Interpretations." *Journal of the Greater Indian Society*, 1 (1934), pp. 105–17.

Pannikar, R. "The Crisis of Mādhyamika and Indian Philosophy Today." *Philosophy East and West*, 16:3–4, pp. 117–31.

Robinson, Richard H. "Some Logical Aspects of Nāgārjuna's System." *Philosophy East and West*, 6:4 (1957), pp. 291–308.

———. "The Classical Indian Axiomatic." *Philosophy East and West*, 17:1–4 (1967), pp. 139–54.

———. "Did Nāgārjuna Really Refute All Philosophical View?" *Philosophy East and West*, 22:3 (1972), pp. 325–31.

Raju, P.T. "The Principle of Four-cornered Negation in Indian Philosophy." *Review of Metaphysics*, 7 (1953–54), pp. 694–713.

Ramanan, K. Venkata. "A Fresh Appraisal of the Mādhyamika Philosophy." *Visvabharati Quarterly*, 27 (1961–62), pp. 230–38.

Ruegg, D. Seyfort. "The Uses of the Four Positions of the Catuṣkoṭi and the Problem of the Description of Reality in Mahāyāna Buddhism." *Journal of Indian Philosophy*, 5 (1977), pp. 1–71.

Saigusa, Mitsuyoshi. "Daichidoron ni tokareta roku haramitsu ni tsuite" 大智度論に説かれた六ハラミツについて. *Indogaku Bukkyōgaku Kenkyū*, 2:2 (1954), pp. 188–92.

———. "Ryūju no kū ni tsuite" 龍樹の空について. *Indogaku Bukkyōgaku Ronshū*, Tokyo: Sanseidō, 1954, pp. 277–90.

———. "法 und Dharma in Kumārajīva's Mādhyamikakārikā." *Indogaku Bukkyōgaku Kenkyū*, 13:1 (1965), pp. 419–12. (Western Section)

———. "Daichidoron shoshū geju to chūron ju" 大智度論所収偈頌と中論頌. *Indogaku Bukkyōgaku Kenkyū*, 15:1 (1966), pp. 85–97.

Sarkar, A.K. "Nāgārjuna: On Causation and Nirvāṇa." *Dr. S. Radhakrishnan Souvenior Volume*, Darshana, Moradabad, India, 1963, pp. 395–404.

Sastri, N.A. "Nāgārjuna on the Buddhist Theory of Causation." *Prof. K.V. Rangaswami Aiyangar Commemoration Volume*, Madras, 1940, pp. 485–92.

Schayer, Stanislaw. "Altindische Antizipationen der Aussagenlogik." *Bulletin de l'Academie Polonaise, classe de philologie* (1933), pp. 90–96.

———. "Das Mahāyānistische Absolutum nach der Lehre der Mādhyamikas." *Orientalistische Literaturzeitung*, 38 (1935), pp. 401–15.

Siderits, Mark, et al. "Zeno and Nāgārjuna on Motion." *Philosophy East and West*. 26:3 (1976), pp. 281–99.

Sprung, Mervyn. "Non-Cognitive Language in Mādhyamika Buddhism." *Buddhist Thought and Asian Civilization*, ed., by L. Kamamura and K. Scott, Berkeley: Dharma Publishing, 1977, pp. 241–53.

———. "The Problem of Being in Mādhyamika Buddhism." *Developments in Buddhist Thought*, ed. by Roy C. Amore, Waterloo: Wilfrid Laurier University Press, 1979, pp. 8–25.

Stambaugh, Joan. "Emptiness and the Identity of Saṃsāra and Nirvāṇa." *Journal of Buddhist Philosophy*, 2 (1984), pp. 51–64.

Streng, Frederick J. "The Buddhist Doctrine of two Truths as Religious Philosophy." *Journal of Indian Philosophy*, 1 (1971), pp. 262–71.

———. "Metaphysics, Negative Dialectic, and the Expression of the Inexpressible." *Philosophy East and West*, 25 (1975), pp. 429–47.

———. "The Process of Ultimate Transformation in Nāgārjuna's Mādhyamika." *The Eastern Buddhist*, 11:2 (Oct. 1978), pp. 12–32.

Tanaka, Junshō. "Kūgan no ronri" 空観の論理. *Indogaku Bukkyōgaku Kenkyū*, 2:1 (1953), pp. 230–32.

———. "Kūgan no hatten" 空観の發展. *Nakano Kyōju Koki Kinen Ronbunshū*, Kōyasan University, 1960, pp. 83–104.

Trundle Jr., Robert. "Beyond the Linguistic and Conceptual: A Comparison of Albert Camus and Nāgārjuna." *Darshana International*, 16 (1976), pp. 1–11.

Tucci, Giuseppe, "Two Humns of the Catuḥ-stava of Nāgārjuna." *Journal of Royal Asiatic Society* (1932), pp. 309–25.

Ui, Hakuju. "Daichidoron ni okeru hosshin setsu" 大智度論に於ける法身説. In his *Indo Tetsugaku Kenkyū*, Vol. 4, Tokyo: Iwanami Shoten, 1965, pp. 401–24.

Vetter, Tilmann. "Die Lehre Nāgārjunas in den Mūla-Madhyamakakārikā." *Epiphanie des Heils*, Wien, 1982, pp. 87–108.

Vidyabhusana, S.C. "The Mādhyamika School." *Journal of the Buddhist Text Society*, 2 (1895), pp. 3–9, 3 (1896), pp. 9–23.

———. "History of the Mādhyamika Philosophy of Nāgārjuna." *Journal of the Buddhist Text Society*, 4 (1897), pp. 7–20.

Wayman, Alex. "The Buddhist 'Not this, Not this.'" *Philosophy East and West*, 11:3 (1961), pp. 99–114.

———. "Contributions to the Mādhyamika School of Buddhism." *Journal of the American Oriental Society*, 89:1 (1969), pp. 141–52. A review on F. Streng's book.

———. "Who Understands the Four Alternatives of the Buddhist Texts?" *Buddhist and Western Philosophy*, ed. by Nathan Katz, New Delhi: Sterling Publishers Private Limited, 1981, pp. 450–72.

Yasui, Kōsai. "Chūgan setsu no tachiba to shite no nitai setsu" 中観説の立場としての二諦説. *The Annual Report of Researches of the Otani University*, 8 (1955), pp. 59–143.

Books

Bareau, André. *L'absolu en philosophie bouddhique: évolution de la notion d'asaṃskṛta*. Paris, 1951. pp. 174–86 express Nāgārjuna's use of "emptiness."

Bukkyō Shisō Kenkyūkai, ed. *Kū* 空. 2 Vols. Kyoto: Heirakuji, 1981, 1982.

Cheng, Hsueh-li. *Nāgārjuna's Twelve Gate Treatise*. Dordrecht: D. Reidel, 1982.

Conze, Edward. *Buddhist Thought in India*. London: George Allen & Unwin Ltd., 1962, pp. 238–49.

———. *Buddhist Wisdom Books*. London: George Allen and Unwin Ltd., 1958.

Frauwallner, Erich. *Die Philosophie des Buddhismus*. Berlin: Akademie Verlag, 1969.

Gard, Richard A. *Mādhyamika Buddhism*. Introductory lectures on its History and Doctrines. Bangkok: Mahāmukūta University Press, 1956.

Gokhale, Vasdev. *The Hundred Letters* (Akṣara Śatakam). A Mādhyamika text by Aryadeva, after Chinese and Tibetan materials. Tr. by V. Gokhale. Heidelberg, 1930.

Hatani, Ryōtai. *Sanron kaidai to honyaku* 三論解題と翻譯; in *Kokuyaku Issaikyō, Chūganbu*, Vol. I. Tokyo: Daitō Shuppan Sha, 1930. The volume also includes Japanese translations of the *Chung-lun*, *Pai-lun* and the *Shih-erh-men lun*.

Hiragawa, A. et al. ed. *Chūgan shisō* 中観思想. Tokyo: Shunjūsha, 1982.

Inada, Kenneth K. *Nāgārjuna, A Translation of His Mūlamadhyamakakārikā with an Introductory Essay*. Tokyo: Hokuseidō, 1970.

Jayatilleke, K.N. *Early Buddhist Theory of Knowledge*. London: Allen & Unwin, 1963.

Kajiyama, Yūichi. *Studies in Buddhist Philosophy: Selected Papers*. Kyoto: Rinsen Book Co., Ltd., 1989.

Kajiyama, Yūichi, et al. *Kū no ronri: chūgan* 空の論理:中観. Tokyo: Kadokawa Shoten, 1969.

———. *Daichidoron*. Tokyo: Chūokoronsha, 1989.

Kalupahana, David J. *Nāgārjuna: The Philosophy of the Middle Way*. New York: State University of New York Press, 1986.

Lancaster, L. ed. *Prajñāpāramitā and Related Systems*. Berkeley Buddhist Studies Series. Printed in Korea, 1977.

Lamotte, Étienne. *Le Traité de la grande Vertu de Sagesse de Nāgārjuna*, Vol. 3. Louvain: Université de Louvain, 1970.

Lindtner, chr. *Nagarjuniana*. Delhi: Motilal Banarsidass. 1987.

Matilal, B.K. *Epistemology, Logic and Grammar in Indian Philosophical Analysis*. The Hague: Mouton, 1971.

Mitsuyoshi, Saigusa. *Nāgārjuna's Mūlamadhyamakahārikās: Texts and Translations*. Tokyo: Daisanbunmei Sha, 1985.

Miyamoto, Shōson. *Kompon chū to kū* 根本中と空. Tokyo: Daiichi Shobō, 1943.

———. *Chūdo shisō oyobi sono hatatsu* 中道思想及びその發達. Tokyo and Kyoto: Hōzōkan, 1944.

Murti, T.R.V. *The Central Philosophy of Buddhism*. London: George Allen and Unwin Ltd., 1955.

Nagao, Gadjin, M. *Chūgan to yuishiki* 中観と唯識. Tokyo: Iwanami Shoten, 1978.

Ng, Yu-kwan. *Fo-chiao ti kai-nien yü fang-fa* 佛教的概念與方法. Taiwan: The Commercial Press, Ltd., 1988.

Pandeya, Ramchandra. *Indian Studies in Philosophy*. Delhi: Motilal Banarsidass, 1977.

Prebish, C.S. ed. *Buddhism, a Modern Perspective*. State University of Pennsylvania Press, 1975.

Ramanan, K. Venkata. *Nāgārjuna's Philosophy*, As presented in the *Mahāprajñāpāramitā-śāstra*. Tokyo: Charles E. Tuttle Co., Inc., 1966.

Robinson, Richard H. *Early Mādhyamika in India and China*. Madison: The University of Wisconsin Press, 1967.

Ruegg, D. Seyfort. *The Literature of the Madhyamaka School of Philosophy in India*. Wiesbaden: Harrassowitz, 1981.

Saigusa, Mitsuyoshi. *Studien zum Mahāprajñāpāramitā (upadeśa) śāstra*. Tokyo: Hokuseidō Verlag, 1969.

———. *Daichidoron no monogatari* 大智度論の物語. Tokyo: Regulus Library, 1974.

Santina, Peter D. *The Madhyamaka Schools in India*. Delhi: Motilal Banarsidass, 1986.

Sharma, Chandradhar. *Dialectic in Buddhism and Vedānta*. Banaras: Nand Kishore and Brothers, 1952.

Sprung, Mervyn, ed. *The Problem of Two Truths in Buddhism and Vedānta*. Dordrecht: D. Reidel, 1973.

Sprung, Mervyn, ed. *The Question of Being*. Pennsylvania State University Press, 1978.

———. *Lucid Exposition of the Middle Way. The Essential Chapters from the Prasannapadā of Candrakīrti*. London and Henley: Routledge & Kegan Paul, 1979.

Stcherbatsky, Theodor. *The Conception of Buddhist Nirvāṇa*. The Hague: Mouton & Co., 1965. Appendices contain English translations of Nāgārjuna's *Mādhyamika-kārikā* (Chapters I & XXV) and Candrakīrti's *Mādhyamika-vṛtti* (Prasannapadā, Chapters I & XXV).

Streng, Frederick J. *Emptiness. A Study in Religious Meaning*. Nashville and New York: Abingdon Press, 1967. Appendix A: Translation of the *Mūlamadhyamakakārikā*; Appendix B: Translation of the *Vigrahavyāvartanī*.

Sueki, Takehiro. *Tōyō no gōri shisō* 東洋の合理思想. Tokyo: Kōdansha, 1970.

T'ang, Yung-t'ung. *Han wei liang-chin nan-pei-ch'ao fo-chiao shih* 漢魏兩晉南北朝佛教史. 2 Vols. Peking: Chung-hua, 1955.

Tachikawa, Musashi. *Kū no kōzō* 「空」の構造. Tokyo: Regulus Library, 1986.

Tsunemoto, Kenyū. *Kūgan tetsugaku* 空観哲学. Tokyo: Daiichi Shobō, 1942.

Tucci, Giuseppe, *Pre-Diṅnāga Buddhist Texts on Logic from Chinese Sources*. Baroda: Oriental Institute, 1929.

Ueda, Yoshifumi. *Daijō bukkyō shisō no kompon kōzō* 大乗仏教思想の根本構造. Kyoto: Hyakkaen, 1957.

———. *Daijō bukkyō no shisō* 大乗仏教の思想. Tokyo: Regulus Library, 1977.

Ui, Hakuju. *Sanron kaidai to honyaku* 三論解題と翻譯, *Kokuyaku Daizōkyō*; Rombu, Vol. v. Tokyo: Kokumin Bunko Kankō-kai, 1921.

———. *Tōyō no ronri* 東洋の論理. Tokyo: Aoyama Shoin, 1950.
———. *Ui Hakuju chōsaku senshū* 宇井伯壽著作選集. Vol. 4. Tokyo: Daitō Press, 1974.
Vaidya, P.L. *Études sur Āryadeva et son Catuḥśataka: Chapitres VIII–XVI.* Paris, 1923. Includes a chapter titled "Le Mādhyamika et la Madhyamāpratipad."
Walleser, Max. *Die Mittlere Lehre des Nāgārjuna. Nach der chinesischen Version übertragen.* Heidelberg, 1912.
Warder, A.K. *Indian Buddhism.* Bombay: Motilal Banarsidass, 1970.
Yamaguchi, Susumu. *Chūgan bukkyō ronkō* 中観佛教論攷. Tokyo: Kōbundo Shobō, 1944.
———. *Hannya shisō shi* 般若思想史. Kyoto: Hōzōkan, 1951.
Yamaguchi, Yusuke. *Kū to benshōhō* 空と辯證法. Tokyo: Risōsha, 1939.
Yasui, Kōsai. *Chūgan shisō no kenkyū* 中観思想の研究. Kyoto: Hōzōkan, 1961.
Yin-shun. *Chung-kuan-lun-song chiang-chi* 中觀論頌講記. Taipei: Hui-jih Chiang-t'ang, 1963.
———. *Hsing-k'ung-hsüeh t'an-yüan* 性空學探源. Taipei: Hui-jih Chiang-t'ang, 1963.
———. *Chung-kuan chin-lun* 中觀今論. Taipei: Hui-jih Chiang-t'ang, 1971.
———. *K'ung chih t'an-chiu* 空之探究. Taipei: Cheng-wen Press, 1985.

Related to Chih-i

Articles:

Andō, Toshio. "Tendai shikan no chūshin mondai" 天台止觀の中心問題. *Indogaku Bukkyōgaku Kenkyū*, 2:2 (1954), pp. 216–18.
Awatani, R. "Tendai santai setsu to kichizō nitai setsu" 天台三諦説と吉藏二諦説. *Indogaku Bukkyōgaku Kenkyū*, 31:1 (1982), pp. 138–39.
———. "Tendai ni okeru ke no shisō" 天台における仮の思想. *Indogaku Bukkyōgaku Kenkyū*, 32:2 (1984), pp. 176–77.
Donner, N.A. "The Great Cessation and Insight, An Annotated Translation of the first Two Rolls of the Sui Dynasty Meditation Text, The *Mo-ho chih-kuan*," unpublished Ph.D. dissertation, British Columbia, 1976.
———. "Chih-i's Meditation on Evil." In David Chappell, ed., *Buddhist and Taoist Practice in Medieval Chinese Society.* Honolulu: University of Hawaii Press, 1987, pp. 49–64.
Fujii, K. "Tendai chigi ni okeru 'nyoraizō' no go no imi" 天台智顗における「如来蔵」の語の意味. *Indogaku Bukkyōgaku Kenkyū*, 30:1 (1981), pp. 339–43.
Hashimoto, Y. "Tendai i ni okeru yuima ni tsuite" 天台義に於ける維摩について. *Indogaku Bukkyōgaku Kenkyū*, 3:2 (1955), pp. 146–47.

Hibi, Nobumasa. "Hokkegengi no santai setsu ni tsuite" 法華玄義の三諦説に就いて. *Ōsaki Gakuhō*, 107 (1957), pp. 12–68.

———. "Makashikan ni okeru shikan no go shu" 摩訶止観における止観の五種. *Indogaku Bukkyōgaku Kenkyū*, 7:1 (1958), pp. 266–69.

Hirai, Shun'ei. "Chūgoku bukkyō ni okeru fukū no gainen" 中国仏教における不空の概念. *Indogaku Bukkyōgaku Kenkyū*, 18:2 (1970).

Hurvitz, Leon. "The Lotus Sūtra in East Asia: A Review of Hokke Shisō" 法華思想. *Monumenta Serica*, 29 (1970–1971), pp. 697–762.

Komatsu, K. "Tendaidaishi chigi no tsūgyō" 天台大師智顗の通教. *Indogaku Bukkyōgaku Kenkyū*, 27:2 (1980), pp. 156–57.

Miyuki, Mokusen. "Chiao-p'an: An Essential Feature of Chinese Buddhism." *Bukkyō Shisōshi Ronshū*, Tokyo: Daizō Shuppan Co., 1964, pp. 79–91.

Muranaka, Y. "Tendai kyōgi ni okeru shimon" 天台教義における四門. *Indogaku Bukkyōgaku Kenkyū*, 17:1 (1968), pp. 295–97.

Nitta, M. "Tendai no bodaishin ni tsuite" 天台の菩提心について. *Indogaku Bukkyōgaku Kenkyū*, 12:2 (1964), pp. 207–10.

———. "Chigi no jissō ninshiki no tenkai riyū ni tsuite" 智顗の実相認識の展開理由について. *Indogaku Bukkyōgaku Kenkyū*, 19:2 (1971), pp. 113–17.

———. "Chigi ni okeru sangan, santai setsu no keisei o meguru hito kōsatsu" 智顗における三観、三諦説の形成をめぐる一考察. *Indo Shisō to Bukkyō*, Tokyo, 1973, pp. 485–96.

———. "Chigi ni okeru 'yuimagyō-so' senjūtsu no shisōteki imi" 智顗における「維摩経疏」選述の思想的意味. *Indogaku Bukkyōgaku Kenkyū*, 22:2, (1974), pp. 122–27.

Nomoto, K. "San shu sangan no seiritsu" 三種三観の成立. *Indogaku Bukkyōgaku Kenkyū*, 26:2 (1978), pp. 180–81.

Ōno, E. "Tendai sōsokuron no tokujitsu" 天台相即論の特質. *Indogaku Bukkyōgaku Kenkyū*, 28:2 (1980), pp. 275–80.

Satō, Tetsuei. "Tendai daishi ni okeru engyō gyōi no keisei" 天台大師における圓教行位の形成. *Indogaku Bukkyōgaku Kenkyū*, 10:2 (1962), pp. 101–05.

———. "Tendai daishi ni okeru shi shu sammai no keisei katei" 天台大師における四種三昧の形成過程. *Indogaku Bukkyōgaku Kenkyū*, 12:2 (1964), pp. 52–58.

Sekiguchi, J. "Sō'o dōshin to tendai shikan hōmon" 雙峰道信と天台止観法門. *Indogaku Bukkyōgaku Kenkyū*, 2:2 (1954), pp. 121–26.

Sekiguchi, Shindai. "Goji hakkyō kyōhan no kigen" 五時八教教判の起元. *Taishō daigaku kenkyū kiyō*, 61 (1975), pp. 1–16.

Senseki, K. "Tendai sandaibu no inyō kyōron ni tsuite" 天台三大部の引用経論について. *Indogaku Bukkyōgaku Kenkyū*, 33:1 (1984), pp. 161–64.

Shioiri, R. "Santai shisō no kichō to shite no ke" 三諦思想の基調としての假. *Indogaku Bukkyōgaku Kenkyū*, 5:2 (1957), pp. 110–19.

———. "Tendai i ni okeru shitai ni tsuite" 天台義における四諦について. *Indogaku Bukkyōgaku Kenkyū*, 12:2 (1964), pp. 113–21.

Tamura, Yoshirō. "Tendai tetsugaku o chūshin to shite mita zettai no tankyū" 天台哲学を中心としてみた絶対の探究. *Bukkyō Shisōshi Ronshū*. Tokyo: Daizō Shuppan Co., 1964, pp. 783–98.

Tanaka, Junshō. "Tendai no kū" 天台の空. *Mikkyō Bunka*, 53–54 (1961), pp. 34–43.

Wakaisugi, K. "Tendai chigi no busshō setsu" 天台智顗の仏性説. *Indogaku Bukkyōgaku Kenkyū*, 28:1 (1979), pp. 362–65.

Books

Andō, Toshio. *Tendai shōgu shisō ron* 天台性具思想論. Kyoto: Hōzōkan, 1953.

———. *Tendai shisō shi* 天台思想史. Kyoto: Hōzōkan, 1959.

———. *Tendaigaku: Kompon shisō to sono tenkai* 天台学:根本思想とその展開. Kyoto: Heirakuji, 1968.

———. *Tendaigaku ronshū: Shikan to jōdo* 天台学論集:止観と浄土. Kyoto: Heirakuji, 1975.

Chan, Wing-tsit. *A Source Book in Chinese Philosophy*. Princeton: Princeton University Press, 1972.

Chang, Chung-yuan. *Original Teachings of Ch'an Buddhism*. New York: Vintage Books, 1971.

Chappell, David W. ed. *T'ien-T'ai Buddhism: An Outline of the Fourfold Teachings*. Tokyo: Daiichi Shobō, 1983.

De Bary, W.T. ed., *The Buddhist Tradition in India, China and Japan*. New York: Vintage Books, 1972.

Fung, Yu-lan. *A History of Chinese Philosophy* (tr. by Derk Bodde). 2 Vols. Princeton: Princeton University Press, 1953.

Hibi, Nobumasa. *Tōdai tendaigaku kenkyū* 唐代天台学研究. Tokyo: Sankibō Busshorin, 1975.

Hirai, Shun'ei. *Hokke mongu no seiritsu ni kansuru kenkyū* 法華文句の成立に關する研究. Tokyo: Shunjūsha, 1985.

Hurvitz, Leon. *Chih-I, An Introduction to the Life and Ideas of a Chinese Buddhist Monk*. Bruxelles: Juillet, 1962.

Ikeda, Rosan. *Makashikan kenkyū josetsu* 摩訶止観研究序説. Tokyo: Daito Shuppansha, 1986.

Inaba, Enjō. *Tendai shikyōgi shinshaku* 天台四教儀新釋. Kyoto: Hōzōkan, 1925.

Kusaka, Daichi. *Taigaku shishin* 台学指針. Kyoto: Hyakkaen, 1937.

Kyōdo, Jikō. *Tendai daishi no shōgai* 天台大師の生涯. Tokyo: Regulus Library, 1975.

Miyamoto, Shōson, ed. *Bukkyō no kompon shinri* 佛教の根本真理. Tokyo: Sanseidō, 1957.

Mou, Tsung-san. *Chih-ti-chih-chüeh yü chung-kuo che-hsüeh* 智的直覺與中國哲學. Taipei: Commercial Press, 1971.

———. *Hsien-hsiang yü wu-tzu-shen* 現象與物自身. Taiwan: Student Book Co., Ltd., 1975.

———. *Fo-hsing yü po-je* 佛性與般若. 2 Vols. Taiwan: Student Book Co., Ltd., 1977.

———. *Ts'ung Lu Hsiang-shan tao Liu Chi-shan* 從陸象山到劉蕺山. Taiwan: Student Book Co., Ltd., 1979.

Nitta, Masaaki. *Tendai jissōron no kenkyū* 天台実相論の研究. Kyoto: Heirakuji Shoten, 1981.

———. *Tendaigaku nyūmon* 天台学入門. Tokyo: Regulus Library, 1988.

———. *Makashikan* 摩訶止観. Tokyo: Daizō Shuppansha, 1989.

Ōchō, Enichi. *Hokekyō josetsu* 法華經序説. Kyoto: Hōzōkan, 1967.

———, ed. *Hoke shisō* 法華思想. Kyoto: Heirakuji, 1969.

Ogawa, Ichijō. *Busshō shisō* 佛性思想. Kyoto: Buneidō, 1982.

Ogawa, K. *Chūgoku nyoraizō shisō kenkyū* 中国如来蔵思想研究. Tokyo: Chūsan Shobō, 1976.

Sakamoto, Yukio, ed. *Hokekyō no shisō to bunka* 法華經の思想と文化. Kyoto: Heirakuji, 1968.

———. *Hokekyō no chūgokuteki tenkai* 法華經の中国的展開. Kyoto: Heirakuji, 1972.

Sasaki, Kentoku. *Tendai kyōgaku gaisetsu* 天台教学概説. Kyoto: Hyakkaen, 1925.

———. *Tendai kyōgaku* 天台教学. Kyoto: Hyakkaen, 1978.

Satō, Tetsuei. *Tendai daishi no kenkyū* 天台大師の研究. Kyoto: Hyakkaen, 1961.

———. *Zoku tendai daishi no kenkyū* 続天台大師の研究. Kyoto: Hyakkaen, 1981.

Sekiguchi, Shindai. *Tendai shōshikan no kenkyū* 天台小止観の研究. Tokyo: Sankibō Busshorin, 1961.

———. *Makashikan: zen no shisō genri* 摩訶止観:禅の思想原理. Tokyo: Inwanami Shoten, 1966.

———. *Tendai shikan no kenkyū* 天台止観の研究. Tokyo: Iwanami Shoten, 1969.

Sekiguchi, Shindai, ed. *Tendai shikyōgi* 天台四教儀. Tokyo: Sankibō Busshorin, 1968.

Shimaji, D. *Tendai kyōgaku shi* 天台教学史. Incorporated in *Gendai Bukkyō Meichō Zenshū*, Vol. 9, Bukkyō ippan (1), ed. by Nakamura Hajime, et al., Tokyo: Ryūmonkan, 1972.

Sueki, Takehiro. *Tōyō no gōri shisō* 東洋の合理思想. Tokyo: Kōdansha, 1970.

Swanson, Paul. *Foundations of T'ien-t'ai Philosophy: The Flowering of the Two Truths Theory in Chinese Buddhism*. Berkeley: Asian Humanities Press, 1989.

Tada, Kōshō. *Hokkegengi* 法華玄義. Tokyo: Daizo Shuppansha, 1991.

Takakusu, Junjirō. *The Essentials of Buddhist Philosophy*. Honolulu: Office Appliance Co., Ltd., 1956.

Take, Kakuchō. *Tendai kyōgaku no kenkyū* 天台教学の研究. Kyoto: Hōzōkan, 1988.

Tamaki, Kōshirō. *Shin hasoku no tenkai* 心把捉の展開. Tokyo: Sankibō-busshorin, 1961.

Tamura, Yoshirō, et al. *Zettai no shinri: tendai* 絶対の真理：天台. Tokyo: Kadokawa Shoten, 1969.

———. *Hokekyō* 法華經. Tokyo: Chūokōronsha, 1969.

———. *Chigi* 智顗. Tokyo: Daizō Shuppansha, 1981.

T'ang, Chun-i. *Chung-kuo che-hsüeh yüan-lun yüan-hsing p'ien* 中國哲學原論原性篇. Hong Kong: New Asia Institute, 1968.

———. *Chung-kuo che-hsüeh yüan-lun yüan-tao p'ien* 中國哲學原論原道篇. Vol. 3, Hong Kong: New Asia Institute, 1974.

T'ang, Yung-t'ung. *Sui-t'ang fo-chiao-shih kao* 隋唐佛教史稿. Peking: Chung-hua, 1982.

Yanagida, Seizan, et al. *Mu no tankyū: Chūgoku zen* 無の探求：中国禅. Tokyo: Kadokawa Shoten, 1969.

Dictionaries and Guides

Daitō Shuppansha, ed. *Japanese-English Buddhist Dictionary*. Tokyo: Daitō Shuppansha, 1979.

Edgerton, Franklin. *Buddhist Hybrid Sanskrit Grammar and Dictionary*, Vol. II: Dictionary, Delhi: Motilal Banarsidass, 1970.

Liang, Shih-ch'iu, ed. *A New Practical Chinese-English Dictionary*. Hong Kong: The Far East Book Co., 1982.

Mochizuki, Shinkō, ed. *Bukkyō daijiten* 佛教大辭典. 10 Vols. Tokyo: Seikai Seiten, 1981.

Monier-Williams, Monier. *A Sanskrit-English Dictionary*. Delhi, Patna, Varanasi: Motilal Banarsidass, 1974 (A reprint in India).

Nakamura, Hajime, et. al., ed. *Shin butten kaidai jiten* 新佛典解題事典. Tokyo: Shunjūsha, 1965.

Nakamura, Hajime. *Bukkyōgo daijiten* 仏教語大辞典. 3 Vols. Tokyo: Shoseki, 1975.

———. ed., *Shin bukkyō jiten* 新佛教辞典. Tokyo: Seishin Shobō, 1976.

Ng, Yu-kwan. *Fo-chiao ssu-hsiang ta ts'u-tien* 佛教思想大辭典. Taiwan: The Commercial Press, Ltd., 1992.

Reynolds, Frank E. et al. *Guide to Buddhist Religion*. Boston: G.K. Hall & Co., 1981.

Soothill, W.E. et al. ed. *A Dictionary of Chinese Buddhist Terms*. Taiwan: Buddhist Culture Service, 1971.

Taya, Raishun, et al. *Bukkyōgaku jiten* 佛教学辞典. Kyoto: Hōzōkan, 1974.

INDEX